Evaluating and Promoting Nonfiction for Children and Young Adults

Evaluating and Promoting Nonfiction for Children and Young Adults

Don Latham

ROWMAN & LITTLEFIELD
Lanham • Boulder • New York • London

Published by Rowman & Littlefield
An imprint of The Rowman & Littlefield Publishing Group, Inc.
4501 Forbes Boulevard, Suite 200, Lanham, Maryland 20706
www.rowman.com

86-90 Paul Street, London EC2A 4NE

Copyright © 2025 by The Rowman & Littlefield Publishing Group, Inc.

All rights reserved. No part of this book may be reproduced in any form or by any electronic or mechanical means, including information storage and retrieval systems, without written permission from the publisher, except by a reviewer who may quote passages in a review.

British Library Cataloguing in Publication Information Available

Library of Congress Cataloging-in-Publication Data

Names: Latham, Don, 1959- author.
Title: Evaluating and promoting nonfiction for children and young adults / Don Latham.
Description: Lanham : Rowman & Littlefield Publishers, [2025] | Includes bibliographical references and index.
 Summary: "Evaluating and Promoting Nonfiction for Children and Young Adults isn't another bibliography that will quickly become outdated. Instead, it situates nonfiction resources within the recent emphasis on reading nonfiction as a way of enhancing critical thinking and combating susceptibility to "fake news.""— Provided by publisher.
Identifiers: LCCN 2024040342 (print) | LCCN 2024040343 (ebook) | ISBN 9781538175552 (cloth) | ISBN 9781538175569 (paperback) | ISBN 9781538175576 (ebook)
Subjects: LCSH: Libraries—Special collections—Children's literature. | Libraries—Special collections—Young adult literature. | Children's libraries—Collection development. | Young adults libraries—Collection development. | Children's literature—History and criticism. | Young adult literature—History and criticism. | Children—Books and reading—United States. | Teenagers—Books and reading—United States.
Classification: LCC Z688.C47 L38 2025 (print) | LCC Z688.C47 (ebook) | DDC 025.2/187625—dc23/eng/20240928
LC record available at https://lccn.loc.gov/2024040342
LC ebook record available at https://lccn.loc.gov/2024040343

∞™ The paper used in this publication meets the minimum requirements of American National Standard for Information Sciences—Permanence of Paper for Printed Library Materials, ANSI/NISO Z39.48-1992.

For Scott and Anya

Contents

Acknowledgments		ix
Introduction		xi
	Terms and Definitions	xii
	Books on Nonfiction	xiv
	Nonfiction's Status Problem	xvii
	This Book	xix
Chapter 1:	History of Nonfiction for Children and Young Adults	1
	Instruction	3
	People, Places, and Events	5
	Science and Technology	10
Chapter 2:	Awards and Reviews	17
	Awards	17
	Reviews	26
Chapter 3:	Nonfiction and Information Needs of Children and Young Adults	37
	Developmental Needs	38
	Information Behavior	41
	Reading Practices	45
Chapter 4:	Nonfiction and Literacies	53
	What Do We Mean by "Literac(ies)"?	54
	Multimodal Literacy	58
Chapter 5:	Nonfiction Genres	69
	Biography and Memoir	72
	History	77
	Science and Technology	79
Chapter 6:	Formats	87
	Picture Books	87
	Graphic Nonfiction	93
	Audiobooks and E-books	98

Chapter 7:	Promoting Nonfiction	105
	Services	106
	Programs	108
	Evaluation	118
Chapter 8:	The Freedom to Read Nonfiction	125
	Censorship	125
	Selection	127

Appendix A: Awards for Children's and Young Adult Nonfiction	131
Appendix B: Review Resources	137
Appendix C: Literacies and Standards	141
Appendix D: Nonfiction Books Cited	143
Bibliography	155
Index	171
About the Author	189

Acknowledgments

I would like to thank Florida State University for granting me a sabbatical for the completion of this book; Charles Harmon, my editor, for his thoughtful guidance; and Scott Thorp for his good will, encouragement, and unwavering support.

Introduction

How we think about nonfiction depends in large part on how we think about children. Case in point: Jo Carr, in her book on nonfiction for children and young people, offers this provocative quotation, sometimes attributed to Rabelais: "A child is not a vase to be filled, but a fire to be lit."[1] In this view, nonfiction serves not as a repository of facts, but as a catalyst and children are quite capable of engaging in critical thinking in response to this catalyst. It might seem that nonfiction, as an area of study, would be a straightforward enterprise, generally free from controversy, easy to define and to defend. But nothing could be further from the truth. In fact, nonfiction raises many questions that scholars, librarians, and educators have all answered in different ways.

In this book I intend to delve into those questions. The primary audience for this book is made up of school and public librarians, but the book will also be useful to academic librarians who support programs in library and information science, teacher education, and children's literature. It also may be of interest to teachers who are looking for advice in developing their classroom collections. This book provides an overview of the variety of nonfiction available for children and young adults, situates nonfiction resources within the recent emphasis on reading nonfiction as a way of enhancing critical thinking, and offers strategies for evaluating nonfiction for the purposes of developing collections, providing readers' advisory, and designing programs using nonfiction for children and young adults.

In this chapter I will consider the question "What do we mean by the term 'nonfiction'?" (spoiler alert: there is no easy answer) and then describe how the book is organized. But first I want to explain what I mean by the terms "children" and "young adults." For the term "children" I will adopt the definition used by the Association for Library Service to Children (ALSC) for their Robert F. Sibert Informational Book Medal: birth to age fourteen years.[2] For the term "young adult" I will adopt the definition used by the Young Adult Library Services Association (YALSA) for their Award for Excellence in Nonfiction: ages twelve to eighteen years.[3] Also, for the sake of brevity I will use the term "nonfiction" to refer to "nonfiction for children and young adults" except in cases where I want to make a distinction between the two age groups or between the two, on the one hand, and nonfiction for adults, on the other.

TERMS AND DEFINITIONS

So what do we mean by "nonfiction"? Before we try to define it, we must consider the term itself. For one thing, it is not universally agreed upon as the best term. While some prefer "nonfiction," others advocate for "information" or "informational" books. As Penny Colman, herself a nonfiction writer, explains, there are problems with both terms. Some people find the "non" in nonfiction to be off-putting because it connotes a negative. Historian Barbara Tuchman describes the term as "despicable" because she does not like being described as "a Non-something: I feel quite specific."[4] The terms "informational books" (which Colman traces to Zena Sutherland) and "information books" (which she traces to Margery Fisher) are problematic too, because they imply that other kinds of books do not contain information, and some people assume the terms apply only to reference books and textbooks. Kathy Latrobe and Judy Drury, in their book *Critical Approaches to Young Adult Literature*, claim that young adults prefer the term "nonfiction" although they do not provide any documentation to support this claim.[5] ALSC uses the term "informational book" for their nonfiction medal while YALSA and the National Council of Teachers of English (NCTE) use the term "nonfiction" for their respective awards. It seems safe to say in most contexts the terms can be used interchangeably.

A related term, "hybrid" book, refers to a work that contains both fictional and nonfictional elements. Other terms used for this kind of work are "faction" and "blended book."[6] A prime example is The Magic School Bus book series by Joanna Cole and Bruce Degen.[7] Each book uses a fictional story in which Ms. Frizzle, the teacher, takes her class on an adventure by way of the magical vehicle. Along the way, the students learn information about various aspects of science (the solar system, the human body, a hurricane, etc.). Other examples include picturebooks in which a fictional, generic child learns about real things like making fry bread with the family (in Kevin Noble Maillard and Juana Martinez-Neal's *Fry Bread: A Native American Family Story*) or attending a Pride parade (in Gayle E. Pitman and Kristyna Litten's *This Day in June*). In these books, the fictional elements serve to draw the reader in, while the nonfictional elements ground the stories in real life. One question raised by these books is how much fiction is too much, to the point that we cannot reasonably call a book "nonfiction." Another is how likely are young children to be able to distinguish between the fictional and the nonfictional elements—and, moreover, does it really matter?

If the terminology is somewhat varied, the definitions are even more so. In fact, in their entry on "Nonfiction Literature for Children" in the *Handbook of Research on Children's and Young Adult Literature*, Barbara Kiefer and Melissa Wilson report that they "found it difficult to find a comprehensive or even a clear definition of nonfiction."[8] Still, by looking at some of the definitions that have been put forth over the years, we might arrive at a more complete and more nuanced definition, and a good place to start is with the major awards for nonfiction for young people. NCTE's Orbis Pictus Award defines nonfiction books "as those written, designed, and organized to interpret documentable, factual material for children."[9] Similarly, ALSC's Robert F. Sibert Informational Book Medal defines informational books "as those written and illustrated to present, organize, and interpret documentable, factual material."[10] YALSA's Award for Excellence in Nonfiction for Young Adults does not provide a definition but does describe the qualities a book must have: "excellent writing, research, presentation and readability for young adults."[11] Other sources offer useful guidance as well. *The Cambridge Guide to Children's Books* defines information books this way: "A wide category of texts specifically designed in print, graphics and illustrations to interest, inform, instruct and thus extend the knowledge of young people about subjects, events and ideas they encounter during their years of formal education."[12] In *Nonfiction Writers Dig Deep*, Melissa Stewart and her co-authors define nonfiction broadly so as to include "expository nonfiction/informational writing, narrative nonfiction, memoir, graphic/comics nonfiction, fact-based poetry, and fact-based pseudonarratives."[13] (This last term is essentially another term for hybrid texts, as discussed above.) Colman offers this succinct definition: "Nonfiction is writing about reality (real people, places, events, ideas, feelings, things) in which nothing is made up."[14] In *A Critical Handbook of Children's Literature*, Rebecca Lukens focuses on how nonfiction works rather than on what it is: "The successful nonfiction book manages to supply information and yet make the reader sense that discovery is open-ended. There is more to be known, and finding out is exciting. Because the attitude of wonder is stimulated, we assimilate the facts and come to understand the concept."[15] Along those lines, Joe Sutliff Sanders argues that nonfiction should be conceptualized as a "literature of questions" rather than a "literature of fact." It should invite critical engagement and stimulate a dialogue between the reader and the text. He writes, "A nonfiction that defines itself as truth bearer is one that cannot tolerate cracks in its authority, one that cannot make itself vulnerable to the inquiry and thoughtful tests of readers."[16] Kylene Beers and Robert Probst add another wrinkle: the responsibility of the reader to enter into that dialogue and not to accept any text at face value. Their definition captures a key aspect of nonfiction: "Nonfiction is that body of work in which the author *purports* to tell us about the real world, a real experience, a real person, an idea, or a belief" (emphasis added).[17] I like Beers and Probst's definition because it highlights what a nonfiction work *claims* to be, and I suspect many would agree with Sanders and with Beers and Probst that a nonfiction text should make this purporting clear, and readers should always recognize that what they are reading is a representation, an interpretation, not absolute truth. If you will excuse the pun, the fact remains that "facts" can and do change, and there are myriad interpretations of "facts."

So what are we talking about when we talk about nonfiction? One way to think about it is to consider what it includes and what it excludes. Broadly defined, nonfiction is everything that is not fiction—so that would include such things as poetry, drama, folklore, and mythology. However, most people would not include those genres in nonfiction. True, they are not fiction, but they are also not informational either, at least in terms of their primary purpose. So what to do? It is tempting to turn to the Dewey Decimal Classification (DDC) for guidance since that system is widely used in school and public libraries in the United States and, indeed, in many other countries as well. We might think we could safely consider the 800 Class—Literature—to cover everything that is not nonfiction, but we run into problems right away. Literary criticism, which is nonfiction, falls into the 800 Class as do essays, speeches, and letters, which are nonfiction too. Folklore and mythology, on the other hand, fall outside of the 800 Class, so we also cannot count on everything outside of 800 being nonfiction. We are left, then, with a laundry list approach, and fortunately, as far as that strategy is concerned, other scholars have paved the way for us. Rosemary Chance, for example, offers these examples of what she calls "informational books": "Biography, autobiography, memoir, nonfiction, science, history, facts, self-help, true crime, true survival, true stories, atlases, dictionaries, encyclopedias."[18] The term "facts" almost certainly refers to compendiums such as *The Guinness Book of World Records* (now *Guinness World Records*).[19] But the term "nonfiction" seems out of place here unless Chance is using it as a catch-all term to cover other kinds of informational books not included in her list. Other scholars opt for fewer, broader categories. Barbara Lounsberry offers four categories: lives, events, places, and ideas.[20] Carrie Hintz and Eric Tribunella, in their introductory text on children's literature, identify four categories as well, though not exactly the same four: conduct literature, life writing, history writing, and science and discovery.[21] The point is nonfiction is both deep and wide and any attempt to provide an exhaustive list is almost certainly futile. Still, it is helpful to have examples of the more common types so that we can say, like U.S. Supreme Court Justice Potter Stewart famously said of pornography, in a quite different context, "I know it when I see it."[22]

BOOKS ON NONFICTION

It seems that every decade or so for the past fifty-plus years, a book on nonfiction for children and young adults has appeared. Of course, a great many more books on children's and young adult literature in general have been published, and most if not all of them contain a chapter or at least a section on nonfiction, usually no more than that. But I want to focus on book-length studies of nonfiction exclusively, for doing so will reveal important contributions as well as interesting trends. The first such book, and one now considered a classic, is Margery Fisher's *Matters of Fact: Aspects of Non-fiction for Children* (1972).[23]

It is here that the term "information book" is introduced, and the distinction between fiction and nonfiction spelled out:

> In a novel the story—the fiction, perhaps I should say—comes first and has priority: facts of whatever kind, exist to support it. The writer of an information book sets out to help towards knowledge, and the techniques he uses, which may well include story-telling, will be subordinate to this end.[24]

Fisher argues that any nonfiction book should be accurate, clear, stimulating, logically organized, and written at a level appropriate for its intended audience.[25] She goes on to say, however, that "there is more to an information book than its technical aspect. Each one should contain fact, concept, and attitude."[26] The notion that a nonfiction book should be based on fact seems fairly self-evident, but what does she mean by concept and attitude? Concept is "a generalisation toward which the facts are arranged";[27] in other words, it is a statement about the topic or a thesis (although Fisher does not use that term). Attitude is the author's attitude toward the topic, or what we might call the author's point of view. After a relatively brief introduction, Fisher devotes the remainder of her substantial book (it runs to nearly 500 pages) to four major types of nonfiction books: foundations (books focused on single topics); multiple subjects (books, such as encyclopedias, that contain multiple entries); biography; and careers (which Fisher admits is a relatively narrow part of nonfiction, but one of great importance to most young people). Though we may take exception to Fisher's categories for having too much overlap (might not a book on architects, for example, fall into all four categories?), we must also acknowledge her discussion of individual nonfiction works is both thoughtful and expansive.

Ten years later, Jo Carr compiled a collection of essays in the book *Beyond Fact: Nonfiction for Children and Young People* (1982).[28] In the introductory section, provocatively titled "Nonfiction Writing: Books as Instruments of Intelligence," Carr says that "an outstanding nonfiction book" is like a great teacher (her term): "Truly inspired and masterfully written, it can lead us, by way of facts and beyond facts, to awakened understanding."[29] To put it another way, such books should "teach children how to think, not what to think."[30] She organizes the collected essays into four broad topical categories: science, history, biography, and controversy. Aside from the fact that this last category seems to imply that science, history, and biography are somehow not controversial, Carr's divisions are useful, if not mutually exclusive, ways of looking at the broad landscape of nonfiction. Moreover, her emphasis on writing that makes readers think prefigures later scholars who insist that good nonfiction must be more than simply a literature of facts.

In the early nineties, Betty Carter and Richard Abrahamson published *Nonfiction for Young Adults from Delight to Wisdom* (1990).[31] A collaboration between a former school librarian-turned-LIS scholar (Carter) and an education scholar (Abrahamson), the book is organized around criteria that should be considered in selecting nonfiction: interest, accuracy, content, style, organization, format, and potential uses. Interspersed are "conversations" with various nonfiction writers (almost all of whom are men). In their introduction Carter and Abrahamson state that part of the bias against nonfiction is due to the lack of professional attention it has received. Their primary purpose is to mitigate that bias by describing nonfiction's literary qualities and discussing its importance for young adults.[32] Skilled writers employ these literary qualities to both delight readers and, under the best circumstances, lead them to new-found wisdom—hence the title of the book. Carter and Abrahamson represent an important contribution to scholarship on nonfiction by focusing on the art of nonfiction writing and by including the voices of nonfiction writers.

Beginning in the late nineties and continuing into the twenty-first century, several books appeared with a particular focus on the role of nonfiction in primary and secondary school classrooms. Though aimed primarily at teachers, these books offer insights to librarians, especially school librarians, in how nonfiction is and can be integrated into the K-12 curriculum. In 1997 *Making Facts Come Alive: Choosing & Using Nonfiction Literature K-8* was published, and a second edition followed soon thereafter (the 2003 edition is the one I will reference here). Edited by Rosemary Bamford and Janice Kristo, this book offers essays from various scholars on how to evaluate nonfiction and how to use it with students of different ages. In addition to the expected discussions of accuracy, organization, and style, there are essays on new directions and challenges in nonfiction, access features and graphics, and early, emergent, and transitional readers. Other essays examine quality nonfiction in different subject areas, including social studies, science, mathematics, and the arts. The book also contains interviews with several nonfiction writers and, as is typical with books aimed at teachers, practical advice about how to encourage students to engage with nonfiction. Scholars who subsequently have written about nonfiction frequently cite the essays contained in this book, suggesting it has clearly had an influence. A later but related book is Kylene Beers and Robert Probst's *Reading Nonfiction: Notice & Note Stances, Signposts, and Strategies* (2016).[33] Beers and Probst situate their discussion of nonfiction within the larger context of what it means, and why it is important, to be information literate in a democratic society. In addition, they offer advice about how to teach students to interrogate an author's stance (viewpoint, possible bias, attitude toward the reader) as well as their own stance and how to identify signposts, what we might call "red flags," in the text (for example, contradictions, extreme language, absolute language). Finally, Joe Sutliff Sanders, in *A Literature of Questions: Nonfiction for the Critical Child* (2018),[34] offers his own take on the issue of children's critical engagement with nonfiction. Whereas Beers and Probst focus on teachers' responsibility to help children become critical readers, Sanders argues that it is the text's responsibility to facilitate such reading. Citing the work of Paolo Freire on critical pedagogy, Sanders explains, "[I]n those places where a text is willing to allow *critical engagement*, it opens itself to dialogue rather than maintaining the privilege of monologue."[35] Texts that do this are examples of "good" nonfiction; texts that do not do this are not. In my own view, successful critical engagement requires three kinds of active participants: authors to invite it, teachers (and librarians and parents) to encourage it, and young readers to embrace it.

NONFICTION'S STATUS PROBLEM

An oft-repeated refrain among people who write about nonfiction is that it has been relegated to second-class status in the world of children's literature. Some of these writers are nonfiction authors themselves; others are teachers, reviewers, and librarians. But they all tend to focus on one or more of three key issues: nonfiction works rarely win the big children's literature prizes, teachers prefer fiction over nonfiction, and many people, including parents, believe young people do not like nonfiction. Let us look at each of these in turn.

In 1976 the nonfiction author Milton Meltzer published what has now become a famous article in *The Horn Book*, asking the question "Where Do All the Prizes Go? The Case for Nonfiction."[36] Needless to say, Meltzer's answer to his perhaps rhetorical question was "not to nonfiction." Noting that the very first Newbery Medal, in 1922, went to a nonfiction work, Hendrik Van Loon's *Story of Mankind*, he pointed out that very few nonfiction books since then had won the Newbery, and the same was true of the Boston Globe–Horn Book Award and the National Book Award in the children's literature category. (Apparently, he did not examine the list of Randolph Caldecott Medal winners although if he had, he would have come to much the same conclusion.) Why is this the case, Meltzer wondered. The fault, he argued, lay with the perception—among reviewers, scholars, and prize committees—that nonfiction was not literature. He then went on to make the case that the best nonfiction writing is characterized by its organization, selection of facts, the author's point of view, the inclusion of other viewpoints, and most of all the writer's "personal voice" and "quality of vision."[37]

Forty years later Anita Silvey, also a nonfiction author, asked the same question in her blog, "Where Do All the Prizes Go?"[38] Here she acknowledges Meltzer's "ground-breaking article" and notes that several awards specifically for nonfiction have been established since then, including a nonfiction category for the Boston Globe–Horn Book Awards, the Children's Book Guild of Washington, DC's Nonfiction Award, ALSC's Robert F. Sibert Informational Book Medal, and the YALSA Award for Excellence in Nonfiction. (She might have mentioned NCTE's Orbis Pictus Award as well.) Still, she comes to a similar conclusion Meltzer came to forty years earlier: the major children's literature awards still regularly go to works of fiction, with very few exceptions.

Another issue contributing to nonfiction's second-class status is the fact that what is taught in most U.S. K-12 classrooms, aside from textbooks, is fiction. This may be because teachers believe fiction is what they are supposed to teach, their perception that fiction is what students prefer, and their own predilections. Colman has written eloquently about her indignation, as a nonfiction author, at being told by teachers (and librarians, editors, and parents) that "[r]eading nonfiction ... is not 'real reading'" because it lacks the qualities of "real" literature.[39] This perception is reflected in Beverly Kobrin's entry on "Information Books" in *Children's Books and Their Creators* that "there is no classic nonfiction" (although she does point out that "the qualities that make good nonfiction books are classic").[40] For her part, Colman argues that good nonfiction is no less literary than good fiction; in order to write both "it is necessary to employ many of the same literary techniques and to pay close attention to the narrative, structure, point of view, language, syntax, sequence, pace, tone, and voice."[41] To Colman's point, one could argue that such literary devices, along with ideas they are conveying, can be analyzed in the classroom using nonfiction as easily as fiction. To be sure, the emphasis has shifted from fiction to nonfiction, especially in some secondary schools in the United States, due to the Common Core State Standards Initiative. While the standards are not without their critics and have not been uniformly adopted across the United States, they have exerted influence including their emphasis on students in grades six through twelve reading, analyzing, and responding to nonfiction materials. Consequently, several books, like the aforementioned Beers and Probst's *Reading Nonfiction: Notice & Note*, have appeared in recent years designed to help teachers facilitate students' engagement with nonfiction texts.

A third issue affecting nonfiction's second-class status is the widespread perception that young people do not like it. Actual evidence supporting this perception is mixed. No doubt, some young people probably do not like nonfiction, and, as Colman points out, the term "information book" does not help because it conjures images of encyclopedias and textbooks.[42] Ray Doiron in a three-year study of Canadian students in grades one through six, found that indeed all students were more likely to check out fiction for recreational reading (60% to 40%) and boys were more likely than girls to check out nonfiction.[43] The nonfiction author Jay Matthews, citing Renaissance Learning's 2017 *What Kids Are Reading* report, laments the fact that only about 30 percent of K-12 students are reading nonfiction.[44] A few years later he found the situation was not any better. While nonfiction reading increased from 11 percent in 2003 to 25 percent in 2020, almost no nonfiction titles appeared on each grade's top twenty books list.[45]

But some young people not only like nonfiction, they actually prefer it. In a rejoinder to Matthews' 2020 article, nonfiction authors Cynthia Levinson,

Melissa Stewart, and Jennifer Swanson offer anecdotal evidence they have collected from children during school visits, indicating that many children do, in fact, like nonfiction.[46] They also cite a study of first graders, in which Kathleen Mohr found that "an overwhelming majority" preferred information picturebooks, particularly ones about animals.[47] When it comes to teens, librarians Jamie Watson and Jennifer Stencel report that in sharing books with hundreds of so-called reluctant readers, "it is the nonfiction books that teens select from our boxes of books; it is nonfiction that gets passed around and returned much worse for the wear; and it is nonfiction that engages a group enough to talk about issues inside the book."[48] So do children and teens like or dislike nonfiction? As is often the case with such dichotomous questions, the answer depends on the individual reader and it depends on whom you ask.

THIS BOOK

This book will explore the various issues related to nonfiction with an emphasis on how understanding those issues can help librarians in developing collections and promoting nonfiction to children and young adults. In the spirit of what many consider to be the best kind of nonfiction, rather than providing pat answers and overly prescriptive advice, I instead hope to invite readers to engage with the ideas presented by including multiple perspectives, highlighting agreements and disagreements among scholars, identifying opportunities and challenges, and opening spaces for critical dialogue. A couple of caveats: the works of nonfiction that I will discuss will be primarily, though not exclusively, works published in the United States. I will also refrain from offering "best of" lists. Such lists are always evolving as new works are added, so I will point to those lists rather than repeating them here. I will, however, provide a select and admittedly idiosyncratic list of nonfiction representing different genres, formats, and age groups. Finally, I will focus on trade nonfiction. I will consider a few reference works that might be described as "trade" reference works, such as many of the books in DK Eyewitness Series aimed at middle grade readers. I will not discuss textbooks as they are typically provided to students by schools but are not part of libraries' collections.

Finally, I'd like to say a few words about how this book is organized. In the Introduction we have explored different views on what nonfiction is and why it is important. Chapter 1 discusses the history of nonfiction for children and young adults. Chapter 2 looks at awards, lists, and review sources as they relate to works of nonfiction. Chapter 3 considers nonfiction in relation to the information needs and information behaviors of children and young adults. Chapter 4 provides an overview of several literacy frameworks that represent potentially useful tools—both for librarians and for young people—for evaluating nonfiction. Chapter 5 focuses on common genres of literary nonfiction, including biography and memoir, history, and science and technology. Chapter

6 examines various formats for nonfiction—picturebooks, graphic nonfiction, audiobooks, and e-books. Chapter 7 discusses ways of developing programs and engaging in readers' advisory using nonfiction. Chapter 8 considers censorship efforts surrounding nonfiction. The appendixes provide one-stop shopping for lists of helpful resources: awards, review sources, and literacy resources. Endnotes will not be provided for children's and young adult books cited; however, full citations are available in Appendix D at the end of the book. The exception is the historical titles that are discussed in chapter 1. Many of these are no longer in print and are only available (if at all) in archives.

To understand the present state—and status—of nonfiction, it helps to understand the ever-changing context(s) in which nonfiction has developed. Thus, in the next chapter we turn our attention to the history of nonfiction for children and young adults.

NOTES

1. Jo Carr, ed., *Beyond Fact: Nonfiction for Children and Young People* (Chicago: American Library Association, 1982), 5.
2. Association for Library Service to Children, "Robert F. Sibert Informational Book Medal," accessed September 11, 2023, https://www.ala.org/alsc/awardsgrants/bookmedia/sibert.
3. Young Adult Library Services Association, "Nonfiction Award," accessed September 11, 2023, https://www.ala.org/yalsa/nonfiction-award.
4. Penny Colman, "A New Way to Look at Literature: A Visual Model for Analyzing Fiction and Nonfiction Texts," *Language Arts* 84, no. 3 (2007): 258.
5. Kathy H. Latrobe and Judy Drury, *Critical Approaches to Young Adult Literature* (New York: Neal-Schuman, 2009).
6. Colman, "A New Way," 261.
7. Full citations for children's and young adult books that are cited in the text will be provided in a separate bibliography at the end of the book. The exception is the historical titles that are discussed in chapter 1. Many of these are no longer in print and are only available (if at all) in archives.
8. Shelby Anne Wolf, *Handbook of Research on Children's and Young Adult Literature* (New York: Routledge, 2011), 291.
9. National Council of Teachers of English, "Orbis Pictus Award," accessed September 12, 2023, https://ncte.org/awards/orbis-pictus-award-nonfiction-for-children/.
10. Association for Library Service to Children.
11. Young Adult Library Services Association.
12. Victor Watson, ed. *The Cambridge Guide to Children's Books in English* (Cambridge, UK: Cambridge University Press, 2001), 368.
13. Melissa Stewart, ed. *Nonfiction Writers Dig Deep: 50 Award-Winning Children's Book Authors Share the Secret of Engaging Writing* (Champaign, IL: National Council of Teachers of English, 2020), 4.

14. Penny Colman, "Point of Departure," in *Handbook of Research on Children's and Young Adult Literature*, ed. Karen Coats Shelby Wolf, Patricia Enciso, and Christine Jenkins (New York: Routledge, 2011), 300.
15. Rebecca J. Lukens, *A Critical Handbook of Children's Literature*, fifth ed. (New York: HarperCollins, 1995), 272.
16. Joe Sutliff Sanders, *A Literature of Questions: Nonfiction for the Critical Child* (Minneapolis: University of Minnesota Press, 2018), 40.
17. Kylene Beers and Robert E. Probst, *Reading Nonfiction: Notice & Note Stances, Signposts, and Strategies* (Portsmouth, NH: Heinemann, 2016), 21.
18. Rosemary Chance, *Young Adult Literature in Action: A Librarian's Guide* (Westport, CT: Libraries Unlimited, 2008), 95.
19. Guiness World Records, in *Guiness World Records* (London: Guiness World Records, 1955-).
20. Barbara Lounsberry, "Anthology Introduction," in *Writing Creative Nonfiction: The Literature of Reality*, ed. Gay Talese and Barbara Lounsberry (New York: HarperCollins, 1996), 29.
21. Carrie Hintz and Eric L. Tribunella, *Reading Children's Literature: A Critical Introduction* (Boston, MA: Bedford/St. Martin's, 2013), 274-91.
22. *Jacobellis v. Ohio,* 378 U.S. 184 (1964).
23. Margery Fisher, *Matters of Fact: Aspects of Non-Fiction for Children* (New York: Crowell, 1972).
24. Ibid., 11.
25. Ibid., 12.
26. Ibid., 12.
27. Ibid., 12.
28. Carr, *Beyond Fact*.
29. Ibid., 4.
30. Ibid., 4.
31. Betty Carter and Richard F. Abrahamson, *Nonfiction for Young Adults from Delight to Wisdom* (Phoenix, AZ: Oryx Press, 1990).
32. Carter and Abrahamson, ix.
33. Beers and Probst, *Reading Nonfiction*.
34. Sanders, *A Literature of Questions*.
35. Sanders, 12.
36. Milton Meltzer, "Where Do All the Prizes Go? The Case for Nonfiction," *The Horn Book Magazine* 52, no. 1 (1976).
37. Ibid., n.p.
38. Anita Silvey, "Where Do All the Prizes Go?," accessed September 13, 2023, https://www.anitasilvey.com/blog/2016/09/19/where-do-all-the-prizes-go/.
39. Penny Colman, "Nonfiction Is Literature, Too," *The New Advocate* 12, no. 3 (1999): 215.
40. Anita Silvey, ed. *Children's Books and Their Creators: An Invitation to the Feast of Twentieth-Century Children's Literature* (New York: Houghton Mifflin, 1995), 342.
41. Colman, "Nonfiction Is Literature, Too," 215.
42. Colman, "A New Way," 258.
43. Ray Doiron, "Boy Books, Girl Books: Should We Re-Organize Our School Library Collections?," *Teacher Librarian* 30, no. 3 (2003): 15.

44. Jay Matthews, "Read It and Weep: Students Still Aren't Embracing Nonfiction, Despite Campaign," *The Washington Post*, November 24, 2017.
45. "Will My Grandkids Still Love Me If I Buy Them Nonfiction? The Movement to Deepen Childhood Reading Faces the Challenge of Captain Underpants," *The Washington Post*, December 11, 2020.
46. Cynthia Levinson, Melissa Stewart, and Jennifer Swanson, "Hey, Grownups! Kids Really Do Like Nonfiction," *The Publishers Weekly*, Januray 7, 2021, n.p.
47. Kathleen Mohr, "Children's Choices for Recreational Reading: A Three-Part Investigation of Selection Preferences, Rationales, and Processes," *Journal of Literacy Research* 38, no. 1 (2006): 81.
48. Jamie Watson and Jennifer Stencel, "Reaching Reluctant Readers with Nonfiction," *Young Adult Library Services* (2005): 8.

1

History of Nonfiction for Children and Young Adults

The history of nonfiction for children and young adults, like the history of children's literature in general, reflects social, cultural, economic, and technological changes over time. As Anne Scott MacLeod explains,

> [From the seventeenth through the nineteenth centuries] children's literature in America followed the evolution of its society. It absorbed and recorded major changes in the American outlook: a slow shift from Puritan preoccupations with spiritual meaning, to a more generalized Protestant concern for personal morality, and from that morality to a largely secular interest in social behaviour.[1]

The amount of literature written for children grew steadily in the eighteenth and nineteenth centuries for several reasons. These centuries saw a growing middle class (with more money to spend), an increase in the number of schools, and a rise in literacy rates although more so for whites than any other group.[2] In the nineteenth century technological advances in printing made it easier and cheaper to print books, and the expansion of the railroad made it easier to distribute them.[3] In the seventeenth and eighteenth centuries most of the literature provided to American children had originally been published in England and then reprinted or, in some cases, adapted. However, this began to change in the nineteenth century as more writers, both women and men, became interested in writing for children. A variety of motivations was at work here: some wanted to be part of the emerging field of children's literature, some believed in the Romantic notion of childhood, and all hoped to make money.[4]

Still, being a children's writer was not considered very prestigious. However, this began to change in the first part of the twentieth century.[5] There were multiple reasons for this. One was the influence of Lucy Sprague Mitchell, founder of the innovative Bank Street College of Education, who wrote the *Here and Now Storybook* (1921) in which she advocated for young children's interest in the real, the "here and now," rather than exclusively fantasy.[6] Nonfiction, of course, is especially well-suited to appeal to this interest. Other factors that contributed to the growth of children's literature during this period was the establishment of school libraries, the establishment of children's reading rooms in public libraries, the training of children's librarians, the employment of children's book editors at major publishers, an increase in reviews of children's books, and the establishment of children's book awards.[7] In the middle part of the twentieth century children's literature, and especially nonfiction, benefitted from the U.S. government's increased support for school libraries as a result of political and social motivations. The launch of the Soviet satellite, Sputnik, in 1957 fueled fears that the United States was losing the Cold War. As a result, Congress passed the National Defense Education Act (1958) that, among other things, provided funding for school libraries to purchase more science and technology books. And, of course, publishers responded by increasing the production of such books.[8] In 1964 additional funding was appropriated for school libraries via the Elementary and Secondary Education Act which was part of President Lyndon Johnson's Great Society Program.[9] Because the civil rights movement in the United States was at its height during this time, there was a great deal of interest in beefing up school library collections of African American history and biography, and the congressional funding helped make this possible.[10] This funding, however, dried up in the late 1960s and early 1970s, having a negative effect on the production and sales of new nonfiction titles.[11] A resurgence of nonfiction occurred in the 1980s thanks in part to advances in printing and photographic technology. These innovations allowed authors to include lots of high quality visuals in their books without publishers having to dramatically increase prices.[12] In the late twentieth and early twenty-first centuries, the advent of digital technology has led to even more exciting innovations in both print and digital nonfiction publications and a concomitant interest among scholars and educators in young people's visual literacy. Other innovations are evident as well, especially an increased attention to social issues, diverse voices, and reclaimed histories of historically marginalized groups.

To gain a more in-depth understanding of the history of nonfiction for young people, let us look at the more prevalent types of nonfiction and consider how they have evolved. Although there have been many changes over the centuries, all of these types, some dating back (at least) to the Late Middle Ages, have analogs in the nonfiction being published for young people today. Specifically, we will look at books of instruction (including courtesy and conduct books), biography and history, science and technology, and travel. Our focus will be primarily on English and American books published up through the mid-twentieth century. We will look at more recent books in later chapters.

INSTRUCTION

Almost every discussion of the history of nonfiction for children and young adults begins with John Amos Comenius' *Orbis Sensualium Pictus*, or *The Visible World in Pictures*. Published in 1658, the book served as a picturebook for younger readers and as a Latin textbook for older children.[13] The idea was that all readers would enjoy the pictures of the natural world, while older readers would be presented with illustrations labeled in their native language along with the Latin equivalents.[14] Containing 150 woodcut illustrations, the book depicts various aspects of both the material and the abstract worlds.[15] As described by the editors of *The Norton Anthology of Children's Literature*,

> The volume progresses through objects in the visible world, the solar system, natural history, human anatomy, trades and professions, daily life, and amusements, and concludes with more abstract matters, such as government, justice, ethics, philosophy, and religion.[16]

Comenius was an innovative Czech educator who believed that children learned best through illustrations of the real world.[17] As such, he espoused pansophy, that is, "education teaching universal God-centered knowledge."[18] Sylvia Vardell notes that the access features of the book are similar to the things we now routinely expect to see in nonfiction texts: chapter headings, labels for illustrations, and an index.[19] Though the first English edition of the book was published in 1659 just a year after the original edition,[20] and was used in England and the United States through the late eighteenth and early nineteenth centuries, the book was never widely used in English-speaking schools.[21] Nonetheless, the book has come to have an iconic status in children's literature studies and is regarded by many as the first children's book.[22]

Another important book of instruction was Benjamin Harris's *The New England Primer* (c. 1690), widely used in schools in America in the seventeenth and eighteenth centuries.[23] Harris was an anti-Catholic writer and bookseller who fled England in 1686 and settled in Boston.[24] He based *The Primer* on a work he had previously published before leaving England, *The Protestant Tutor* (1683).[25] The book was so popular that by 1830 it had gone through 450 editions.[26] Whether it is fair to call *The Primer* nonfiction is debatable. In part it was an alphabet book with illustrations, not all that different from today's alphabet books, but it contained other parts as well. As Leonard Marcus explains, the book contained certain key parts regardless of the edition:

> While an illustrated alphabet in rhyme, the shorter catechism, and selections of prayers and Bible verses remained the unchanging core of *The New-England Primer*, variations in the text from edition to edition were common and became a barometer of changing cultural codes and priorities.[27]

One example of these variations that Marcus cites is the K rhyme. In the 1727 edition, the rhyme was "Our King the good/No man of blood." By 1797, this had been changed to "The British King/Lost states thirteen." And by 1819, the reference to a king had been replaced with "The Youth's delight/To fly their kite."[28]

As a side note, an interesting phenomenon that emerged during the eighteenth century (and perhaps earlier) was the production, usually by mothers, of materials to aid them in instructing their children at home. Jane Johnson was one such mother, who, during the 1740s, created more than 400 cards, booklets, and tiles for the purpose of educating her sons before they were old enough to be sent off to formal schooling.[29] There is no reason to think that Johnson was unique among her peers as a practitioner of homeschooling and creator of homegrown educational materials; what is unique is the fact that these artifacts have survived for nearly four hundred years.

Another kind of book related to instruction was what we would now call a "reference book," something intended to be consulted rather than read in a linear fashion. In fact, *Orbis Pictus*, though clearly intended as a book of instruction, might also be considered a kind of reference book. Sylvia Vardell astutely compares it to what we now call a visual encyclopedia, "the Renaissance counterpart to today's [DK] 'Eyewitness series.'"[30] Other reference-type books appeared over the years. In 1800 Richmal Mangnall published her *Historical and Miscellaneous Questions for the Use of Young People*. Set up as a series of questions and answers, it was intended to be used by teachers in instructing their pupils.[31] We might see this as a forerunner to today's "fact and trivia" books that are so popular with young people. A true reference work for children appeared in the early part of the twentieth century in the form of Sir Arthur Mee's *The Children's Encyclopedia* (known as *The Book of Knowledge* in the United States) (1908-1933).[32]

Another kind of instructional book was the courtesy (later called conduct) book. In fact, in the century before *Orbis Pictus* was written, a number of courtesy books were produced for young people, mostly aristocratic males with the goal of teaching them "manners, morals, and Latin."[33] One example can be found in *The Babees Book, or a 'Lytyl Reporte' of How Young People Should Behave*, a series of late medieval manuscripts that were compiled by the Victorian scholar Frederick Furnivall.[34] Such books were intended to prepare boys to serve in courtly society and offered helpful advice such as not to drink with one's mouth full and not to pick one's nose.[35] Among the first books printed in England were William Caxton's *Book of Curtesye* in 1477 and his translation of *The Book of the Knight of the Tower* in 1484, both of which were intended to instruct children—the former for boys, the latter for girls—on how to conduct themselves in a noble household.[36] With the rise of the middle class, a shift occurred from courtesy books (with an emphasis on "courtly" manners) to conduct books (with a focus on how one should behave in everyday life). Some of these books were geared toward boys, teaching them how to conduct themselves in work, society, and politics, and others were geared toward girls, teaching them "good" morals, manners, and appearance.[37] *The Instructor; or, the Young Man's Best Companion*, by George Fisher and published in 1727, provided not only lessons in reading and arithmetic, but also advice on a range of subjects from writing legal documents to gardening and pickling.[38] *The Polite Academy*, published in 1762, offered advice to girls and young women on such things as how to walk, how to dance, and how to curtsy.[39] These kinds of books persisted in England and the United States until well into the nineteenth century. Two examples from the United States are Daniel C. Eddy's *The Young Man's Friend* (1849) and Daniel Wise's *The Young Lady's Counsellor* (1852).[40] And these books were not only "gendered"; some, especially in England, were class-based as well. *Duties of a Lady's Maid* (1825) was for working class girls, while *Lord Chesterfield's Advice to His Son* (1818) was intended for upper-class boys.[41]

These kinds of books are less about individual self-actualization and more about how one can become a contributing member of society. For example, in times of national crisis, books of practical advice have appeared. In the early days of World War II, Munro Leaf, who in *The Story of Ferdinand* (1936) had introduced the world to the beloved pacifist bull, wrote a conduct book for children about how they could help with the war effort. According to an Ellen Lewis Buell's review in the *New York Times Book Review*, *A War-Time Handbook for Young Americans* (1942) offered specific advice such as remaining cheerful and cooperative, "learning the rudiments of first aid, gardening, running errands, collecting salvage, and ... learning about one's community and how to be a good neighbor."[42] It is not too much of a stretch to see conduct books as the forerunners of today's ubiquitous self-help and advice books aimed at children and teenagers on topics ranging from developing healthy eating habits and positive relationships to doing one's part to combat climate change and promote social justice.

PEOPLE, PLACES, AND EVENTS

Courtesy and conduct books were not the only kinds of nonfiction available to young people between the sixteenth and nineteenth centuries. Biographies and character sketches were offered as well, providing exemplars of how one should live or what role one might play in society. John Foxe's *Actes and Monuments*, popularly known as the *Book of Martyrs*, was first published in 1563. Designed to stir up anti-Catholic sentiment, primarily in England, the book was not originally intended for children, but it was nevertheless widely read by them.[43] As Gillian Avery explains, children "were enthralled by the brisk narrative, the dialogue, and above all by the gruesome power of the woodcut illustrations."[44] The same was true of Sir Thomas North's 1579 translation of Plutarch's *Lives of the Noble Greeks and Romans*. Avery again: "Children enjoyed Plutarch's *Lives* not only because of the heroic past that they described, but also because of the vivid narrative, the anecdotes, and the deft choice of detail."[45] In 1762-1763 John Newbery brought out a child-friendly *Plutarch's Lives*, and Benjamin Tabart published *The Juvenile Plutarch* in 1801.[46] Clearly, then as now, children were captivated by compelling stories about real people, whether famous figures from antiquity or Protestant martyrs.

Though neither Plutarch's *Lives* nor Foxe's *Book of Martyrs* was written for children, by the late seventeenth century children had access to biographical works tailored specifically to them. One such work, no doubt inspired by the success of the *Book of Martyrs*, was James Janeway's *A Token for Children being an Exact Account of the Conversion, Holy and Exemplary Lives, and Joyful Deaths, of Several Young Children* (1672). Janeway was a Puritan minister and writer whose purpose, according to M. O. Grenby, was "to warn children against worldly temptations and point out the hard path toward salvation."[47] If this sounds unusually harsh to contemporary ears, it should be noted the book remained popular for nearly 200 years.[48] Moreover, in 1700 it was adapted for American children by no less a personage than Cotton Mather, who one-upped Janeway on both the length and the severity of the title: *A token, for the children of New-England, or, Some examples of children, in whom the fear of God was remarkably budding, before they dyed, in several parts of New-England: preserved and published, for the encouragement of piety in other children.*[49] We can understand Mather's attraction to Janeway's book if we reflect on the larger Puritan enterprise. As Anne Scott MacLeod explains, the Puritans had a singular purpose in writing literature for children:

> It was not what is recognized now as "children's literature"; it was meant entirely for instruction, and religious instruction in a difficult doctrine at that. Yet it was written for children and designed to match children's capabilities and tastes as the authors understood them.[50]

These mini-biographies of real children suited the purpose perfectly.

Another popular genre in the sixteenth and seventeenth centuries was character studies, "brief accounts of emblematic professional, social, and moral types."[51] One of the earliest and most popular was John Earle's *Microcosmographie*. First published in 1628, the book described, not actual individuals, but various types of people: "the Antiquary, the Church-Papist, the Cook, the Pretender to Learning, the Shop-keeper, the Plodding Student, and the like."[52] These kinds of books persisted into the twentieth century—and beyond. For example, E. F. Lucas and Francis D. Bedford's picturebook *Four-and-Twenty Toilers* (1900) depicts various occupations, including shipbuilder, cobbler, veterinarian, and stevedore; Nina Scheider's *While Susie Sleeps* (1948) relates the nocturnal duties of a baker, a farmer, and a milkman; and Lois Lenski's Mr. Small series (1934-1962) features a cowboy, a pilot, and a police officer, among others.[53] It is not too much of a stretch to see the character types in Earle's *Microcosmographie* and these other books as forerunners of the people in *Mister Rogers' Neighborhood*. Children have always been fascinated by what adults do, and especially what they do for a living, so it is not surprising that character studies have been and continue to be a popular genre.

Of course, the popularity of biographies has persisted as well although their purpose and focus have changed to reflect the values of society at any given time. While many biographies of the sixteenth and seventeenth centuries were intended to provide moral and religious instruction, by the nineteenth century, especially in the United States, biographies served a more nationalistic purpose. The young, newly independent country wanted to instruct its young in its national heroes, and Mason Locke "Parson" Weems's *A History of the Life and Death, Virtues and Exploits of General George Washington* (1800) fit the bill perfectly. Weems was a minister and also a traveling bookseller whose book reflected the tremendous esteem in which the first president was held by citizens of the new republic. Weems is credited with some of the famous (and perhaps apocryphal) stories associated with Washington, including the anecdote about the six-year-old boy chopping down his father's cherry tree and then, being noble and good, was unable to lie about it.[54] The good parson also wrote biographies of Francis Marion, Benjamin Franklin, and William Penn.[55] Before establishing himself as a serious writer for adults, Nathaniel Hawthorne also wrote for children, including some nonfiction. *Grandfather's Chair* (1840), *Famous Old People* (1841), and *Liberty Tree* (1841) may be seen as part of the nationalistic project in that these books presented children with entertaining, and partly imagined, stories about people and events from American history.[56] *Biographical Stories for Children* (1842) offered brief biographical sketches of such famous figures as Queen Christina of Sweden, Benjamin Franklin, Oliver Cromwell, and Samuel Johnson.[57] Jacob and John Abbott published a series of popular and critically acclaimed biographies in the middle part of the nineteenth century on such figures as Julius Caesar, Cleopatra, Queen Elizabeth, and Josephine. In fact, their biographies were so well regarded, they received a fan letter from President Abraham Lincoln, who praised the books for their brevity and accessibility.[58] Since the nineteenth century, the popularity of biography has not waned nor has its role diminished in providing lessons from the histories of famous, and sometimes not-so-famous, lives. Early in the twentieth century, for example, E. Boyd Smith published *The Story of Pocahontas and Captain John Smith* (1906), a picturebook for young readers.[59] In 1952 Grosset and Dunlap began publishing its Signature series featuring biographies of famous people from history.[60] And in 1988 Russell Freedman was awarded the Newbery Medal for *Lincoln: A Photobiography* (1987), one of only six nonfiction books—and, as of this writing, the most recent—to win the Newbery. The other five? All were biographies except for one—Hendrik Willem van Loon's *The Story of Mankind* (1921), a history book and the very first Newbery winner.[61]

If the biographies mentioned thus far suggest a disproportionate emphasis on white men, it is because that was largely the case. It would be a mistake, however, to think there were no biographies of individuals belonging to other groups published prior to, say, the mid-twentieth century. As early as 1804, Mary Pilkington's *Memoirs of Celebrated Female Characters* was published in England. In the United States, Laura Richards published biographies of several eminent women, including Florence Nightingale (1909), Elizabeth Fry (1916), and Abigail Adams (1917).[62] In 1934, Cornelia Meigs won the Newbery Medal for *Invincible Louisa: The Story of the Author of Little Women* (1933).[63] Moreover, as Kiefer and Wilson note, "Biography was one of the first genres to represent people of color to children." They cite as examples biographies of Nehru and Sun Yat Sen, published in the 1940s, and Catherine Owens Peare's *Mary McLeod Bethune*, published in 1951.[64] Also published in 1951 is Elizabeth Yates's *Amos Fortune, Free Man* (1951), which won the Newbery Medal in 1952. *Amos Fortune* is a fictionalized biography based on the true story of Amos Fortune, an African prince who was captured and sold into slavery at the age of fifteen. After spending most of his life as an enslaved person, he was finally able to buy his freedom at the age of sixty.[65] There were biographies by African American authors as well. Beginning with the Harlem Renaissance, leading African American writers and thinkers felt that African American children needed to become aware of their history and their proud heritage, and they began writing historical and biographical works in order to address that need. An important venue for this enterprise early on was *The Brownies' Book*, the first magazine created specifically for African American young people. The magazine was founded for the purpose of providing a corrective to the racist stereotypes seen in many mainstream children's magazines of the time, like the popular *St. Nicholas*.[66] *The Brownies' Book* (subtitled *A Monthly Magazine for Children of the Sun*) featured, in addition to fiction and poetry, nonfiction stories on the history and accomplishments of Africans and African Americans, including some children.[67] Jessie Redmon Fauset, one of the founding editors (along with W. E. B. DuBois and Augustus Granville Dill), recruited well-known authors to write for the magazine. Langston Hughes, Nella Larsen, and Georgia Douglas Johnson all contributed to it at different times.[68] Some of the biographical subjects were Phillis Wheatley (the first published African American woman), Sojourner Truth (an abolitionist and women's rights activist), and Bert Williams (a famous Vaudeville performer).[69] Though it was short-lived—it lasted from January 1920 to December 1921—the magazine was highly regarded in the African American community for its quality and its impact. African American writers would go on to publish a number of nonfiction books highlighting the history and achievements of African Americans. Arna Bontemps, for example authored biographies aimed at teenagers; among his subjects were Frederick Douglass, Booker T. Washington, and George Washington Carver. And Langston Hughes (with Steven C. Tracy) wrote a biography of the groundbreaking opera singer Marian Anderson, *Marian Anderson: Famous Concert Singer* (1954).[70]

Biography and history are closely intertwined and share a similar goal of informing children about their own history and culture as well as the history and culture of others. Both genres became prevalent during the eighteenth century. John Newbery published *A New History of England, from the Invasion of Julius Caesar to the Present Time* (1761) and soon thereafter appeared Oliver Goldsmith's *An History of England, in a Series of Letters from a Nobleman to His Son* (1764).[71] William Godwin produced *The History of England, for the Use of Schools and Young Persons* in 1806, and a few years later Louisa Brown offered her poetic take on the British monarchs in *Historical Questions on the Kings of England, in Verse* (1815).[72] Elizabeth Penrose, known as "Mrs. Markham," wrote *A History of England from the First Invasion by the Romans to the End of the Reign of George III* (1823) and followed that up with *A History of France* (1828). Mrs. Markham was known for expurgating the more distasteful parts of history, the "horrors" and conflicts, because she considered them unsuitable subjects for children.[73] On the other side of the Atlantic, history books for American children began appearing around this same time. One of the most famous was Samuel G. Goodrich's *Tales of Peter Parley about America* (1827), the first of a series on U.S. history. The prolific Jacob Abbott wrote a series of books on American history, from *Aboriginal America* (1860) to *War of the Revolution* (1864).[74] Thomas Wentworth Higginson, now mostly remembered as Emily Dickinson's friend and mentor, was also an author and a staunch abolitionist. After the Civil War he published *Young Folks' History of the United States* (1875), which was widely reviewed and widely praised.[75] In the United States, the twentieth century saw continued interest in historical writing for children and not just American history. Eva March Tappan, an American author, published *The Story of the Greek People* in 1908[76] and *The Story of the Roman People* in 1910.[77] And as previously mentioned, the first Newbery Medal winner was a work of history, Hendrik Willem van Loon's *The Story of Mankind* (1921). Random House began issuing its Landmark Books series in 1950. Initially focused on American history, the series was expanded two years later to include world history as well.[78] By the mid-twentieth century, Harlem Renaissance writers were producing books for children on African American history. Arna Bontemps, for example, wrote *The Story of the Negro* (1948), which had the distinction of being named a Jane Addams Children's Book Award winner as well as a Newbery Honor Book.[79] Langston Hughes also wrote historical works for children, publishing, among others, *The First Book of the Negroes* (1952) and *First Book of Africa* (1966).[80]

In addition to being interested in famous people and historical events, children have long been curious about new and unfamiliar places, and travel books have helped satisfy this curiosity. The rise of the middle class and advances in modes of transportation (i.e., steamships and railroads) meant that people in the eighteenth and nineteenth centuries had more money and leisure time to devote to travel and more efficient means of doing so. It is no surprise then that books on travel became more prevalent.[81] An early example is Thomas

Boreman's *Gigantick Histories* (1740-1743). Ironically titled, these volumes were actually miniature guidebooks to London.[82] According to Evelyn Wenzel, travel books were "the most ubiquitous informational material" of the mid-to late-nineteenth century in the United States, and most followed the same pattern: "a family or an adult escorting a group of children takes a series of trips to a foreign land (usually several countries of Europe); the children are instructed by the adult who, of course, attends to morals as well as to mind."[83] Many of these books were published as a series. Some representative titles that were popular in the nineteenth century included Samuel G. Goodrich's *Tale of Peter Parley about America* (1827), Jacob Abbott's *Rollo's Travels* (1840), Horace Scudder's *Doings of the Bodley Family in Town and Country* (1875), Thomas W. Knox's *The Boy Travellers in the Far East, or Adventures of Two Youths in a Journey to Japan and China* (1879), and Edward Everett Hale and Miss Susan Hale's *A Family Flight through France, Germany, Norway and Switzerland* (1881).[84]

SCIENCE AND TECHNOLOGY

Young people have long had a fascination with topics related to science and technology. Animal books, especially, have been and continue to be popular. An early example is Thomas Boreman's *A Description of Three Hundred Animals* (1730). Influenced by medieval bestiaries, the book features animals both real and imagined, from tigers to frogs and unicorns to monsters.[85] Other lavishly illustrated books, like Thomas Bewick's *General History of Quadrapeds* (1790) and Robert Mudie's *The Feathered Tribes of the British Isles* (1814), though intended primarily for adults, were surely enjoyed by children as well.[86] The publisher Benjamin Tabart offered *The Wonders of the Microscope* (1804), which featured detailed illustrations from Robert Hooke's adult book *Micrographia* (1665) and became a bestseller.[87] Margaret Gatty, the Victorian children's writer and science writer, used her books to argue against Darwin's theory of evolution. Her *Parables from Nature* (1855), for example, depicted God as being present in nature and nature as a rich source for moral lessons.[88] Moreover, the book described many aspects of the natural world, not just animals, suggesting that children were potentially interested in a wide range of science-related topics. In the United States, the prolific Jacob Abbott, though best known for his biographies and history books, also wrote a series of science books: *Heat, Light, Force*, and *Water and Land* (1871-1872).[89] An especially unique take on the topic can be seen in Arabella B. Buckley's *The Fairy-Land of Science* (1879), in which she depicts the forces of energy as sprites.[90] In the twentieth century, many science experts produced books for children in the natural and the physical sciences. Harvard astronomy professor William Maxwell Reed, for instance, wrote *The Stars for Sam* (1931) for his young nephew.[91] As previously noted, the passage of the National Defense Education Act in 1958 led to publishers producing many new science book series, including the popular and innovative Let's Read and Find Out series from the publisher Thomas Y. Crowell. Aimed at younger readers (kindergarten through second grade), the books taught basic science concepts using accessible vocabulary and colorful pictures.[92] More recently, advances in the technology for color printing have led to a number of visually stunning science books.[93] Some examples include Seymour Simon's *Saturn* (1985) and *Jupiter* (1985), which features NASA photographs that are in the public domain, Patricia Lauber's *Volcano: The Eruption and Healing of Mount St. Helens* (1986),[94] Nic Bishop's *Spiders* (2007), and Sy Montgomery and Nic Bishop's *Kakapo Rescue: Saving the World's Strangest Parrot* (2010). In terms of innovative narratives, we need look no further than Joanna Cole and Bruce Degen's Magic School Bus series. Using a fictional frame story of school children going on fantastical field trips, the books provide a healthy measure of nonfiction scientific information as well. The series, which began with *The Magic School Bus at the Waterworks* (1986), became enormously popular and remains a staple even today (the most recent title was published in 2020).[95] Scientific advances mean there are always new frontiers to be explored through books. Growing awareness of crucial issues facing humankind—such as climate change, ecological disasters, and deadly diseases—has generated new books to introduce children to these topics.

Closely related to scientific advancements are technological innovations, and often one drives the other. Not surprisingly, many young people are intrigued by technology—both its current state and its future potential—but this is certainly not a new development. As machines became more prevalent in the twentieth century, books on machinery proliferated as well. Evelyn Wenzel notes that a reading list from 1939 recommended the following titles: *Big Fellow, the Story of a Road-Making Machine*, *Story of the Submarine*, *Historic Railroads*, *The Dirigible Book*, and *Automobiles*.[96] During World War II, books that showcased the nation's military hardware, like Creighton Peet and Fritz Kredel's *Defending America*, were popular, especially among older boys.[97] Books on the technology being developed for space travel coincided with the race to the moon in the 1960s. Nowadays, books on computers and other digital technologies are plentiful. And, of course, books on the history of famous technologies and their sociological implications can be both enlightening and engaging. Examples include Russell Freedman's *The Wright Brothers: How They Invented the Airplane* (1991), Sue Macy's *Wheels of Change: How Women Rode the Bicycle to Freedom (with a Few Flat Tires Along the Way)* (2011), and Steve Sheinkin's *Bomb: The Race to Build—and Steal—the World's Most Dangerous Weapon* (2012).

As we have seen, the nonfiction genres popular with children today have a long and rich history. Forms and formats have changed, and as in previous centuries topics and approaches have evolved to be more inclusive and reflect the concerns and values of the twenty-first century. In many ways we are now in a golden age of children's nonfiction. The increasing attention nonfiction has received in the last thirty or forty years has been spurred in part by the establishment of nonfiction awards and a steady growth in the number of reviews. Those are the topics to which we shall turn our attention in the next chapter.

NOTES

1. Anne Scott MacLeod, "Children's Literature in America from the Puritan Beginnings to 1870," in *Children's Literature: An Illustrated History*, ed. Peter Hunt (Oxford, UK: Oxford University Press, 1995), 129.
2. Ibid., 109.
3. Ibid., 119.
4. Laura Laffrado, *Hawthorne's Literature for Children* (Athens: University of Georgia Press, 1992), 1.
5. Evelyn L. Wenzel, "Historical Backgrounds," in *Beyond Fact: Nonfiction for Children and Young People*, ed. Jo Carr (Chicago: American Library Association, 1982), 24.
6. Ibid., 22.
7. Ibid., 24–25.
8. James Cross Giblin, "More Than Just the Facts: A Hundred Years of Children's Nonfiction," *The Horn Book Magazine* 76, no. 4 (2000): 418–19.
9. Michael Cart, *Young Adult Literature: From Romance to Realism*, fourth ed. (Chicago: ALA Neal-Schuman, 2022), 201.
10. Giblin, 419.
11. Cart, 201.
12. Ibid., 202.
13. Sylvia M. Vardell, *Children's Literature in Action: A Librarian's Guide* (Westport, CT: Libraries Unlimited, 2008), 235.
14. Jack Zipes et al., eds., *The Norton Anthology of Children's Literature: The Traditions in English* (New York: W. W. Norton & Company, 2005), 7.
15. Ibid., 7.
16. Ibid., 7.
17. Vardell, 235.
18. Zipes et al., 7.
19. Ibid., 235.
20. Ibid., 235.
21. Zipes et al., 7.
22. Ibid., xxvii.
23. Humphrey Carpenter and Mari Prichard, *The Oxford Campanion to Children's Literature* (Oxford, UK: Oxford University Press, 1999), 376.
24. Leonard A. Marcus, *Minders of Make-Believe: Idealists, Entrepreneurs, and the Shapiing of American Children's Literature* (New York: Houghton Mifflin, 2008), 3.
25. Carpenter and Prichard, 376.
26. Marcus, 3.
27. Ibid., 3.
28. Ibid., 3.

29. M. O. Grenby, "The Origins of Children's Literature," in *The Cambridge Companion to Children's Literature*, ed. M. O. Grenby, and Andrea Immel (Cambridge, UK: Cambridge University Press, 2009), 11.
30. Vardell, 235.
31. Zipes et al., 1420.
32. Ibid., 1422.
33. Zipes et al., xxvii.
34. Ibid., 1416.
35. Ibid., 1416.
36. Grenby, "The Origins of Children's Literature," 4.
37. Zipes et al., 1417.
38. Grenby, 4.
39. Zipes et al. 1417.
40. Ibid., 1418.
41. Ibid., 1418.
42. Ellen Lewis Buell, "A War-Time Handbook for Young Americans," review of A War-Time Handbook for Young Americans, *The New York Times Book Review* 1942, 9.
43. Gillian Avery, "The Beginnings of Children's Reading to C.1700," in *Children's Literature: An Illustrated History*, ed. Peter Hunt (Oxford, UK: Oxford University Press, 1995), 21.
44. Ibid., 21.
45. Ibid., 19.
46. Carpenter and Prichard, 252.
47. Grenby, 4-5.
48. Ibid., 5.
49. Cotton Mather, *A Token, for the Children of New-England* (Boston: Timothy Green, 1700), Digital Collections, Yale University Library, accessed October 17, 2023, https://collections.library.yale.edu/catalog/15497368.
50. MacLeod, "Children's Literature in America from the Puritan Beginnings to 1870," 103.
51. Seth Lerer, *Children's Literature: A Reader's History from Aesop to Harry Potter* (Chicago: University of Chicago Press, 2008), 85.
52. Ibid., 85.
53. Lois Palmer, "While Susie Sleeps," review of While Susie Sleeps, *The New York Times Book Review*, April 4, 1948, 29; Wenzel, "Historical Backgrounds," 23.
54. "Mason Locke Weems," *Wikipedia*, accessed October 17, 2023, https://en.wikipedia.org/wiki/Mason_Locke_Weems.
55. Ibid.
56. Laffrado, *Hawthorne's Literature for Children*, 1, 6.
57. Ibid., 1, 41.
58. "Makers of History," *Heritage History*, accessed October 20, 2023, https://www.heritage-history.com/index.php?c=library&s=ser-dir&f=series_makershistory.
59. Wenzel, 22.
60. Marcus, *Minders of Make-Believe*, 190.
61. Association for Library Service to Children, "Newbery Medal & Honor Books, 1922-Present," American Library Association, accessed October 18, 2023, https://

www.ala.org/alsc/sites/ala.org.alsc/files/content/awardsgrants/bookmedia/newberymedal/newbery-medals-honors-1922-present.pdf.
62. Carpenter and Prichard, 252.
63. Ibid., 252.
64. Barbara Kiefer and Melissa I. Wilson, "Nonfiction Literature for Children: Old Assumptions and New Directions," in *Handbook of Research on Children's and Young Adult Literature*, ed. Shelby Anne Wolf et al. (New York: Routledge, 2010), 293.
65. "Amos Fortune, Free Man," *Wikipedia*, accessed October 19, 2023, https://en.wikipedia.org/wiki/Amos_Fortune,_Free_Man.
66. Zipes et al., 1516.
67. Ibid., 1516.
68. "The Brownies' Book," *Wikipedia*, accessed October 19, 2023, https://en.wikipedia.org/wiki/The_Brownies%27_Book.
69. "Arna Bontemps," *Wikipedia*, accessed October 19, 2023, https://en.wikipedia.org/wiki/Arna_Bontemps.
70. "Langston Hughes," *Wikipedia*, accessed October 20, 2023, https://en.wikipedia.org/wiki/Langston_Hughes.
71. Carpenter and Prichard, 252.
72. Ibid., 252.
73. "Mrs. Markham," *Wikipedia*, accessed October 19, 2023, https://en.wikipedia.org/wiki/Mrs_Markham.
74. "Jacob Abbott," *Wikipedia*, accessed October 20, 2023, https://en.wikipedia.org/wiki/Jacob_Abbott#American_History_Series.
75. Wenzel, "Historical Backgrounds," 20.
76. Ibid., 26.
77. "Eva March Tappan," *Wikipedia*, accessed October 19, 2023, https://en.wikipedia.org/wiki/Eva_March_Tappan.
78. Marcus, *Minders of Make-Believe*, 187-90.
79. "Arna Bontemps."
80. "Langston Hughes."
81. Wenzel, "Historical Backgrounds," 20.
82. Eric J. Johnson, "Chronology," in *The Cambridge Companion to Children's Literature*, ed. M. O. Grenby and Andrea Immel (Cambridge, UK: Cambridge University Press, 2009), xviii.
83. Wenzel, "Historical Backgrounds," 18.
84. Ibid., 19.
85. "A Description of Three Hundred Animals," British Library, accessed October 23, 2023, https://www.bl.uk/collection-items/a-description-of-three-hundred-animals.
86. M. O. Grenby and Andrea Immel, eds., *The Cambridge Companion to Children's Literature* (Cambridge, U. K.: Cambridge University Press, 2009), xix-xx.
87. Zipes et al., 1419-20.
88. "Margaret Gatty," *Wikipedia*, accessed October 23, 2023, https://en.wikipedia.org/wiki/Margaret_Gatty.
89. Wenzel, "Historical Backgrounds," 20.
90. Ibid., 21.
91. Ibid., 25.
92. Giblin, "More Than Just the Facts: A Hundred Years of Children's Nonfiction," 419.

93. Marcus, *Minders of Make-Believe*, 307.
94. Ibid., 307.
95. Ibid., 308.
96. Wenzel, "Historical Backgrounds," 24.
97. Marcus, *Minders of Make-Believe*, 169, 71.

2

Awards and Reviews

Librarians generally take a multi-pronged approach to evaluating children's and young adult materials to include in their collections. Nothing can beat reading and evaluating a book for oneself, but we're all limited by our own biases and, in any case, we can't read everything. Fortunately, there are other sources to draw on, including colleagues, patrons, award lists, and reviews. A book that has received positive reviews, garnered awards, and been highly recommended deserves serious consideration for being added to our library's collection. By the same token, if a book has received none of those things, we might conclude our limited budget resources are better spent elsewhere. If a book has received some positive and some negative response, then we'll have to scrutinize it more closely and decide whether it is a good fit for our library and patrons. Toward that end, this chapter will consider various awards and review sources related to nonfiction for children and young adults, and will discuss the pros and cons inherent in both. Subsequent chapters will discuss specific criteria librarians can use in evaluating nonfiction books.

AWARDS

The prizing of children's and young adult literature is a two-sided medal, so to speak, having both positive and negative consequences. On the plus side, awards can promote quality literature for young people, enhance literacy among young people, and result in greater recognition and economic benefits for authors and publishers of award-winning books. On the negative side, as Kenneth Kidd and Joseph Thomas point out in their edited volume *Prizing Children's Literature*, awards may not actually lead to the production of "good" literature and can be elitist in favoring authors and illustrators from (or approved of by) the dominant culture. Furthermore, the proliferation of awards (currently there are over 300 awards for English-language texts and authors) has rendered the awards virtually meaningless.[1] Nonetheless, they admit that, in spite of these problems, "prizing has been a remarkably effective mechanism for publicity, sales, and scandal, if not also for the production of 'literature,' in the form of instant, modern classics."[2] As a tool for collection development, awards lists (including almost always honor books as well) are enormously useful, but certainly not the be-all and end-all of the selection process. In using any tool, it's best to understand what it does well and what its potential pitfalls are.

Awards for children's and young adult literature have a proud history, with the children's awards having a much longer history than their young adult counterparts. As Kidd and Thomas point out, librarians along with publishers and editors played a key role in establishing and administering these awards, more so than teachers, with the result that the awards helped enhance the stature of both children's literature and the profession of librarianship.[3] The American Library Association (ALA) awarded the first John Newbery Medal in 1922 and the first Randolph Caldecott Medal in 1938. Given ALA's leadership role in instituting and implementing these awards, it's surprising they were such latecomers to the nonfiction party. In this section, we will look at the awards that are exclusively for nonfiction, then the awards that have a nonfiction category, and finally at awards that do not have a nonfiction category but consider nonfiction to be eligible in their other categories.

One of the earliest awards created exclusively for children's nonfiction is The Children's Book Guild Nonfiction Award. The first award was given in 1977—to the author and illustrator David Macauley. The award is administered by the Children's Book Guild of Washington, DC, the members of which are professionals in the DC metro area who are involved in the various disciplines related to children's literature. Unlike many awards that focus on a single book, this award "honors an author or author-illustrator whose total work has contributed significantly to the quality of nonfiction for children."[4] Authors must be American, and illustrators are eligible only if they have written as well as illustrated their books.[5] Recent winners have included such esteemed nonfiction authors as Sy Montgomery (science writer), Candace Fleming (biography, history, science), Carole Boston Weatherford (history), Steve Sheinkin (suspenseful history), and Don Brown (graphic nonfiction). The award criteria and a full list of winners are available on the award website. This is an especially useful list for collection development purposes as it provides an easy way for librarians to see who's who in the world of children's and young adult nonfiction. One downside is that the list provides only names, no biographies or lists of books; you'll have to go elsewhere, such as to author and publisher websites, for that information. But the list is a great place to start.

The next major prize for children's and young adult nonfiction was the Orbis Pictus Award, established by the National Council of Teachers of English (NCTE) and first given in 1990. The inaugural award went to *The Great Little*

Madison (1989) by Jean Fritz. Part of the Unforgettable Americans series, *The Great Little Madison* is a biography for intermediate-level readers of the Founding Father and fourth president of the United States. The term "Orbis Pictus," as was noted in the previous chapter, was the title of Johannes Amos Comenius's 1658 work, considered by many to be the first work of children's literature and children's nonfiction. Library educator Sylvia Vardell, in her excellent discussion of Comenius's book, mentions that she served on the proposal committee for NCTE's nonfiction award and that she was the one who suggested the name "Orbis Pictus."[6] The award is intended for a book published or distributed in the United States or its territories in the preceding year "which has as its central purpose the sharing of information" and which is "written, designed, and organized to interpret documentable, factual material for children."[7] Poetry, adaptations of adult books, reissues, historical fiction, and folklore are not eligible, and the award criteria explicitly state that the committee should consider potential contribution to the K–8 curriculum, roughly ages five to thirteen years. Up to five honor books are named each year and up to eight additional recommended books. The complete list of winners, honor books, and recommended books is available on the award website. Over thirty years' worth of titles are now available, so this is a rich resource for librarians interested in beefing up their nonfiction collections.

It was ten years later that ALA established its first award for children's nonfiction. The Robert F. Sibert Medal was first given in 2001, and the winner was Marc Aronson's *Sir Walter Raleigh and the Quest for El Dorado* (2000), a biography of the Elizabethan poet, courtier, and adventurer. The award is named for the long-time president of Bound to Stay Bound Books, Inc., an organization whose primary mission is "[t]o provide through constant improvement, the best juvenile books, media products and related services to the libraries of North America, as closely matched to their needs as possible and as economically as possible."[8] The award, which is administered by the Association for Library Service to Children (a division of ALA), goes to an informational book published in the United States in English the preceding year, and all of the authors and illustrators credited on the title page must be citizens or residents of the United States.[9] In theory, the award can go to any nonfiction book intended for children ages birth through 14 years; however, in practice, the award has typically gone to books for intermediate or young adult readers. Along with the winner, honor books are usually named as well. The list of winners and honor books and the award criteria are available on the award website.

The YALSA Award for Excellence in Nonfiction for Young Adults has the distinction of being the most recently established nonfiction award (as well as the award with the longest name). Administered by the Young Adult Library Services Association (also a division of ALA), the award was first given in 2010—to Deborah Heiligman's *Charles and Emma: The Darwins' Leap of Faith*

(2009), a dual biography of the famous naturalist and his devoutly religious wife. The award is intended for a nonfiction title, available in English in the United States, for young adults, which YALSA defines as ages 12 to 18 years. Up to five finalists are named in early December, and the winner is announced in January. The award criteria state, among other things, that "[t]he title must include excellent writing, research, presentation and readability for young adults."[10] Interestingly, nothing is said about illustrations although one might interpret "presentation" as including graphics. The full set of award criteria and a list of winners and finalists are available on the award website.

A genre-specific nonfiction book award is the Norman A. Sugarman Children's Biography Award, administered by the Cleveland Public Library. Established in 1998, the award is given biennially to an author and/or illustrator of a new biography for children grades K-8; typically honor awards are given as well. The award criteria and the most recent winners and honor books are available on the award website.[11] A complete list of winners and honor books is available on the Sugarman Award page on the TeachingBooks website.[12]

A subject-specific book award is the Mathical Book Prize, given by the Simons Laufer Mathematical Sciences Institute in partnership with the National Council of Teachers of English and the National Council of Teachers of Mathematics and in cooperation with the Children's Book Council. Book prizes, which typically go to both fiction and nonfiction titles, are given in five categories based on grade level: pre-K, K-2, 3-5, 6-8, and 9-12. A downloadable list of winners for each year going back to 2015 is available on the Mathical Book Prize website.[13] Two additional resources for identifying subject-specific nonfiction titles are not awards per se but rather lists of notable books in the sciences and the social sciences. The National Science Teaching Association in cooperation with the Children's Book Council publishes a list of Outstanding Science Trade Books for Students K-12 each year. Lists for each year going back to 1996 are available on the association's website.[14] The National Council for the Social Studies, also in cooperation with the Children's Book Council, publishes a list of Notable Social Studies Trade Books for Young People each year. Membership in the association is required to access the most recent lists, but a database of titles from the 2000-2019 lists (as of this writing) is freely available on the association website. The database allows browsing by reading level or by National Social Studies Standards Theme.[15]

Some awards that are not exclusively for nonfiction do have nonfiction categories, and their lists of winners and honor books can be useful resources for collection development. The Boston Globe-Horn Book Awards were first given in 1967 in two categories, Picture Book and Fiction and Poetry.[16] They have had a nonfiction category since 1976,[17] the same year Milton Meltzer's famous essay appeared in *The Horn Book*, lamenting the lack of prizes for children's nonfiction. In retrospect, we might wonder whether Meltzer's complaint spurred the administrators of the Boston Globe-Horn Book Awards to establish a nonfiction category or his essay served as a cleverly timed promotion for an award that was already in the works. It may have been a bit of both. In any case, the first winner was Alfred Tamarin and Shirley Glubok's *Voyaging to Cathay: Americans in the China Trade* (1976), a look at the early years of contact between the United States and China from the late eighteenth to the early nineteenth century. The award guidelines stipulate that to be eligible for consideration, books must have been published in the United States between June 1 of the previous year and May 31 of the current year. The award committee is made up of three judges appointed by the editor-in-chief of *The Horn Book* each year.[18] Specific criteria are not provided on the award website, but a list of previous winners and honor books is.

Another award with a nonfiction category is The Golden Kite Awards, administered by the Society of Children's Book Writers and Illustrators. In fact, there are two nonfiction categories: Nonfiction Text for Younger Readers and Nonfiction Text for Older Readers (although 2018 was the first year the Nonfiction award was split into two categories). The first nonfiction award was given in 1978—to Robert McClung's *Peeper, First Voice of Spring* (1977), a book about tree frogs.[19] Titles for consideration may be submitted by authors, illustrators, and publishers. Books must have been written in or translated into English and must have been published during the previous year.[20] A list of winners in all categories is available on Wikipedia's "Golden Kite" page.

Many other awards for children's and young adult literature do not have a separate category for nonfiction, but they do consider nonfiction to be eligible in the categories they do have. It is worth keeping an eye out for nonfiction titles among these award winners and honor books. The major awards in the United States are the John Newbery Medal for best work of literature for children up to age 14, the Randolph Caldecott Medal for best picturebook for children up to age 14 (although in practice most winners are for children between the ages of four and seven), and the Michael L. Printz Award for best book for young adults, ages 12 to 18. As already noted, although the first Newbery Medal went to an informational book, the award committees since then have been stingy about giving the award to a nonfiction work (though a number of nonfiction works have been named honor books). As Jonathan Hunt notes, the Caldecott committees have been more generous in recognizing nonfiction books among both winners and honor books.[21] The Printz is a much more recently established award, having first been given in 2000. To date, only one work of nonfiction has won the award, John Lewis, Andrew Aydin, and Nate Powell's *March: Book Three* (2016), a graphic memoir of Lewis' experiences in the Civil Rights Movement.

Two helpful collection development tools are ALSC's Book and Media Awards Shelf[22] and YALSA's Book Finder.[23] Both will allow you to search by award, author, genre, and award year although they do have certain limitations. Books of poetry, for example, often show up tagged as "nonfiction," and honor books are sometimes tagged as winners. Overall, though, they're both enormously useful resources for collection development.

A non-ALA affiliated award is the Charlotte Zolotow Award for the author of the best children's picturebook published each year. Administered by the Cooperative Children's Book Center in the School of Education at the University of Wisconsin–Madison, the award has been given since 1998. A list of winners, honor books, and highly commended titles is available on the award's website.[24] By far, most of the winners and honor books are works of fiction, but occasionally a nonfiction title appears. The 2016 award, for example, went to Margarita Engle and Rafael López's *Drum Dream Girl: How One Girl's Courage Changed Music* (2015), the story of how Millo Castro Zaldarriaga became the first female drummer in Cuba and went on to become world famous.

Other awards worth exploring for nonfiction winners and honor books include those with a special focus, or as Kidd and Thomas call them, awards that "prioritize social vision."[25] The ones affiliated with ALA are indexed in the Book and Media Awards Shelf and the Book Finder, discussed above. The Coretta Scott King Book Awards, administered by ALA's Coretta Scott King Book Awards Round Table, are given each year to "outstanding African American authors and illustrators of books for children and young adults that demonstrate an appreciation of African American culture and universal human values."[26] As Michelle Martin points out in her excellent study of African American children's picturebooks, the Coretta Scott King Author Awards have typically gone to novels, biographies, and other kinds of informational books; the Illustrator Awards, on the other hand, have come from a wider variety of genres[27] (although, to be sure, biography and history are certainly represented). To take one example, a recent winner of both the Author and Illustrator Awards is a work of history, *Unspeakable: The Tulsa Race Massacre* (2021) by Carole Boston Weatherford and Floyd Cooper.

The Pura Belpré Award is presented each year "to a Latino/Latina writer and illustrator whose work best portrays, affirms, and celebrates the Latino cultural experience in an outstanding work of literature for children and youth."[28] The award, which is administered by ALSC, YALSA, and REFORMA (the National Association to Promote Library and Information Services to Latinos and the Spanish-Speaking), has had both fiction and nonfiction winners and honor books. A recent Honor Book for Youth Illustration, for example, is a biography, *Phenomenal AOC: The Roots and Rise of Alexandria Ocasio-Cortez* (2022) by Anika Aldamuy Denise and Loris Lora.

The Stonewall Book Awards, administered by ALA's Rainbow Round Table, has been giving the Mike Morgan and Larry Romans Children's and Young Adult Literature Award since 2010. Intended to recognize excellence in LGBTQIA+ books, this annual award includes winners and honor books.[29] Though most of the recent recipients have been works of fiction, a few years ago Robin Stevenson's *Pride: Celebrating Diversity & Community* (2016) was named an honor book. Perhaps nonfiction will gain more traction in the years to come (there is a separate nonfiction category for adult books).

Rise: A Feminist Book Project for Ages 0–18 (formerly known as the Amelia Bloomer Project) is an initiative of ALA's Social Responsibilities Round Table and the Feminist Task Force. Since 2002, the project has been compiling a list "of well-written and well-illustrated books with significant feminist content, intended for young readers (ages birth through 18)."[30] There are categories for early readers, middle grade, and young adult, and within each of these categories are subcategories for fiction and nonfiction. A recent early reader nonfiction title is Traci N. Todd and Shannon Wright's *Holding Her Own: The Exceptional Life of Jackie Ormes* (2023) about the first Black woman cartoonist to be nationally syndicated in the United States. A recent middle grade title is Jill Doerfler and Matthew J. Martinez's *Deb Haaland: First Native American Cabinet Secretary* (2022).

Other organizations that are not officially part of ALA offer children's and young adult literature awards as well. The American Indian Library Association, for example, sponsors the American Indian Youth Literature Award. Given biennially, the awards include winners and honor books, some of which are nonfiction. A recent honor book is a picturebook biography, Traci Sorell and Natasha Donovan's *Classified: The Secret Career of Mary Golda Ross, Cherokee Aerospace Engineer* (2021).

Three children's literature awards are administered by the Asian/Pacific American Librarians Association (APALA): Young Adult/Youth Literature, Children's Literature, and Picture Books. The purpose of these awards (along with APALA's two adult literature awards—Fiction and Nonfiction) are "to honor and recognize individual works of Asian/Pacific American experiences (either historical or contemporary) and/or Asian/Pacific American cultures by Asian/Pacific Islander American authors and illustrators."[31] A recent Picture Book Award winner is *Paper Son: The Inspiring Story of Tyrus Wong, Immigrant and Artist* (2019) by Julie Leung and Chris Sasaki, a biography of the Chinese American immigrant and animator.

The Américas Award was established in 1993 by the Consortium of Latin American Studies Programs (CLASP)

> to encourage and commend authors, illustrators and publishers who produce quality children's and young adult books that portray Latin America, the Caribbean, or Latinx cultures in the United States, and to provide teachers with recommendations for classroom use.[32]

To be eligible, a book must have been published in the United States, but it can be in English, Spanish, Portuguese, or an indigenous language of the Americas.[33] Two awards may be given each year—to a primary reading-level book and to a secondary-reading-level book, and honorable mentions can be named as well. Though fiction has predominated, nonfiction titles are sometimes selected. A few years ago, Duncan Tonatiuh's *Funny Bones: Posada and His Day of the Dead Calaveras* (2015) received an honorable mention. Written on a secondary reading level, the book tells the story of José Guadalupe Posada and the Day of the Dead skeletons he created.

Each year the Association of Jewish Libraries presents the Sydney Taylor Book Award "to outstanding books for children and teens that authentically portray the Jewish experience." Awards are given in three categories: Picture Books, Middle Grade, and Young Adult.[34] A recent winner in the Picture Book category is Sue Macy and Stacy Innerst's *The Book Rescuer: How a Mensch from Massachusetts Saved Yiddish Literature for Generations to Come* (2019), a biography of Aaron Lansky who has spent decades scavenging for any book written in Yiddish.

The Arab American National Museum administers the Arab American Book Award, which is intended to recognize a book that is "written, edited, or illustrated by an Arab American, and/or highlight[s] the Arab American experience." "Arab American" is defined "as anyone who has ancestry in any of the 22 Arab countries."[35] There is a category for Children's/Young Adult Literature. A 2023 honor book is Rashida Tlaib, Adam Tlaib, Miranda Paul, and Olivia Aserr's *Mama in Congress: Rashida Tlaib's Journey to Washington* (2022), the story of one of the first Muslim women elected to the U.S. Congress. Award criteria and lists of winners and honor books are available on the award website.

The Walter Dean Myers Awards, administered by the We Need Diverse Books organization, are given in two categories, Teen and Younger Readers. To be eligible for one of the awards, the work must be published in English and available in the United States, the author (or at least one of the authors) must be diverse, and the main character of the book must be diverse. "Diverse" is defined as being a member of one or more of the following groups: "person of color, Native American, LGBTQIA+, person with a disability, marginalized religious or cultural minority in the United States."[36] Additional criteria as well as a list of winners and honor books are provided on the award website. A recent Honor Book in the Younger Readers category is a work of nonfiction: a biography in verse and prose of the famous science fiction author Octavia Butler, Ibi Zoboi's *Star Child: A Biographical Constellation of Octavia Estelle Butler* (2022).

Thus far, the "social vision" awards we've looked at are intended to honor literary achievement in relation to various racial, ethnic, or gender identities. One award that honors an idea rather than an identity is the Jane Addams Children's Book Award. Administered by the Jane Addams Peace Association, the award is given each year to recognize "children's books of literary and aesthetic excellence that effectively engage children in thinking about peace, social justice, global community, and equity for all people."[37] Awards are given in two categories, Books for Younger Children and Books for Older Children. It is not unusual for a work of nonfiction, usually history or biography, to win the award.

Two recent winners in the Books for Younger Children category are *Choosing Brave: How Mamie Till-Mobley and Emmett Till Sparked the Civil Rights Movement* (2022) by Angela Joy and Janelle Washington and *Separate Is Never Equal: Sylvia Mendez and Her Family's Fight for Desegregation* (2014) by Duncan Tonatiuh.

The National Book Awards, administered by the National Book Foundation, are devoted to the idea, broadly speaking, that books and reading are good for society. The foundation's stated mission is "to celebrate the best literature published in the United States, expands its audience, and ensure that books have a prominent place in our culture."[38] Most of the categories are for literature aimed at adults, but there is one for Young People's Literature. A recent winner was Dan Santat's graphic memoir, *A First Time for Everything* (2023), about a life-changing trip he took to Europe when he was in middle school.

In developing a nonfiction collection, it is also worth consulting awards lists for books not initially published in the United States. One such award is the Mildred L. Batchelder Award, administered by ALSC and intended to recognize

> an American publisher for a children's book considered to be the most outstanding of those books originating in a country other than the United States and in a language other than English and subsequently translated into English for publication in the United States during the preceding year.[39]

Though fiction predominates, nonfiction books are sometimes selected. The 2023 winner, for example, is *Just a Girl: A True Story of World War II* (2022), Lia Levi's memoir of what it was like growing up as a Jewish girl in Italy in the years leading up to World War II. A list of winners and honor books dating back to 1968 is available on the award website.

A similar and equally useful resource is not an award list per se, but rather a list of outstanding books selected by the United States Board on Books for Young People (USBBY), the U.S. national section of the International Board on Books for Young People. Each year since 2006, USBBY has published in the February issue of *School Library Journal* and on the award website the Outstanding International Books List. For the purposes of the list, USBBY defines an "international book" as "a book published or distributed in the United States that originated or was first published in a country other than the U.S."[40] Appearing on the 2023 list is Richard Conyngham's *All Rise: Resistance and Rebellion in South Africa 1910-1948: A Graphic History* (2022). The book tells six stories of South Africans who resisted the oppressions of the colonial government with each story being illustrated by a different South African artist.

Many U.S. states have awards and/or honor lists, some of which contain titles selected by young people themselves. And other countries, of course, have their own book awards, and these are worth consulting, especially if one is interested in strengthening their library's collection on a particular culture or nationality. Canada, for example, has the Governor General's Literary Awards, including categories for Young People's Literature—Text and Young People's Literature—Illustrated Books. The U.K. has the Carnegie Medal for Writing and the Carnegie Medal for Illustration (formerly the Kate Greenaway Medal). A complete survey of awards and honors—in the United States and in other countries—is beyond the scope of this chapter. For those wishing to explore further, a highly useful resource is ALA's web page "Other Book Awards - from other organizations."[41] It provides links to awards from other ALA divisions, ALA affiliates, and other organizations not affiliated with ALA.

I would never suggest that, just because a nonfiction book has won an award or been named an honor book, it should be included in every library's collection, but I do believe that such a book, if it fits a particular library's collection development parameters, should be given serious consideration. Award lists are useful tools that can make the work of evaluating nonfiction titles much more efficient. At the same time, it's important to remember that, just because a nonfiction book hasn't won an award or been named an honor book, it doesn't mean the book doesn't belong in a library's collection. Not every book can win an award or receive an honor, and, in fact, most of the nonfiction books that do are either biographies or histories, which means that other genres like science, sports, arts, and self-help are often overlooked. That's where reading reviews can be especially helpful.

REVIEWS

Reviews of children's and young adult books have been published for decades, and, again, librarians have led the way in serving as reviewers and promoting "high-quality" literature, however one might define that term. As with awards, most reviews have been devoted to fiction with a few devoted to poetry, traditional literature (such as folktales), and, increasingly, nonfiction. Meltzer in his article "Where Do All the Prizes Go?" famously lamented the neglect of nonfiction by the major children's literature awards. (At the time he was writing—1976—there really were no major awards to speak of for young adult literature.) What's often forgotten, though, is that Meltzer also made some pointed comments about published reviews of children's nonfiction. He expressed dismay that most reviewers of nonfiction tend to focus on how much information is in the book and how accurate or current it is. Much less frequently, he encountered reviews that compared books to others on the same subject and discussed whether there was more to the book than just the presentation of facts.[42] What more might one hope for? Meltzer explains,

> I would want to ask how well it is organized. What principle of selection animated the writer; what is the writer's point of view; does the writer

acknowledge other opinions of value? And then, beyond all this, what literary distinction, if any, does the book have? And here I do not mean the striking choice of word or image but the personal style revealed. I ask whether the writer's personal voice is heard in the book.[43]

Reviews of nonfiction gradually got more insightful and indeed played a role in the development of nonfiction for children and young adults. As James Cross Giblin points out, in his aptly titled article "More Than Just the Facts," by the 1980s reviewers (and authors, too, like Jean Fritz and Russell Freedman) were calling for nonfiction writers to stop fictionalizing scenes and dialogue in children's biographies and instead rely on a subject's actual words as found in the historical record.[44] At around the same time, reviewers, especially Hazel Rochman writing in *Booklist*, began insisting that writers include source notes in their nonfiction books for children.[45] By the 1990s, nonfiction books were regularly including supplementary materials and an index,[46] a trend that may very well have been spurred by Rochman's, and others', reviews.

Librarians developing nonfiction collections for adults have richer review resources available to them than do librarians developing nonfiction collections for children and young adults. Barbara Kiefer and Melissa Wilson note that while reviews of adult nonfiction books are typically around 800 words, those for children's and young adult nonfiction titles are more like 200-250 words.[47] Also, while the *New York Times* and *Publishers Weekly* have separate bestseller lists for adult fiction and adult nonfiction, they do not have a separate nonfiction category for children's and young adult bestsellers.[48] It's also the case that fewer nonfiction than fiction titles get reviewed. While this may be due in part to the number of titles published in each genre, it may also reflect editors' genre preference in terms of the titles they assign to be reviewed. To take just one example: in the Children's section of the November 27, 2023, issue of *Publishers Weekly*, there were 14 fiction reviews and only two nonfiction reviews.

There is an art to writing children's and young adult nonfiction reviews—and an art to reading them as well. For helpful advice that serves both purposes, one need look no further than Kathleen T. Horning's *From Cover to Cover: Evaluating and Reviewing Children's Books*.[49]

Horning discusses six features that should be examined in evaluating a nonfiction book: authority and responsibility of the author, organization, illustrations, design, writing style, and documentation of sources.[50] Kiefer and Wilson, under the heading "New Directions for the Study of Nonfiction Children's Literature," offer a similar list of features along with three additional ones: text patterns (narrative, but also comparison and contrast, cause and effect, sequence, description, and definition), formats (for example, alphabet books, photo-essays, and survey books), and, citing Colman,[51] books that represent a mix of fiction and nonfiction (The Magic School Bus series is one example).[52]

Another element to be considered is the extent to which a book invites inquiry as opposed to presenting facts in an absolute, authoritarian way. As Joe Sutliff Sanders says,

> Children's nonfiction has long been considered a literature of answers.... But there is a growing sense that children's nonfiction ought to be instead a literature of questions, and it is out of this perception of the genre that its real potential for critical engagement grows.[53]

According to Sanders, successful nonfiction foregrounds gaps in the record, disagreements among sources, and differing interpretations. Finally, nonfiction books should be evaluated on the extent to which—and how—they portray diversity. Roberta Price Gardner, Suzanne Knezek, and Thomas Crisp note that many people, incorrectly, think of nonfiction as "neutral and apolitical." In fact, "within children's nonfiction, there is continual significance assigned to white, monolingual, heteronormative histories, subjects, and perspectives."[54] It is important for reviewers to consider whether a book is representing diversity in an accurate, sensitive way, if indeed it is representing diversity at all. This paragraph may read like a laundry list of features, perhaps a bit overwhelming, but of course not every review will (or can) address each one. Some are more applicable to certain books than are others. It might be helpful to think of these features as falling into three broad admittedly overlapping categories: those that promote text literacy, those that promote visual literacy, and those that promote cultural literacy. We will consider these literacies in more depth in chapter 4.

Some aspects of nonfiction book reviews can be problematic, and it's important we acknowledge and address those before moving on. One is recommended age range. Sometimes this is presented in years (for example, ages 9 to 12 years); sometimes as grade levels (for example, 4th to 7th grade). This is related to, but not exactly the same as, reading level, which is sometimes referred to as Lexile Measure and is listed as a number with the letter "L" after it (for example, 650L). The Lexile Measure for a book is determined by analyzing things like sentence length and word frequency.[55] Publishers may or may not assign age range, grade levels, and/or reading level. Most reviewers will include age range and/or grade level; they may or may not include reading level. And any given reviewer's numbers may or may not agree with the publisher's. It gets even more confusing when several different reviewers offer different numbers, based on their own assessments. That's why it's important to read more than one review of any given title. If there's consensus across several reviews about the age, grade, and reading level, then you can feel confident in where you decide to shelve the book (with children's books or with young adult books) and to whom you recommend it. If there's disagreement in these numbers across the reviews, then you'd probably better examine the book yourself before making a final determination. But reading level isn't the only factor in determining appropriateness for a particular age group or grade level. Content is (at least) equally important, but what's considered appropriate content for different age ranges varies from community to community. Reviews, if they do nothing else, should provide a clear indication of a book's content. Then, considering content and reading level as well as other factors, librarians can make decisions about any given book's suitability within their particular context.

Another potentially gnarly issue with nonfiction reviews is the somewhat fluid nature of nonfiction itself. Normally, we think of nonfiction and fiction as polar opposites, but, as Colman points out, "nonfiction and fiction can have many similar and overlapping characteristics, that nonfiction can have an intense author's voice, that fiction can have informational and expository text."[56] She argues that we should think of fiction and nonfiction as existing on a continuum, and any particular book (for example, hybrid books, like The Magic School Bus series) might fall somewhere in between.[57] These kinds of books can pose problems for reviewers and perhaps even more so for book review editors. Where, for example, would one place a review of Jacqueline Woodson's memoir in verse, *Brown Girl Dreaming* (2014)? In poetry or nonfiction? What about a review of a picturebook biography, such as Julia Finley Mosca and Daniel Rieley's *The Girl Who Thought in Pictures: The Story of Dr. Temple Grandin* (2017)? Would it go under picturebooks or nonfiction? The editors of *The Horn Book* discuss this very conundrum in a recent article titled "How Do You Solve a Problem Like Nonfiction?"[58] Some examples of hard-to-categorize books include books where animals are personified but do not talk. If the primary purpose is to convey information, then they are put in the nonfiction section. Interestingly, books about the natural world that are written in verse are usually placed in poetry while biographies and memoirs in verse are placed in nonfiction. According to the editors, recent picturebook biographies can be especially challenging because "the definition seems to be stretching, as the lines between fact and fiction are blurring; we've seen a good number of first-person perspectives lately, along with a resurgence of invented dialogue and authorial speculation."[59] Other kinds of books, the so-called hybrid books, pose a challenge as well. A case in point is Kevin Noble Maillard and Juana Martinez-Neal's *Fry Bread: A Native American Family Story* (2019). The main story, aimed at younger readers, is about a grandmother making fry bread with her family and talking about its meaning in their culture, while the extensive end notes, aimed at older readers, provide detailed information about the history, cultures, and traditions of Native peoples. Because of the main story, the editors of *The Horn Book* decided to place the review of the book in the picturebooks section. They admit, however, that insisting on a strict definition of nonfiction may very well have a deleterious effect: by doing so, they wonder, "Whose stories would we continue to overlook, question, erase, and invalidate?"[60] The lesson in all of this for librarians engaged in developing nonfiction collections is that the reviews of some nonfiction books may not necessarily appear in a section labeled "nonfiction." In other words, it pays to look around.

Review sources fall into basically three categories: subscription periodicals, subscription databases, and freely available web resources. Among the subscription periodicals devoted exclusively to children's and young adult books, three of the most venerable are *The Horn Book Magazine*, *The Bulletin of the Center for Children's Books*, and *School Library Journal*. *The Horn Book Magazine* has been publishing reviews of as well as articles about children's and young adult books since 1924—including nonfiction for all age ranges up to 18 years. *The Horn Book Guide*, started in 1989, publishes reviews of (among other things) series nonfiction. There is an online searchable Guide/Reviews Database that "offers short, critical reviews by trusted professionals of recommended hardcover trade books published in the United States for young people."[61] A fair amount of material is available through the website, but full access requires a subscription. *The Bulletin of the Center for Children's Books* is the review journal for the Center for Children's Books located in the School of Information Sciences at the University of Illinois Urbana-Champaign. *The Bulletin* states that it "is the only major reviewing periodical for children's literature whose entire reviewing staff meets regularly, reads and discusses everyone's reviews for the issue."[62] Also, each year *The Bulletin* selects books in several categories, including nonfiction, for their Blue Ribbon Awards. This is typically a fairly substantial list and is definitely a useful tool for developing nonfiction collections. The 2022 Blue Ribbons, for example, included eleven books in the nonfiction category. *School Library Journal* is a popular review resource for both school and public librarians. For 70 years, *School Library Journal* has been "evaluat[ing] a broad range of resources, from books and digital content to databases, in 6000+ reviews published annually."[63] An especially useful resource is the supplement *Series Made Simple*, published a couple of times a year and focusing exclusively on series nonfiction. Each issue is made up of articles devoted to books on a wide variety of nonfiction topics. The fall 2023 issue, for example, includes Kate Rao's "What a Wonderful World: Geography Series Nonfiction" and Liz Bosarges' "Minds and Mindfulness: Health Series Nonfiction."[64]

Several general review periodicals review books for adults as well as children's and young adult books. One popular review periodical among librarians is *Booklist*, an ALA publication that's been publishing reviews for 100 years. To receive the print version or access the digital version of the magazine, one must be a subscriber, but anyone can access a wealth of content through *Booklist Online*.[65] *Kirkus Reviews* is another longstanding and highly regarded resource that reviews children's books and teen and young adult books, as well as adult titles. Some content is freely available on the website, but full access requires a subscription.[66] And many librarians rely on *Publishers Weekly* for reviews of a range of books, including children's. In addition to offering book reviews, *Publishers Weekly* also compiles bestseller lists in various categories. There are bestseller lists for children's fiction and children's picturebooks but not one for children's nonfiction.[67] National newspapers, such as the *New York Times*, publish reviews of children's and young adult titles although typically only a few titles are covered in any given issue. The *New York Times Book Review*, for example, published every Sunday, usually reviews two to four titles for children and/or young adults each week.[68]

In addition to review periodicals, there are several subscription databases that provide, among other things, reviews of books. The *Children's Literature Comprehensive Database* offers a suite of products related to children's and young adult literature. The supporting content includes access to "600,000+ non-biased, professional reviews from 52 reputable resources, including organizations, universities, and children's literature educators."[69] The *Literature Resource Center* is a Gale product and provides access to reviews, literary criticism, and author biographies for children's, young adult, and adult titles.[70] *Book Review Digest Plus* is an EBSCO product that mines review journals, newspapers, and popular magazines for book reviews. It bills itself as providing "extensive coverage of books for children and teens with a suggested grade range."[71] *NoveList*, a suite of EBSCO products, is a favorite among many librarians. It provides recommendations, book lists, and book discussion guides created by librarians.[72]

Of course, subscription resources cost money, so most libraries have to be selective about which, if any, of them to subscribe to. Fortunately, there are also freely available review resources to draw from. *Diverse BookFinder* states that its vision is "to be a go-to resource for librarians, educators, parents, book creators, and publishers who seek to create collections in which all children can see themselves—and each other—reflected in the picture books they read."[73] *Social Justice Books* offers a "[c]ritically reviewed selection of multicultural and social justice books for children, young adults, and educators."[74] Another widely used review source is *Common Sense Media*, which provides reviews and ratings of books, movies, television, apps, and games. One of their key missions, as stated on their website, is to recommend

> age-appropriate media that kids can enjoy and families and teachers can feel good about: movies and books with diverse characters, made by diverse creators. Apps and games that don't collect kids' personal data. Great online learning activities. And so much more—all using our ratings based on research and child development guidelines.[75]

While not everyone agrees with the practice of rating books, some parents (and some librarians) appreciate the extra guidance provided by ratings. The *Cooperative Children's Book Center* at the University of Wisconsin–Madison is a highly respected resource for book reviews, book lists on various topics, and end-of-year CCBC Choices. The CCBC-Recommended Book Search allows you to search a database of all the recommended books going back to 2008 and selected titles prior to that, going back to 1980.[76] Other online resources for reviews of children's and young adult books include *The Children's Book Review*,[77] *Children's Literature*,[78] and *Through the Looking Glass Children's Book Reviews*.[79]

Goodreads is also a popular source for reviews of all kinds of books.[80] The reviews are written by members of the Goodreads community, and there are categories for children's and young adult books and subcategories within those two broad categories. However, there is no easy way to search for nonfiction in either category. If you know a specific title, you can search on that, but if you want to browse, say, nonfiction for middle grade readers, there's no obvious way to do that. *Amazon* is another popular online resource for accessing excerpts from published reviews as well as comments from non-professional reviewers.[81] The drop-down menu in the upper left corner of the home page allows you to select "Shop by Department"; selecting "Books" will allow you to choose "Children's Books" and then the age range you're interested in. And *Book Riot* offers "the largest independent editorial book site in North America and home to a host of media, from podcasts to newsletters to original content, all designed around diverse readers and across all genres."[82]

We all like to read as much as we can, but even when we've read a book, consulting other opinions, by examining awards lists and reading reviews, allows us to compare our own evaluation with the evaluations of others. And, of course, we can't read everything, and that's where awards and reviews can be especially helpful in developing nonfiction collections for children and young adults. At the end of the day, however, it's not just about the books—or even mostly about the books. It's really about the clients we serve, the children and young adults whose information needs and information preferences we want to anticipate so that we can address them effectively through our collections and services. In the next chapter, we will look at the information needs and information behaviors of children and young adults and consider how nonfiction relates to those needs and behaviors.

NOTES

1. Kenneth B. Kidd and Joseph T. Thomas, "A Prize-Losing Introduction," in *Prizing Children's Literature: The Cultural Politics of Children's Book Awards*, ed. Kenneth B. Kidd and Joseph T. Thomas (New York: Routledge, 2017), 3.
2. Ibid., 3.
3. Ibid., 4–5.
4. The Children's Book Guild of Washington, DC, "Nonfiction Award," accessed November 21, 2023, https://www.childrensbookguild.org/nonfiction-award.
5. Ibid.

6. Sylvia M. Vardell, *Children's Literature in Action: A Librarian's Guide* (Westport, CT: Libraries Unlimited, 2008), 235.
7. National Council of Teachers of English, "Orbis Pictus Award," accessed September 12, 2023, https://ncte.org/awards/orbis-pictus-award-nonfiction-for-children/.
8. Bound to Stay Bound Bookstore, "Mission," accessed November 24, 2023, https://www.btsb.com/about-us/mission/.
9. Association for Library Service to Children, "Robert F. Sibert Informational Book Medal," accessed November 24, 2023, https://www.ala.org/alsc/awardsgrants/bookmedia/sibert.
10. Young Adult Library Services Association, "Yalsa Award for Excellence in Nonfiction for Young Adults," accessed November 22, 2023, https://www.ala.org/yalsa/nonfiction.
11. Cleveland Public Library, "Norman A. Sugarman Children's Biography Award," accessed December 2, 2023, https://cpl.org/aboutthelibrary/subjectscollections/youth-services/norman-a-sugarman-childrens-biography-award/.
12. TeachingBooks, "Norman A. Sugarman Children's Biography Award, 1998–2022," accessed December 2, 2023, https://www.teachingbooks.net/tb.cgi?wid=142.
13. Simons Laufer Mathematical Sciences Institute, "Mathical Book Prize," accessed December 1, 2023, https://www.mathicalbooks.org/.
14. National Science Teaching Association, "Outstanding Science Trade Books for Students K-12," accessed December 1, 2023, https://www.nsta.org/outstanding-science-trade-books-students-k-12.
15. National Council for the Social Studies, "Notable Social Studies Trade Books for Young People Books 2000–2019," accessed December 1, 2023, https://www.librarycat.org/lib/NCSS.
16. Boston Globe–Horn Book Awards, accessed November 26, 2023, https://www.hbook.com/story/about-the-boston-globe-horn-book-awards.
17. Ibid.
18. Ibid.
19. Wikipedia, "Golden Kite Award," accessed November 26, 2023, https://en.wikipedia.org/wiki/Golden_Kite_Award.
20. Society of Children's Book Writers and Illustrators, "The Golden Kite Awards," accessed November 26, 2023, https://www.scbwi.org/awards-and-grants/for-pal-published/golden-kite-awards.
21. Jonathan Hunt, "Where Do All the Prizes Go? Thoughts on the State of Informational Books," *The Horn Book Magazine* 81, no. 4 (2005).
22. Association for Library Service to Children, "Book & Media Awards Shelf," accessed Novermber 27, 2023, https://alsc-awards-shelf.org/.
23. Young Adult Library Services Association, "Book Finder," accessed November 27, 2023, http://booklists.yalsa.net/.
24. Cooperative Children's Book Center, "Charlotte Zolotow Award," accessed December 3, 2023, https://ccbc.education.wisc.edu/literature-resources/charlotte-zolotow-award/.
25. Kidd and Thomas, "A Prize-Losing Introduction," 3.
26. Coretta Scott King Book Awards Round Table, "Coretta Scott King Book Awards," accessed November 27, 2023, https://www.ala.org/rt/cskbart.

27. Michelle H. Martin, *Brown Gold: Milestones of African American Children's Picture Books, 1845–2002* (New York: Routledge, 2004).
28. Association for Library Service to Children, "Pura Belpré Award," accessed November 27, 2023, https://www.ala.org/alsc/awardsgrants/bookmedia/belpre.
29. Rainbow Round Table, "Stonewall Book Awards," accessed November 27, 2023, https://www.ala.org/rt/rrt/award/stonewall.
30. Feminist Task Force and Social Responsibilities Round Table, "Rise: A Feminist Book Project for Ages 0–18," accessed June 13, 2024, https://risefeministbooks.wordpress.com/.
31. Asian/Pacific American Librarians Association, "Literature Award Guidelines & Nominations," accessed November 27, 2023, https://www.apalaweb.org/awards/literature-awards/literature-award-guidelines/.
32. Consortium of Latin American Studies Programs, "Américas Award," accessed November 28, 2023, http://claspprograms.org/americasaward.
33. Ibid.
34. Association of Jewish Libraries, "Award Overview," accessed November 27, 2023, https://jewishlibraries.org/sydney_taylor_book_award/.
35. Arab American National Museum, "The Arab American Book Award," accessed November 28, 2023, https://arabamericanmuseum.org/book-awards/.
36. We Need Diverse Books, "The Walter Awards," accessed November 27, 2023, https://diversebooks.org/programs/walter-awards/.
37. Jane Addams Peace Association, "What Is the Jane Addams Children's Book Award," accessed November 27, 2023, https://www.janeaddamschildrensbookaward.org/book-award/.
38. National Book Foundation, accessed November 27, 2023, https://www.nationalbook.org/.
39. Children Association for Library Service to, "Mildred L. Batchelder Award," accessed November 28, 2023, https://www.ala.org/alsc/awardsgrants/bookmedia/batchelder.
40. United States Board on Books for Young People, "2023 Outstanding International Books List," accessed November 28, 2023, https://www.usbby.org/outstanding-international-books-list.html.
41. Association for Library Service to Children, "Children's Book Awards - from Other Orgnanizations," accessed November 28, 2023, https://www.ala.org/alsc/awardsgrants/bookmedia/childrens-book-awards-other-organizations.
42. Milton Meltzer, "Where Do All the Prizes Go? The Case for Nonfiction," accessed November 29, 2023, https://www.hbook.com/story/where-do-all-the-prizes-go-the-case-for-nonfiction-2.
43. Ibid.
44. James Cross Giblin, "More Than Just the Facts: A Hundred Years of Children's Nonfiction," *The Horn Book Magazine* 76, no. 4 (2000): 418.
45. Ibid., 418.
46. Ibid., 418.
47. Barbara Kiefer and Melissa I. Wilson, "Nonfiction Literature for Children: Old Assumptions and New Directions," in *Handbook of Research on Children's and Young Adult Literature*, ed. Shelby Anne Wolf et al. (New York: Routledge, 2010), 292.

48. Ibid., 293–94.
49. Kathleen T. Horning, *From Cover to Cover: Evaluating and Reviewing Children's Books*, rev. ed. (New York: HarperCollins, 2010).
50. Ibid., 27–46.
51. Penny Colman, "A New Way to Look at Literature: A Visual Model for Analyzing Fiction and Nonfiction Texts," *Language Arts* 84, no. 3 (2007).
52. Kiefer and Wilson, "Nonfiction Literature for Children: Old Assumptions and New Directions," 294–97.
53. Joe Sutliff Sanders, *A Literature of Questions: Nonfiction for the Critical Child* (Minneapolis: University of Minnesota Press, 2018), 44.
54. Roberta Price Gardner, Suzanne M. Knezek, and Thomas Crisp, "Introduction: Diverse Nonfiction in Prek–8 Classrooms," in *Reading and Teaching with Diverse Nonfiction Children's Books: Representations and Possibilities*, ed. Thomas Crisp, Suzanne M. Knezek, and Roberta Price Gardner (Champaign, IL: National Council of Teachers of English, 2021), xv–xvi.
55. MetaMetrics, "Lexile Framework for Reading," accessed December 3, 2023, https://lexile.com/educators/tools-to-support-reading-at-school/tools-to-determine-a-books-complexity/the-lexile-analyzer/.
56. Colman, "A New Way to Look at Literature: A Visual Model for Analyzing Fiction and Nonfiction Texts," 267.
57. Ibid., 260.
58. The Horn Book, "How Do You Solve a Problem Like Nonfiction?," *The Horn Book* 96, no. 3 (2020).
59. Ibid., n.p.
60. Ibid., n.p.
61. The Horn Book, "Guide/Reviews Database," accessed December 2, 2023, https://www.hornbookguide.com/site/.
62. The Bulletin of the Center for Children's Books, "About the Bulletin," accessed December 2, 2023, https://bccb.ischool.illinois.edu/about-us/.
63. *School Library Journal*, "About Us," accessed December 2, 2023, https://www.slj.com/page/About-Us.
64. *School Library Journal*, "Series Made Simple," accessed December 2, 2023, https://www.slj.com/section/reviews/seriesmadesimple.
65. American Library Association, "Booklist," accessed December 3, 2023, https://www.booklistonline.com/Default.aspx.
66. Kirkus Media LLC, "Kirkus Reviews," accessed December 3, 2023, https://www.kirkusreviews.com/.
67. PWxyz LLC, "Publishers Weekly," accessed December 3, 2023, https://www.publishersweekly.com/pw/home/index.html.
68. *New York Times*, "New York Times Book Review," accessed December 3, 2023, https://www.nytimes.com/column/childrens-books.
69. CLCD, "Clcd Supporting Content," accessed December 3, 2023, https://clcd.com/clcd-supporting/.
70. Gale, "Gale Literature Resource Center," accessed December 3, 2023, https://www.gale.com/c/literature-resource-center.
71. EBSCO, "Book Review Digest Plus," accessed December 3, 2023, https://www.ebsco.com/products/research-databases/book-review-digest-plus.

72. "About Novelist," accessed December 3, 2023, https://www.ebsco.com/novelist/about/our-curated-content.
73. Diverse BookFinder, "Our Vision & Mission," accessed June 13, 2024, https://diversebookfinder.org/our-missionvision/.
74. Teaching for Change, "Social Justice Books," accessed May 17, 2024, https://socialjusticebooks.org/booklists/.
75. Common Sense, "Media Choice," accessed December 3, 2023, https://www.commonsensemedia.org/what-we-stand-for/media-choice.
76. Cooperative Children's Book Center, "Ccbc Recommended-Books Overview," accessed December 3, 2023, https://ccbc.education.wisc.edu/literature-resources/ccbc-recommended-books-2/.
77. *The Children's Book Review*, "The Children's Book Review," accessed June 16, 2024, https://www.thechildrensbookreview.com/.
78. CLCD, "Children's Literature," accessed June 16, 2024.
79. Through the Looking Glass Children's Book Reviews, "Through the Looking Glass Children's Book Reviews," accessed June 16, 2024, https://lookingglassreview.com/books/.
80. Goodreads, "Goodreads," accessed December 3, 2023, https://www.goodreads.com/?ref=nav_home.
81. Amazon, "Amazon," accessed December 3, 2023, https://www.amazon.com/.
82. Riot New Media Group, "About Book Riot," accessed December 3, 2023, https://bookriot.com/about/.

3

Nonfiction and Information Needs of Children and Young Adults

Thus far, we have examined various definitions of "nonfiction," discussed the history of nonfiction for children and young adults, and described major awards and review sources for nonfiction books. Now it is time to turn our attention to children and young adults themselves, the audience for whom these books are written. Specifically, I want to consider how nonfiction resources can address the information needs of children and young adults, focusing on their developmental needs, information behavior, and reading practices. But before diving in, we should think about what we mean by "information needs." Though there is no universally agreed-upon definition of the term, Donald Case and Lisa Given offer a concise and useful one: "An *information need* is a recognition that your knowledge is inadequate to satisfy a goal that you have. There are also unconscious precursors to needs, such as *curiosity*."[1] In keeping with Case and Given's definition, I will use the term "information need" to refer not only to information needed to complete a task (such as a school assignment) or to make a decision (such as where to go to college), but also to information desired to satisfy one's curiosity about people, places, things, and ideas (such as a biography of a famous hip-hop artist). For any given patron at any given time, an information need may be "needed information" or it may skew more toward what we think of as pleasure reading. Either way, it helps to talk with patrons (or their caregivers) about perceived needs and also be familiar with the larger context in which they are seeking information—in other words, where they are on their journey from childhood to adulthood.

DEVELOPMENTAL NEEDS

One way to better understand the information needs of children and young adults is to consider the insights provided by developmental psychology. According to the American Psychological Association, developmental psychology "focus[es] on human growth and changes across the lifespan, including physical, cognitive, social, intellectual, perceptual, personality and emotional growth."[2] Two early pioneers in developmental psychology were Jean Piaget and Lev Vygotsky, and they offered somewhat different views of human development. Piaget tended to see development as more of an individual, internal process whereas Vygotsky believed that social factors played a greater role.[3] Piaget divided cognitive development into four stages. In the Sensorimotor stage (ages birth to two years), children learn about the world through movement and sensations. In the Preoperational stage (ages two to seven years), they begin to acquire language and thus to think symbolically. In the Concrete Operational stage (ages seven to 11 years), their thinking becomes more logical and more organized, and they become capable of using inductive logic. And in the Formal Operational stage (ages 12 and up), they become capable of abstract thinking and using deductive logic.[4] Vygotsky's contribution was in recognizing the social dimension of cognitive development, and his concept of the Zone of Proximal Development is still frequently cited. The Zone of Proximal Development, according to Vygotsky, is

> the distance between the actual development level [of the learner] as determined by independent problem solving and the level of potential development as determined through problem solving under adult guidance, or in collaboration with more capable peers.[5]

In other words, children can achieve more—and achieve it more efficiently—with help from parents, teachers, peers, and, of course, librarians.

Other developmental models have been proposed as well, with two of the more influential being those of Robert J. Havighurst and Erik Erikson. Havighurst saw development largely as a matter of successfully achieving key tasks at various stages of life. As he explained,

> A developmental task is a task which arises at or about a certain period in the life of the individual, successful achievement of which leads to his happiness and to success with later tasks, while failure leads to unhappiness in the individual, disapproval by society, and difficulty with later tasks.[6]

One needs to be at the right age in order to achieve a particular task, which is something Havighurst called the "teachable moment."[7] He divided the entire lifespan into six stages, but since we are concerned with ages birth to 18 years in this book, I will briefly describe only the first three. Infancy and early childhood, birth to six years, is a stage characterized by walking and talking, foundations of literacy (what we now call "emergent literacy"), and toilet training.[8] Later childhood, ages six to 13 years, involves developing skills for ordinary games, learning to get along with other children, moving toward independence, and developing basic skills in reading, writing, and arithmetic.[9] Adolescence, ages 13 to 18 years, includes accepting one's physical body as it changes, preparing for intimacy and family life, preparing to make a living, and acquiring values and ethics.[10] Erikson saw each stage of development less in terms of accomplishing key tasks and more in terms of resolving key conflicts so as to develop psychological strengths needed for being successful in life.[11] He divided human development into eight stages, the first five of which will concern us here. In Infancy (birth to 18 months), the child is completely dependent on caregivers, and the conflict associated with this stage is trust vs. mistrust.[12] Early Childhood (ages two to three years) involves gaining physical control over one's body as in toilet training, for example. The conflict associated with this stage is autonomy vs. shame and doubt.[13] Preschool (ages three to five years) is characterized by asserting power and control in social interactions without overstepping one's bounds. The conflict associated with this stage is initiative vs. guilt.[14] School Age (ages six to 11 years) involves developing a sense of pride in one's abilities and achievements. The conflict associated with this stage is industry vs. inferiority.[15] And Adolescence (ages 12 to 18 years), which Erikson sees as a key stage of development, is when one develops a personal identity. The conflict associated with this stage is identity vs. role confusion.[16]

These "classic" models of human development are still influential although some of their tenets have been supplemented, and in other cases supplanted, by more recent research findings. Brain science research, in particular, has yielded new insights into the development of the adolescent brain. Jennifer Burek Pierce, in her provocatively titled book *Sex, Brains, and Video Games*, notes that recent brain research findings have shown that the brain is not fully developed until a person in their mid-twenties.[17] This insight contradicts Piaget's belief that cognitive maturity was achieved in adolescence.[18] Citing the work of neuroscientist Jay Giedd and others, Pierce explains,

> In particular, the frontal lobe, one part of the cerebrum, is regarded as both important to reasoned decision making and slower to acquire adult properties. Its role in impulse control, risk evaluation, and understanding consequences and goals has significance for the myriad independent choices teens make every day.[19]

Because teenagers' brains are not yet fully wired, they may not be in the best position to make wise choices in complex situations. What is needed, Pierce says, is scaffolding, or support structures, that can help them make choices that are in their best interests.[20] Though she does not mention Vygotsky explicitly, we are reminded of his Zone of Proximal Development when she writes,

> Scientists' findings indicate, then, that despite popular perceptions of teens as independent individuals, young people still benefit from adults' involvement in their lives. Interactions with caring and reflective adults are essential to teens, who still need certain kinds of protection and guidance.[21]

It has long been known that the child's brain undergoes great changes from birth to late childhood. Now we know that the teenage brain is a work in progress as well. Thus, with both groups, insights from developmental psychology and brain science can help us more fully understand and address their information needs at various stages of their development.

Nonfiction can help support children's and young adults' developmental needs in a variety of ways. For toddlers, toilet training is a key developmental task, and fortunately there are many books for young children (and their parents) to help facilitate the process. A couple of examples are Leslie Patricelli's board book *Potty* (2010) and Allison Jandu's *Let's Go to the Potty! A Potty Training Book for Toddlers* (2021). A book on a related topic for slightly older children is David Macaulay and Sheila Keenan's *Toilet: How It Works* (2013). And toilet training books aren't the only instructional books for young children. Early language and cognitive development are key tasks for preschoolers as well, and there are books, including nonfiction, available to help support these tasks. Some of the most common are alphabet, counting, and concept books, and the best of these are both instructional and engaging. Stephen T. Johnson's *Alphabet City* (1995) is a clever take on the typical alphabet book. Johnson's photorealistic illustrations capture found letters in an urban landscape. For example, the legs of a sawhorse represent the letter A. Counting books are popular as well among the younger set, and one notable nonfiction example is *National Geographic Kids Look and Learn: Count!* (2011). The book uses photographs of different numbers of animals to teach kids how to count (three frogs are pictured on the front cover). The Look and Learn series, by the way, features a number of books on such topics as plants, bugs, and colors. Many concept books (i.e., books intended to teach children various concepts) fall into the nonfiction category too. Pamela Hill Nettleton and Becky Shipe's *Look, Listen, Taste, Touch, and Smell: Learning About Your Five Senses* (2004) introduces the concept of the senses and what they're used for.

A key developmental task for school-aged children is forming relationships and learning to get along with other children. Often that task begins at home in the relationship among siblings. Janis Lacovara, Anthony Pinto, and Carlos Varejão's *Brothers and Sisters: The Book for Siblings Who Don't Get Along* (2022) shows children how to develop empathy and resolve conflict within the family.

Growing Friendships: A Kids' Guide to Making and Keeping Friends (2017), by Dr. Eileen Kennedy-Moore and Christine McLaughlin, is aimed at ages six to nine and offers advice on developing five friendship skills: reaching out, stepping back, blending in, speaking up, and letting go.[22] A similar book intended for tweens is Catherine Newman's *What Can I Say? A Kid's Guide to Super-Useful Social Skills to Help You Get Along and Express Yourself* (2022). Newman offers children advice on developing relationships and communication skills so that they can speak up and speak out.

Young adults, too, face several key developmental tasks. As Sandra Hughes-Hassell and Denise Agosto discovered in their study of urban teens, these young people are interested in information related to developing various aspects of their identities: social, emotional, reflective, physical, creative, cognitive, and sexual.[23] A classic resource—and a frequently challenged one—is Robie H. Harris and Michael Emberley's *It's Perfectly Normal: Changing Bodies, Growing Up, Sex, Gender, and Sexual Health* (most recent edition 2021). One reason the book is challenged is that it's aimed at tweens and teens and some adults feel the content is inappropriate for younger readers. A similar book more clearly aimed at teens is Erika Moen and Matthew Nolan's *Let's Talk About It: The Teen's Guide to Sex, Relationships, and Being a Human* (2021). The book contains information on sex, dating, romance, and healthy vs. unhealthy relationships. In addition to learning about about sex and sexuality, teens also need to develop life skills that will allow them to become more independent as they move toward adulthood. Many books are available that offer advice on developing life skills. A perennial favorite is Sean Covey's *The 7 Habits of Highly Effective Teens* (2014). Topics covered include self-image, relationships, achieving goals, finances, and dealing with challenging situations. Most teens are also concerned with what they will do beyond high school, so it's no surprise that books on careers are useful resources to have at hand. While there's plenty of career information online, there is also a plethora of books on the subject. One notable example is DK Publishing's *Careers: The Ultimate Guide to Planning Your Future* (2022). Geared toward middle and high school students, the book presents information on hundreds of careers in the inimitable and highly visual DK style.

INFORMATION BEHAVIOR

We can gain additional insights about children's and young adults' information needs by considering their information behavior. The term "information behavior" was coined by Thomas D. Wilson, and he defined it as "the totality of human behavior in relation to sources and channels of information, including both active and passive information seeking and information use."[24] Information behavior includes information seeking (seeking information for a particular purpose), information searching (interacting with some kind of information system), and information use (incorporating information into one's existing knowledge base).²⁵ In the preface to *Theories of Information Behavior*, Karen E. Fisher, Sanda Erdelez, and Lynne (E. F.) McKechnie cite Wilson's definition and offer their own: "[W]e conceptualize information behavior as including how people need, seek, manage, give, and use information in different contexts."²⁶ While there are many theories and models of information behavior, I will focus on four that have been widely cited and are especially relevant to work with children and young adults. But before doing that, it is worth making a distinction between two different contexts in which information behavior often occurs for young people—formal and informal learning. Formal learning is generally defined as learning that occurs within the context of school, whereas informal learning occurs outside of school. Maureen Callanan, Christi Cervantes, and Molly Loomis, however, argue that the distinction should not be thought of in terms of where learning occurs, but rather should be based on certain characteristics of the learning experience. They identify five dimensions of informal learning: "(1) non-didactive, (2) highly socially collaborative, (3) embedded in meaningful activity, (4) initiated by learner's interest or choice, and (5) removed from external assessment."²⁷ There are times when children and young adults seek information in response to a school assignment (formal learning), and there are other times when they do so in order to solve a problem, make a decision, or satisfy their curiosity (informal learning).

Two models that initially grew out of observations of children in a formal learning context are especially relevant here: Melissa Gross's Imposed Query and Carol Kuhlthau's Information Search Process. An imposed query, Gross explains, is when "people are seeking information not because they have identified an information need themselves, but because they have been set on that course by another."²⁸ Imposed queries are not limited to children and young adults, nor are they limited to academic environments. However, a typical imposed query for both children and young adults is the case of a school assignment. For librarians, it is important to recognize when they are being presented with an imposed query because the person negotiating and transacting the query (the agent) is not the person who developed it (the imposer); as a result, the dynamics are different. Key features of an imposed query are the possibility for mutation of the query as it gets passed along, the fact that the imposer is not present during the transaction to determine the pertinence and relevance of the information, and the possibility that "feelings, beliefs, stereotypes, and understandings held by the agent and the intermediary [i.e., the librarian] about the imposer have the potential to affect positively or negatively the understanding and successful transaction of the query."²⁹ Moreover, successfully transacting the query often involves not just finding the right answer or an appropriate response, but also using resources prescribed by the imposer (such as a book, an article, or a web resource).³⁰ Imposed queries have implications for how reference interviews are conducted as well as for how collections are developed.

Children and young adults, of course, may or may not interact with a librarian while undertaking research in response to an imposed query. Carol Kuhlthau's Information Search Process (ISP) model provides insights into how young people go about searching for information, especially within the school context. Based on her investigations of search behavior, Kuhlthau developed a model with six stages, each of which has a cognitive (what people are thinking), a physical (what they are doing), and an affective (what they are feeling) dimension. The stages are: (1) task initiation, (2) topic selection, (3) exploration, (4) formulation, (5) collection, and (6) presentation. Thoughts generally proceed from ambiguity to specificity and increased interest, actions proceed from seeking relevant information (relevant to the topic) to seeking pertinent information (relevant to the focus), and feelings proceed from uncertainty to initial optimism to confusion, clarity, confidence, and satisfaction (or not).[31] If a young person does interact with a librarian, it can be helpful for the librarian to be familiar with the ISP in order to understand where the person is in the search process and what they are likely feeling—and to be able to reassure the person that these feelings are normal.[32] It can also be helpful to recommend resources appropriate for the particular ISP stage the person is at. For example, it would be helpful to have resources that provide concise, readable overviews of a topic; later in the process, it would be helpful to have more in-depth resources pertinent to a specific focus.

Of course, not all queries are imposed. Children and young adults often search for information in response to self-generated queries with the ultimate goal perhaps of solving a problem, making a decision, or satisfying a curiosity. This kind of information behavior occurs within the realm of informal learning. Two theories that offer insights into self-generated information seeking are Reijo Savolainen's Everyday Life Information Seeking (ELIS) and Eliza Dresang's Theory of Radical Change. According to Savolainen, "ELIS refers to the acquisition of various informational (both cognitive and expressive) elements which people employ to orient themselves in daily life or to solve problems not directly connected with the performance of occupational tasks."[33] In the case of most children and young adults, we might substitute the term "school-related" for the word "occupational" (although many teens hold part-time jobs while also going to school and some older teens drop out of school and go to work). There is a strong social dimension to how one seeks information:

> The ways by which the individual monitors daily events and seek[s] information to solve specific problems are determined by the values, attitudes, and interests characteristic of their way of life. . . . In most cases, the relevance of different information sources and channels is evaluated on the basis of their familiarity and effectiveness in information use situations.[34]

ELIS has been used as a conceptual framework in numerous studies of children's and young adults' information behavior. Two notable examples are Denise Agosto and Sandra Hughes-Hassell's investigation of the information seeking behavior of urban young adults[35] and Eric Meyers, Karen Fisher, and Elizabeth Marcoux's study of the information behavior of preteens.[36] Since a part of everyday life for most people, including children and young adults, is leisure time, it will be useful to consider the concept of serious leisure, as defined by the sociologist Robert Stebbins. Serious leisure, as opposed to casual leisure, involves information seeking and knowledge acquisition.[37] Stebbins divides serious leisure into three basic types: amateurism, volunteering, and hobbies.[38] While children and young adults may take part in any or all of these types of serious leisure, the most obvious type that involves information seeking and knowledge (and skill) acquisition is hobbies. Hobbies include collecting, making, participating in an activity, playing sports and games, and being a liberal arts enthusiast (a fancy term for becoming obsessed with a particular subject, like dinosaurs, for instance).[39]

Dresang's Theory of Radical Change posits three principles of the digital age that help explain many aspects of both information behavior and information resource design:

- *Interactivity* refers to dynamic, user-initiated, nonlinear, nonsequential, complex information behavior, and representation.
- *Connectivity* refers to the sense of community or construction of social worlds that emerge from changing perspectives and expanded associations.
- *Access* refers to the breaking of long-standing information barriers, bringing entrée to a wide diversity of opinion and opportunity.[40]

These principles, according to Dresang, have affected how children's and young adults' information behavior has changed in the digital age, specifically

- How they think, learn, give, receive, and create information.
- How they perceive themselves and others.
- How they access information and seek community.[41]

Dresang also identifies ways books have changed in the digital age, and we will look at that part of Radical Change in the next section.

How, then, does nonfiction relate to formal and informal learning and to imposed and self-generated information-seeking? In theory, any nonfiction book can support formal learning, but in practice most school assignments that require students to consult nonfiction resources focus on biography, history, or science. Let's take women's history as an example. A recent post by Melissa Taylor of Imagination Soup lists sixty women's biographies in eight categories, including Women in STEM, Activists, Athletes, and Musicians, Actors, and

Artists.[42] There one can find an annotated list of biographies for younger and older readers on such figures as NASA mathematician Katherine Johnson, Supreme Court Justice Ruth Bader Ginsburg, First Lady Eleanor Roosevelt, sisters and superstar athletes Venus and Serena Williams, and storyteller and librarian Pura Belpré. Also listed are a number of biography collections, including Vashti Harrison's *Little Dreamers: Visionary Women Around the World* (2018) and Catherine Thimmesh and Melissa Sweet's *Girls Think of Everything: Stories of Ingenious Inventions by Women* (2018).

To be sure, biographies (and histories and books on science) can support informal learning as well. Many children and young adults enjoy reading about their favorite athletes and pop culture stars, others like to read about the Civil War or the Civil Rights Movement, and still others are fascinated with climate change, wildlife, or space travel. In a study of what children in grades K-4 would include if they were allowed to develop a library's collection, Linda Cooper found they all wanted books on animals and sports. Children in grades 3 and 4 also wanted books on outer space, biographies, joke books, and how-to books.[43] Hobbies play an important role in the everyday lives of many children and young adults, and nonfiction books on hobbies can offer important information for this kind of informal learning. A number of years ago, Michael Smith and Jeffrey Wilhelm published an award-winning book with the memorable title *"Reading Don't Fix No Chevys": Literacy in the Lives of Young Men.*[44] The attitude reflected in the title says a lot about how some people perceive what "counts" as reading. After all, while it's true that reading *Pride and Prejudice* won't equip one with the knowledge needed to repair a car, reading *Car and Driver* very well might. With that in mind, it's worth spending a little time thinking about the value of nonfiction books related to hobbies. From Lego to Minecraft and basketball to ballet, the hobbies kids participate in and books about those hobbies are virtually endless. Popular topics include sports of all kinds, gaming, coding, drawing comics and manga, cooking, collecting, making, photography, gardening, playing a musical instrument, dancing, and many, many more. While these kinds of books rarely win awards or make "best of" lists, they are popular with a lot of young people and are worth including in library collections. Libraries fortunate enough to have makerspaces can shelve hobby-related books there or close by.

READING PRACTICES

When we talk about reading and young people, we are usually talking about it in two senses of the word: early on, reading as the decoding of letters, words, and sentences; and then later on, reading for comprehension—or as the old saying goes, "learning to read and then reading to learn." There are also several issues related to reading and young people. Some children have trouble reading because they may have a reading disability and/or they may have fallen behind in learning to read. Others are reluctant readers because they don't find reading as engaging as doing other things. Studies have shown that reading for pleasure decreases as young people move into their teen years because of competing demands, such as assigned reading for school, extracurricular activities, and so forth.[45] Other studies suggest that, overall, girls tend to read more than boys,[46] while boys tend to read more nonfiction than girls.[47] As Paulette Rothbauer explains, for both groups, "narrative forms of reading material such as fiction and biography remain generally more popular than expository forms of nonfiction."[48] Indeed, biography is popular among young people, and, according to Bernard Lukenbill, it "plays an important role in transmitting vital cultural information to youth."[49] He explains,

> If used wisely, [biography] can help youth become better persons and contribute more to the improvement of their world. On a personal level, it can contribute to academic achievement, the growth in self-awareness, and the development of useful social and intellectual skills for later in life.[50]

We see here a connection between reading and the achievement of various developmental tasks. Moreover, there is an implied connection to information behavior as well. In fact, Lukenbill cites social worker Peter K. Gerlach who discusses the importance of youth being able to acquire, evaluate, retain, prioritize, and apply information.[51] Reading biography and, more broadly speaking, reading in general can help young people to further those aims.

How, then, does reading help to meet children's and young adults' information needs and preferences? Setting aside the mechanics of decoding—which are important, of course, but beyond the scope of our discussion—let us consider four aspects of reading that can empower young readers. One is the power of choice. Stephen Krashen has advocated persuasively for what he calls free voluntary reading (FVR), in other words, reading because you want to and not because you have to write a book report or answer a set of questions.[52] Research suggests that allowing children and young adults choice in what they read has several benefits: it improves reading comprehension, it improves writing style, and it helps second language learners achieve greater proficiency.[53] Another important aspect of reading to consider is the role of the reader. Louise Rosenblatt, an early reader-response theorist who studied actual readers rather than implied or constructed readers, described the transactional nature of reading, involving both the reader and the text. Reading, then, is not simply a matter of unlocking the mysteries of the text with no regard to the person doing the unlocking. As Rosenblatt explained,

> The reader approaches the text with a certain purpose, certain expectations or hypotheses that guide his choices from the residue of past

experiences. Meaning emerges as the reader carries on a give-and-take with the signs on the page.... [T]he two-way, reciprocal relation explains why meaning is not "in" the text or "in" the reader. Both reader and text are essential to the transactional process of making meaning.[54]

Creating engaged readers, then, involves respecting readers' choices as to what they read (per Krashen) and recognizing that different readers will react to and interpret the same text in different ways (per Rosenblatt).

A third aspect of promoting reading among children and young adults is the issue of representation. In her now famous article, "Mirrors, Windows, and Sliding Glass Doors," Rudine Sims Bishop explained that books can be windows, providing views of worlds not familiar to the reader; sliding glass doors, allowing the reader to enter the world through their imagination; or mirrors, reflecting the reader's own life and experiences.[55] She argued that it's important for all children to see themselves reflected in respectful ways in the books they read:

> When children cannot find themselves reflected in the books they read, or when the images they see are distorted, negative, or laughable, they learn a powerful lesson about how they are devalued in the society of which they are a part. Our classrooms need to be places where all the children from all the cultures that make up the salad bowl or American society can find their mirrors.[56]

And, I would add, this should occur not just in our classrooms, but in our libraries as well and wherever children and young adults read. A fourth aspect of reading is reading in the digital age. As previously discussed, Dresang identifies three digital age principles that impact information behavior, including reading practices: interactivity, connectivity, and access.[57] Of course, not all children and young adults have equal access to digital technology, but they still live in a digital age that immerses them in these principles. In developing her Theory of Radical Change, Dresang examined a wide variety of contemporary handheld books and identified three types of change that she saw as a response to and an incorporation of digital age principles: Type One: Changing forms and formats; Type Two: Changing perspectives; and Type Three: Changing boundaries.[58] These changes describe how books are using innovative ways of presenting stories and other information (Type One), including a variety of voices (Type Two), and addressing a variety of topics (Type Three).[59] While not all contemporary handheld books reflect these changes, many of them do, and as such they offer digital age reading experiences that many children and young adults find to be both familiar and engaging.

Findings from reading research can be useful to librarians in collecting and promoting nonfiction books to children and young adults. For one thing, since choice is important, it's also important to have a variety of nonfiction books from which young people can choose. As we've seen from Cooper's study, mentioned above, most children like books on animals, sports, and outer space, and books related to hobbies are perennial favorites. In addition to having nonfiction books on a wide range of topics, it is also important to recognize, per Dresang, that today's young people are interested in seeing innovative forms and formats. In that respect, I believe nonfiction books have been in the vanguard for some time now. Many of them feature photographs and other illustrations, sidebars and call-out boxes with supplemental text, and peritextual elements such as glossaries, maps, and suggestions for further reading. These kinds of features promote what Kathleen Burnett and Dresang call "rhizomorphic reading," which is similar to the nonlinear way people read hypertext.[60] DK Publishing's Eyewitness books are especially notable for their innovative design and content, but there are many other fine examples as well. Jason Chin's picturebook *Grand Canyon* (2017), for instance, depicts a child and his father journeying through the various ecological communities in the canyon. The main picture on each page shows a scene from the journey along with the geography associated with that particular community, while pictures in the margins provide additional information about such things as how fossils are created, what happens when rocks break apart, and which animals and plants are characteristic of each community. At the end of the journey, the book opens to a quadruple-page spread showing a stunning vista from the top of the Canyon. Backmatter provides additional information about the canyon along with illustrations, a note from the author, and resources for further reading.

Finally, per Bishop, it's important for libraries to include books that reflect the diversity of the young people they serve—and this is true for both nonfiction and fiction. This may be easier, however, to accomplish in terms of content than authorship. Marc Aronson, in his article "Nonfiction Windows So White," notes that while in 2018 the percentage of nonfiction written by BIPOC (Black, Indigenous, People of Color) authors was only 3.2, by 2020 it had risen to 11.5. Still, Aronson expresses a concern that most of this diverse nonfiction is in the form of biography, history, and social studies with very little in science and mathematics.[61] The reasons for the low numbers are complicated. Aronson speculates that for many BIPOC authors, writing fiction is more lucrative than writing nonfiction, but he also acknowledges that editors can be shortsighted as to what diverse authors "should" be writing about.[62] Still, it's encouraging to see more and more diverse authors writing nonfiction about sometimes difficult but nonetheless important subjects. Two recent books on the Tulsa Race Massacre of 1921 provide heartrending accounts of the bigotry and brutality that led to the destruction of the Greenwood District, known as America's Black Wall Street. Carole Boston Weatherford and Floyd Cooper's *Unspeakable: The Tulsa Race Massacre* (2021) is an award-winning picturebook for ages eight to twelve years. Brandy Colbert's *Black Birds in the Sky: The Story and Legacy* of the 1921 Tulsa Race Massacre (2021) is aimed at teens and is a thoroughly researched book that not only describes the event itself, but also provides helpful historical context.

When it comes to more children being able to see themselves represented in nonfiction books, strides have definitely been made; still, representation of diverse groups can be problematic. In a study of Orbis Pictus Award books with LGBTQIA+ content, Thomas Crisp, Roberta Price Gardner, and Matheus Almeida found that "the creators of these books rely upon heteronormative constructions, queer erasure, and compulsory heterosexuality to minimize (and even eliminate) queerness."[63] As librarians, of course, we can't control the choices publishers and authors make, but we can keep an eye out for nonfiction books that reflect all kinds of diversity, both in content and authorship. Fortunately, many of the awards and lists discussed in the previous chapter provide useful tools for librarians to use in staying current with the latest nonfiction titles related to diversity. One source of material that can help address representation issues can be found in the growing number of graphic memoirs by members of diverse groups. Cece Bell's *El Deafo* (2014) has been widely praised for its depiction of a child living with deafness. Pedro Martín's *Mexikid: A Graphic Memoir* (2023) is a funny and poignant account of the Martín family's road trip to Mexico in the late 1970s. And Maia Kobabe's frequently challenged *Gender Queer: A Memoir* (2019) relates Maia's journey toward self-acceptance and coming out as nonbinary and asexual.

As we have seen, children's and young adults' information needs can be better understood within the context of their developmental needs, information behavior, and reading practices. Having a robust and diverse nonfiction collection is one way librarians can help address these needs. Nonfiction not only helps in addressing children's and young adults' information needs, but it also helps them develop the multiple literacies they need to be successful in today's digital world. In the next chapter we consider the relationship between literacies and nonfiction.

NOTES

1. Donald O. Case and Lisa M. Given, *Looking for Information: A Survey of Research on Information Seeking, Needs, and Behavior*, ed. Jens-Erik Mai, fourth ed., Studies in Information (Bingley, UK: Emerald Group Publishing Limited, 2016), 6.
2. American Psychological Association, "Developmental Psychology Studies Humans across the Lifespan," accessed January 10, 2024, https://www.apa.org/education-career/guide/subfields/developmental#:~:text=Developmental%20Psychology%20Studies%20Humans%20Across,perceptual%2C%20personality%20and%20emotional%20growth.
3. Kendra Cherry, "Piaget's 4 Stages of Cognitive Development Explained," accessed January 10, 2024, https://www.verywellmind.com/piagets-stages-of-cognitive-development-2795457.

4. Ibid.
5. Lev S. Vygotsky, *Mind in Society: The Development of Higher Psychological Processes* (Cambridge, MA: Harvard University Press, 1978), 86.
6. Robert J. Havighurst, *Human Development and Education* (New York: Longmans, Green and Co., 1953), 2.
7. Ibid., 5.
8. Ibid., 9-17.
9. Ibid., 28-41.
10. Ibid., 120-39.
11. Kendra Cherry, "Erikson's Stages of Development," accessed January 10, 2024, https://www.verywellmind.com/erik-eriksons-stages-of-psychosocial-development-2795740.
12. Erik H. Erikson, *Identity: Youth and Crisis* (New York: W. W. Norton & Company, 1968), 96-107.
13. Ibid., 107-14.
14. Ibid., 115-22.
15. Ibid., 122-28.
16. Ibid., 128-35.
17. Jennifer Burek Pierce, *Sex, Brains, and Video Games: Information and Inspiration for Youth Services Librarians*, second ed. (Chicago: American Library Association, 2017), 83.
18. Ibid., 79.
19. Ibid., 82-83.
20. Ibid., 106.
21. Ibid., 107.
22. Dr. Eileen Kennedy-Moore and Christine McLaughlin, *Growing Friendships: A Kids' Guide to Making and Keeping Friends* (New York: Aladdin/Beyond Words, 2017), viii-ix.
23. Sandra Hughes-Hassell and Denise E. Agosto, "Modeling the Everyday Life Information Needs of Urban Teenagers," in *Youth Information-Seeking Behavior II: Context, Theories, Models, and Issues*, ed. Mary K. Chelton and Colleen Cool (Lanham, MD: Scarecrow Press, Inc., 2007), 39-53.
24. T. D. Wilson, "Human Information Behavior," *Informing Science* 3, no. 2 (2000): 49.
25. Ibid., 49-50.
26. Karen E. Fisher, Sanda Erdelez, and Lynne (E. F.) McKechnie, "Preface," in *Theories of Information Behavior*, ed. Karen E. Fisher, Sanda Erdelez, and Lynne (E. F.) McKechnie (Medford, NJ: Information Today, Inc., 2005), xix.
27. Maureen Callanan, Christi Cervantes, and Molly Loomis, "Informal Learning," *WIREs Cognitive Science* 2 (2011): 646.
28. Melissa Gross, "The Imposed Query," in *RQ* (1995), n.p.
29. Ibid., n.p.
30. Melissa Gross, "The Imposed Query and Information Services for Children," in *Journal of Youth Services in Libraries* (2000), n.p.
31. Carol Collier Kuhlthau, "Kuhlthau's Information Search Process," in *Theories of Information Behavior*, ed. Karen E. Fisher, Sanda Erdelez, and Lynne (E. F.) McKechnie (Medford, NJ: Information Today, Inc., 2005), 230-31.
32. Ibid., 233.

33. Reijo Savolainen, "Everyday Life Information Seeking: Approaching Information Behavior in the Context of 'Way of Life,'" *Library and Information Science Research* 17 (1995): 266-67.
34. Ibid., 267.
35. Denise E. Agosto and Sandra Hughes-Hassell, "People, Places, and Questions: An Investigation of the Everyday Life Information-Seeking Behaviors of Urban Young Adults," *Library and Information Science Research* 27 (2005).
36. Eric M. Meyers, Karen E. Fisher, and Elizabeth Marcoux, "Making Sense of an Information World: The Everyday-Life Information Behavior of Preteens," *The Library Quarterly: Information, Community, Policy* 79, no. 3 (2009).
37. Jenna Hartel, "Serious Leisure," in *Theories of Information Behavior*, ed. Karen E. Fisher, Sanda Erdelez, and Lynne (E. F.) McKechnie (Medford, NJ: Information Today, Inc., 2005), 313.
38. Ibid., 314.
39. Ibid., 315.
40. Eliza T. Dresang, "Radical Change," in *Theories of Information Behavior*, ed. Karen E. Fisher, Sanda Erdelez, and Lynne (E. F.) McKechnie (Medford, NJ: Information Today, Inc., 2005), 298. Emphasis in original.
41. Ibid., 299.
42. Melissa Taylor, "60 Inspiring Women's History Month Biographies for Kids," accessed January 18, 2024, https://imaginationsoup.net/childrens-books-biographies-womens-history/.
43. Linda Z. Cooper, "Children's Information Choices for Inclusion in a Hypothetical Child-Constructed Library," in *Youth Information-Seeking Behavior: Theories, Models, and Issues*, ed. Mary K. Chelton and Colleen Cool (Lanham, MD: Scarecrow Press, 2004), 200.
44. Michael W. Smith and Jeffrey D. Wilhelm, *"Reading Don't Fix No Chevys": Literacy in the Lives of Young Men* (Portsmouth, NH: Heinemann, 2002).
45. Vivian Howard and Shan Jin, "Teens and Pleasure Reading: A Critical Assessment from Nova Scotia," in *Youth Information-Seeking Behavior Ii: Context, Theories, Models, and Issues*, ed. Mary K. Chelton and Colleen Cool (Lanham, MD: Scarecrow Press, Inc., 2007), 143.
46. Ibid., 138, 143.
47. Ibid., 139; Lynne (E. F.) McKechnie, "Becoming a Reader: Childhood Years," in *Reading Matters: What the Research Reveals About Reading, Libraries, and Community*, ed. Catherine Sheldrick Ross, Lynne (E. F.) McKechnie, and Paulette M. Rothbauer (Westport, CT: Libraries Unlimited, 2006), 90; Paulette M. Rothbauer, "Young Adults and Reading," ibid., 111.
48. "Young Adults and Reading," 111.
49. W. Bernard Lukenbill, *Biography in the Lives of Youth: Culture, Information, and Society* (Westport, CT: Libraries Unlimited, 2006), 2.
50. Ibid., 2.
51. Ibid., 7-8.
52. Stephen D. Krashen, *The Power of Reading: Insights from the Research*, second ed. (Westport, CT: Libraries Unlimited, 2004), x.
53. Ibid., x.

54. Louise M. Rosenblatt, *Literature as Exploration*, fifth ed. (New York: Modern Language Association, 1995 [1938]), 26–27.
55. Rudine Sims Bishop, "Mirrors, Windows, and Sliding Glass Doors," *Perspectives: Choosing and Using Books for the Classroom* 6, no. 3 (1990): n.p.
56. Ibid., n.p.
57. Dresang, "Radical Change," 298.
58. Ibid., 299.
59. Eliza T. Dresang, *Radical Change: Books for Youth in a Digital Age* (New York: H. W. Wilson, 1999), 19, 24, 26.
60. Kathleen Burnett and Eliza T. Dresang, "Rhizomorphic Reading: The Emergence of a New Aesthetic in Literature for Youth," *The Library Quarterly* 69, no. 4 (1999): 421.
61. Marc Aronson, "Nonfiction Windows So White," *The Horn Book Magazine* 97, no. 2 (2021): 16.
62. Ibid., 16.
63. Thomas Crisp, Roberta Price Gardner, and Matheus Almeida, "The All-Heterosexual World of Children's Nonfiction: A Critical Content Analysis of LGBTQ Identities in Orbis Pictus Award Books, 1990–2017," *Children's Literature in Education* 49, no. 3 (2018): 246.

4

Nonfiction and Literacies

In the previous chapter, we looked at how nonfiction for children and young adults can help address their information needs. In this chapter, we'll consider how it can help foster literacies needed for success in both their academic and personal lives. I'm using the plural form of the word "literacy" because in the last couple of decades we have seen a proliferation of different literacies advocated for by various groups, from health literacy to financial literacy and computer literacy to cultural literacy. To be sure, any nonfiction book is potentially related to a variety of literacies. For example, a nonfiction book on the human body, such as David Macaulay's meticulously illustrated *The Way We Work* (2008), can facilitate the development of science literacy, health literacy, visual literacy, and information literacy, among others. Given this multiplicity, getting the lay of the land in the literacy landscape is a challenging but not impossible task. We will begin with some key definitions and then focus on the literacies most relevant to nonfiction books.

Before going any further, though, I want to acknowledge a couple of issues with the concept of literacies. One is that the term has become so ubiquitous as to become virtually meaningless. Media studies scholar David Buckingham makes this very point, arguing that the term literacy used in conjunction with a content-related adjective, such as "information literacy," may have "finally passed its sell-by date." The problem, Buckingham believes, is that the term "literacy" when used in this way merely means competence, having a set of "functional or instrumental skills" rather than "a much more profound form of cultural awareness and understanding."[1] There is some truth to what he is saying, and I can't help being reminded of Abraham Maslow's observation (perhaps not original to him) that "if the only tool you have is a hammer, it is tempting to treat everything as if it were a nail."[2] However, as we shall see shortly, recent definitions of at least some literacies, like information literacy, do include the social and cultural dimensions that Buckingham finds lacking in other definitions. Another potential issue with literacy is who defines it and for what purpose. If it is defined and used as a way of excluding already marginalized groups, then that's obviously problematic. But if it is defined and used as a way of empowering people, then that's admirable. The approach I will take in this chapter is the latter, as I hope to show how nonfiction resources, specifically books, can help facilitate the development of various literacies in children and young adults, literacies that can enrich their lives and enhance their ability to be full participants in society.

WHAT DO WE MEAN BY "LITERAC(IES)"?

The word "literacy" is usually taken to mean having the ability to read and write. The term is used nowadays in (at least) a couple of different, but related, ways. The *Oxford English Dictionary* defines "literacy" as "[t]he quality, condition, or state of being literate; the ability to read and write," and also "[i]n extended use (usually with a modifying word). The ability to 'read' a particular subject or medium; competence or knowledge in a particular area."[3] One of the examples provided for the second definition is "computer literacy," and we could add many others, like information literacy, media literacy, digital literacy, multimodal literacy, and so on. But let's focus on the first definition for a moment. Many groups now define literacy as going beyond basic reading and writing to reflect the social contexts in which literacy is developed and practiced. UNESCO, for example, characterizes it this way:

> Beyond its conventional concept of reading, writing and counting skills, literacy is now understood as a means of identification, understanding, interpretation, creation, and communication in an increasingly digital, text-mediated, information-rich and fast-changing world.[4]

Moreover, as Frank Serafini explains, literacy is "as much a social practice as it is an individual cognitive skill"; it is "something individuals *do* in particular social contexts, rather than something they *acquire*" (emphasis in original).[5] In the mid-1990s, a group of literacy and media scholars calling themselves the New London Group published a manifesto advocating for a more expansive view of literacy. In this document, titled "A Pedagogy of Multiliteracies," they argued that "the multiplicity of communications channels and increasing cultural and linguistic diversity in the world today call for a much broader view of literacy than portrayed by traditional language-based approaches."[6] This notion of multiliteracies has had an enormous influence on how literacy has been (re)conceptualized in the twenty-first century.

The National Council of Teachers of English (NCTE) document "Definition of Literacy in a Digital Age," while embracing multiliteracies, also points out that literacy has always contained multitudes:

Literacy has always been a collection of communicative and sociocultural practices shared among communities. As society and technology change, so does literacy. The world demands that a literate person possess and intentionally apply a wide range of skills, competencies, and dispositions. These literacies are interconnected, dynamic, and malleable. As in the past, they are inextricably linked with histories, narratives, life possibilities, and social trajectories of all individuals and groups.[7]

The document goes on to describe nine elements associated with literacy in a digital age. While they are all potentially relevant to evaluating and promoting nonfiction books for children and young adults, two seem especially apropos:

- Explore and engage critically, thoughtfully, and across a wide variety of inclusive texts and tools/modalities.
- Determine how and to what extent texts and tools amplify one's own and others' narratives as well as counter unproductive narratives.[8]

Different academic and professional fields tend to emphasize different literacies, depending on the particular focus of the field. Communication, for example, is concerned with media literacy, graphic design with visual literacy, the sciences with science and data literacy, and so on. In library and information science, we tend to focus on information literacy and, more recently, digital literacy as well. Interestingly, the American Association of School Librarians' *AASL Standards Framework for Learners* does not use the term "information literacy" and, in fact, avoids using the term "literacy" at all. The document does, however, emphasize reading, information access, and information technology, so it very much reflects the key elements of information literacy. Briefly, the *AASL Standards Framework* identifies six shared foundations—Inquire, Include, Collaborate, Curate, Explore, and Engage. In addition, there are four domains that cut across all of the foundations—Think, Create, Share, and Grow. Specific competencies are identified at the intersections, for example, at Inquire-Think, Inquire-Create, and so on. The complete *Standards Framework* is available on the AASL website.[9] And, while the document does not use the term "information literacy" explicitly, several of the foundations, domains, and related competencies are relevant to information literacy—in particular Inquire, Curate, and Explore—and engaging with nonfiction resources can play an important role in helping learners develop these competencies. The Association of College and Research Libraries (ACRL) does provide a definition of information literacy in their *Framework for Information Literacy for Higher Education*, and, although the *Framework* is focused on adult learners, that is, college students, the definition, I believe, can be applied to learners of all ages. ACRL defines information literacy as "the set of integrated abilities encompassing the reflective discovery of information, the understanding of how information is produced and valued, and the use of information in creating new knowledge and participating ethically in communities of learning."[10] Again, engaging with nonfiction resources can help learners, regardless of grade level, develop knowledge and skills in each of these areas. The ACRL definition of information literacy relies heavily on the concept of metaliteracy, as defined by Thomas Mackey and Trudi Jacobson. In their book *Metaliteracy: Redefining Information Literacy to Empower Learners*, published two years before the ACRL *Framework* was adopted, Mackey and Jacobson explain that

> [m]etaliteracy expands the scope of traditional information skills (determine, access, locate, understand, produce, and use information) to include the collaborative production and sharing of information in participatory digital environments (collaborate, participate, produce, and share).[11]

Metaliteracy, as they define it, emphasizes metacognition, that is, reflecting on how one learns, and also includes related literacies such as visual literacy, media literacy, and digital literacy.[12]

Indeed, a concept closely related to information literacy is digital literacy, which tends to emphasize the technological aspects of multiliteracies. UNESCO defines digital literacy as

> the ability to access, manage, understand, integrate, communicate, evaluate and create information safely and appropriately through digital technologies.... It includes skills such as computer literacy, ICT literacy, information literacy and media literacy which aim to empower people, and in particular youth, to adopt a critical mindset when engaging with information and digital technologies, and to build their resilience in the face of disinformation, hate speech and violent extremism.[13]

Here we see a direct reference to so-called fake news and other dangers associated especially, though not exclusively, with social media. While nonfiction resources aren't a panacea for online mis- and disinformation, they can sometimes help to provide a corrective. At the very least, comparing information across media can often lead to a more informed view of a particular story or topic. In addition, there are books devoted specifically to the topic of fake news. Lerner Publications, for example, offers a series of books for ages eight to 10 on different types of fake news. The titles include Matt Doeden's *What Are Satire and Parody?* (2019), *What Are Hoaxes and Lies?* (2019), and *What Is Propaganda?* (2019), and Margaret J. Goldstein's *What Are Conspiracy Theories?* (2019). Other publishers offer books aimed at teens, for example, Michael Miller's *Fake News: Separating Truth from Fiction* (2019) and John Grant's *Debunk It! Fake News Edition: How to Stay Sane in a World of Misinformation* (2019).

These various literacies overlap, of course, and arguments can be made for which is the "umbrella" literacy. To me this is the wrong approach. I think a stronger case can be made for interconnections among these literacies, so the more appropriate metaphor is a web of literacies rather than a hierarchy. Two examples will help illustrate the point. One kind of literacy that's being much talked about these days is data literacy, which goes beyond basic math skills (numeracy) to encompass "the ability to read, understand, create, and communicate data as information."[14] Since data is often presented in visual forms, such as charts and graphs, data literacy involves not only information literacy but also visual literacy. These literacies are interwoven in such a way that each depends on and supports the others. Nonfiction books for children and young adults are replete with maps and cutaway drawings, but fewer contain charts and graphs. One author/illustrator who is adept at visualizing data for children is Jason Chin. In *The Universe in You: A Microscopic Journey* (2022), he uses drawings and text to compare an inch to a centimeter, a centimeter to a millimeter, and millimeter to a micron. In *Your Place in the Universe* (2020), he again uses text and drawings to compare the sizes of things. An eight-year-old, we are told, is five times as tall as this book but only half as tall as an ostrich, which in turn is less than half as tall as a giraffe. Through fun and engaging text and illustrations, these books help cultivate data literacy as well as visual literacy.

How these different literacies are practiced can vary depending on the discipline within which they are being practiced—which leads to another kind of literacy that's being much talked about these days: disciplinary literacy. According to Zhihui Fang and Suzanne Coatoam, disciplinary literacy recognizes that "disciplines differ not just in content but also in ways this content is produced, communicated, evaluated, and renovated" and that "being literate in a discipline means understanding both disciplinary content and disciplinary habits of mind (i.e., ways of reading, writing, viewing, speaking, thinking, reasoning, and critiquing)."[15] A great example of how nonfiction books can introduce young readers to disciplinary thinking is Clarion Books' Scientists in the Field series. Aimed at ages eight to 12 years, the books cover topics on different animals (orcas, turtles, snowy owls, octopi, sharks, just to name a few) as well as other aspects of the natural sciences (weather, volcanoes, the Mars rover, trash). To take one example: Sy Montgomery and Nic Bishop's *Saving the Ghost of the Mountain: An Expedition Among Snow Leopards in Mongolia* (2009) is typical of the books in the series. Montgomery and Bishop went along on the expedition, so their book is an eyewitness account of a scientist at work. The book opens with a chapter on the elusive snow leopard and then introduces Tom, the scientist who is leading the expedition, and provides extensive information about his background and training. The book is lavishly illustrated with Bishop's photographs, the text is lively, and "Fact" boxes are interspersed throughout the book (for example, "Fact: Snow leopards spend about a third of their time moving and two-thirds resting"). At the end of the book the reader can find not only an author's note and an illustrator's note, but also advice from Tom for would-be conservationists. This book, like the others in the series, focuses on a particular scientific question or problem and explains how scientists go about addressing it. The overarching question in this book is how do you track an animal that almost never shows itself? *Saving the Ghost of the Mountain* provides an in-depth look at how one scientist approaches that challenge. Martin W. Sandler's *Shipwrecked! Diving for Hidden Time Capsules on the Ocean Floor* (2023) is not part of the Scientists in the Field series, but it too offers a compelling look at how scientists, in this case marine archaeologists, work and think. In the book, Sandler focuses on eight shipwrecks, describing how they were explored, the treasures and artifacts found, and offering related content in sidebar sections (for example, "Sponge Diving" and "Human Remains"). At the end of the book are short descriptions of additional shipwrecks "For Further Exploring." Two books that offer insights into disciplinary thinking while also appealing to young readers' attraction to the gross-out factor are Colleen Paeff and Nancy Carpenter's *The Great Stink: How Joseph Bazalgette Solved London's Poop Pollution Problem* (2021) and Gail Jarrow's *American Murderer: The Parasite that Haunted the South* (2022). *The Great Stink* is aimed at younger readers, ages five to nine, and tells the story of the engineer who devised a plan to clean up the River Thames by building a new sewer system. *American Murderer* is aimed at tweens and teens and tells the story of zoologist Charles Stiles, who discovered that hookworms were what were making people sick in the South and taught people how to protect themselves from these microscopic parasites. The book, which is part of the provocatively named Medical Fiascoes series, features a frightening front cover: the close-up photograph of a hookworm's mouth resembles something straight out of a science fiction movie. The other books in the series, also by Gail Jarrow, are *Blood and Germs: The Civil War Battle Against Wounds and Disease* (2020) and *Ambushed: The Assassination Plot Against President Garfield* (2021).

MULTIMODAL LITERACY

Most of today's nonfiction books for children and young adults could be described as what Frank Serafini calls "multimodal ensembles," in other words, a work made up of more than one mode. As Serafini explains,

> In general, the modes in print-based multimodal ensembles fall into three categories: (1) textual elements, which include all written language; (2) visual images like photography, painting, drawings, graphs, and charts; and (3) design elements like borders, typography, and other graphic elements.[16]

Each mode has its strengths and its limitations.[17] Moreover, different readers may engage with the modes in different ways. Echoing Louise Rosenblatt, Serafini sees reading a multimodal ensemble as a transactional process: "Images and texts mean things because readers bring experiences and understandings of images, language and the world to them when reading."[18]

Joe Sutfliff Sanders also believes that the process is transactional, but he is especially interested in how nonfiction texts invite or refuse critical engagement. As he explains, "[S]earching for where a work of nonfiction invites or refuses critical engagement reveals what ideas that text wants to normalize and what ideologies it is willing to risk by making them vulnerable to the critical attention of children."[19] He uses the word "critical" to refer to "a process by which readers ask questions and test information" and the word "engagement" to refer to "an activity that is collaborative, characterized by a sharing of authority between books and children."[20] While Sanders tends to emphasize the text's role in the transaction, Kylene Beers and Robert Probst focus on the reader's role. According to them,

> Reading nonfiction, in many ways, requires an effort not required in the reading of fiction. We must question the text, question the author, question our own understanding of the topic, and accept the possibility that our views will change as a result of the reading we're doing. All those demands mean that the *reader* has a great responsibility when reading nonfiction.[21] (emphasis in original)

In exploring the transaction between readers and multimodal texts, Serafini's three categories of textual elements, visual images, and design elements can serve as a useful framework. To those three elements, I would add critical literacy and peritextual literacy, both of which I will define below.

First, let's look at text literacy and consider how that works as a transactional process. Myra Zarnowski argues that

> [t]o truly understand nonfiction, students need to know that an author shapes information, a process that is much more than selecting the facts to include. Shaping consists of making decisions about (1) the gist, pattern, or main idea; (2) organizational structure; (3) style of writing; (4) integration of visual information; and (5) use of disciplinary thinking.[22]

With the exception of visual information, all of these elements relate directly to the textual part of a multimodal text. We might think of these elements as what is presented (main idea), how it is presented (organization and style), and how it reflects a particular disciplinary process of thinking and conducting research (historical, scientific, etc.). Child and young adult readers should certainly be able to identify these elements in nonfiction books, but they also need to be able to critically analyze them. As Sanders says, they need to look for places where texts invite or close off critical engagement. Beers and Probst suggest that one way to critically engage with the text is to look for what they call "signposts":

- Contrasts and contradictions
- Extreme or absolute language
- Numbers and statistics
- Quotations
- Vocabulary words they don't know[23]

One book that provides an excellent example of how organization can be used to convey content and illustrate disciplinary thinking is Jill Rubalcaba and Peter Robertshaw's *Every Bone Tells a Story: Hominin Discoveries, Deductions, and Debates* (2010). Each chapter is devoted to the discovery of a hominin, the deductions made about it, and the debates surrounding the discovery and deductions. Each chapter concludes with suggestions for further reading and sources, something that typically appears in the back matter of a book. The content and organization of each chapter not only show how archaeologists think and work, but also emphasize the point that scientific "facts" are often the subject of much debate among the archaeologists themselves. A book that draws attention to the issues surrounding selecting and presenting content is Susan Campbell Bartoletti's *They Called Themselves the K.K.K.: The Birth of an American Terrorist Group* (2010). In "A Note to the Reader" placed on the left directly before the first page of chapter 1 on the right, Bartolleti says that to the extent possible she included the voices of people from the past and images from periodicals of the time. She acknowledges that the language and images are sometimes crude and offensive, but she says that she has "chosen not to censor."[24] Readers can debate the value and potential pitfalls of including such content and compare the various points of view represented by this content with Bartoletti's own point of view.

Attending to the visual images in a multimodal text is another important aspect of critically engaging with that text. Visual literacy, according to B. A. Chauvin, is "the ability to access, analyze, evaluate, and communicate information in any variety of form that engages the cognitive processing of a visual image."[25] Serafini, while interested in all aspects of multimodal texts, has mostly focused on the visual in his research and writings. He suggests that one can read any image from three different perspectives: the perceptual, which focuses on "the literal or denotative contents of an image or series of images"; the structural, which focuses on "spatial and compositional layouts"; and the ideological, which focuses on "the social, political and cultural contexts" in which images are produced and viewed.[26] I find it helpful to think of these perspectives as a series of questions:

- What elements are present in the image? (perceptual)
- How do the elements in the image relate to one another and to the viewer? (structural)
- How do the elements in the image relate to the social, political, and cultural context(s) in which they are produced and viewed? (ideological)

Serafini stresses that "each perspective should be considered necessary but insufficient in and of itself to render a viable interpretation or analysis of multimodal texts."[27] A detailed discussion of how images work is beyond the scope of this chapter, but those interested in learning more will find Serafini's *Reading the Visual* to be an excellent resource.[28]

A key question, as Zarnowski points out, when examining the images in a nonfiction text is "How do the visual elements support and extend the written text?"[29] There are basically two kinds of images that may be included in a nonfiction book: those that are created specifically for the book and those that preexist the book but are acquired to include in the book. Of the latter, modifications may be made, such as making the original larger or smaller, rendering a color image in black and white, or cropping an image to emphasize only a portion of it. None of these practices is necessarily bad as long as the integrity of the image is preserved so that the image is not deliberately distorted. But readers should be aware that these kinds of manipulation can and do occur. A special case is the photograph. Photographs are frequently used in nonfiction books, and many of them, as Sanders notes, offer a kind of quiet authority that discourages the reader/viewer from questioning them.[30] In other words, photographs are often thought of as reflections rather than *interpretations* of reality. As we've seen, Sanders is suspicious of anything that doesn't invite critical engagement, so he encourages readers not to accept a photograph at face value but to pay particular attention to the elements around a photograph, to scrutinize "how books use captions, prose, layout, and other elements to indicate that a photograph is something to be interpreted."[31] He continues by offering a series of questions readers should ask of photographs and the books in which they appear:

> Are we asked to take the photographs as transparent truths? Are we guided to focus on certain information within the photographs? Are we urged to ask questions about the content of the photograph or how the photograph was made? Are we supposed to doubt either the photograph's content or origins? In short, are we supposed to see the photographs, or are we supposed to see through them?[32]

One book that offers a treasure trove of images for this kind of critical analysis is Elizabeth Partridge and Lauren Tamaki's *Seen and Unseen: What Dorothea Lange, Toyo Miyatake, and Ansel Adams's Photographs Reveal about the Japanese American*

Incarceration (2022). In the book Partridge's text and Tamaki's illustrations are interspersed with reprints of photographs from the three photographers mentioned in the title. Lange, we learn, was hired as a photographer for the War Relocation Authority (WRA) although she was much opposed to the incarceration of innocent people. Adams, who was not opposed to the incarceration program per se but felt that detainees who had pledged loyalty to the United States should be released, was also hired by the WRA to take photographs at the Manzanar internment camp. The WRA's purpose in hiring photographers was to show that conditions were not so bad in the various camps although, of course, only a few photographs were released to the public. Miyatake, who was incarcerated at the Manzanar internment camp between 1942 and 1945, took photographs with a camera he had smuggled in (because inmates were not allowed to have cameras). As a way of cultivating visual literacy, readers/viewers can think about whether and how the different photographers emphasized different kinds of images based on their own views and situations. They can consider the relationship between the photographs, which of course were not created for this book, and compare them with Tamaki's illustrations, which were. And they can contemplate the relationship between Partridge's text and the visual images. An author's note and an illustrator's note in the back matter provide additional insight into the making of the book. Readers can analyze the photographs from the different photographers based on something Partridge says in her author's note: "I thought I would use both Dorothea's and Ansel's images to show their different viewpoints. I was fascinated by what Dorothea was forbidden to photograph, and what Ansel chose not to photograph."[33] This would also be an excellent book to pair with George Takei's *They Called Us Enemy* (2019), a graphic memoir (written with Justin Eisinger and Steven Scott and illustrated by Harmony Becker) about his childhood experiences in two different internment camps. In addition to comparing the content of the two books, readers can think about how the visuals and format of a graphic memoir (to be discussed in more detail in chapter 6) compare with the visuals and format of Partridge and Tamaki's book.

Considering the design of a multimodal text is yet another way of critically engaging with the work. In many ways, design is what brings the text and the images together such that they help to make an overall point and achieve an overall effect, or, as Serafini writes,

> [d]esign is an active process of integrating and composing various modes for representing meaning potentials in multimodal ensembles. . . . What was once considered *writing* is now viewed as *assembling* or designing and composing various modes and semiotic resources into apt configurations for representing particular meanings.[34] (emphasis in original)

Design elements include such things as eye-catching front covers, typography, headings and subheadings, sidebars, the positioning of images in relation to one another and to the relevant text, and the use of color and contrast. In a successful book, these elements work together to facilitate learning and pleasure in young readers. To understand how this happens, let's look at a few examples.

For a fun and accessible primer on graphic design, one need look no further than Chip Kidd's *Go: A Kidd's Guide to Graphic Design* (2013). After defining graphic design, Kidd goes on to discuss form, typography, content, and concept, and he concludes by offering ten design projects readers can try at home. Though not specifically focused on book design, practically everything in *A Kidd's Guide* can be applied to book design. This would be an excellent book to read in conjunction with another nonfiction book and to think about why the book designers made the choices they did and what effects those choices have on the reader. A particularly interesting book in terms of design is Ariel Aberg-Riger's *America Redux: Visual Stories from Our Dynamic History* (2023). Made up of photographs and other illustrations, almost all of which Aberg-Riger found in archives, the book examines various aspects of the American experience, such as slavery, women's rights, the fascination with guns and cars, sports, agriculture, manufacturing, and many more. Each section is relatively short, contains many images, and includes text that appears to have been written by hand like that often seen in comic books and graphic novels. In the preface, the author highlights the importance of design in her own reading experiences, lamenting the kinds of history textbooks she read in school: "A history textbook is so impersonal. The type, the layout, the tone. Its design makes the subject feel distant. I love visual storytelling because the opposite is true."[35] She also explicitly invites critical engagement with her book and its design: "Forms change us, and I hope this book changes you. . . . I hope you question these stories, this book. I hope your questions turn into creation—of conversation, or art, of action."[36]

One aspect of design that is often overlooked is the peritext of a nonfiction book, in other words, the front and back matter that can be rich sources of information to supplement the information in the main text. The concept of the peritext originated with Gérard Genette, who defined it as elements of a text that are contained within a book and surround the main part of the text, or what we might call the text proper. Other kinds of discourses relating to the book but existing outside of the physical book itself—things such as author interviews, book reviews, communications between the author and the editor—Genette referred to as the epitext. The two together, peritext and epitext, constitute the paratext.[37] While exploring the epitext related to any given book can be a fascinating project, for our purposes we will focus on the peritext, as it is more closely associated with the main text and consists of elements over which the author and publisher have more control. Understanding what elements make up the peritext and how these elements relate to the main text is itself a kind of literacy, and a useful tool for exploring peritext and promoting critical thinking is Melissa Gross's and my Peritextual Literacy Framework (PLF).[38] The PLF identifies six types of peritext based on function:

- Production—elements that help identify a work and provide information about its creation. Examples include the title, author, illustrator, publisher.
- Promotion—elements that serve to advertise or promote the work. Examples include endorsements, excerpts from reviews of the book, book blurbs.
- Navigational—elements that indicate how a work is organized and how content can be accessed. Examples include the table of contents and the index.
- Intratextual—elements that interface between the work and the reader. Examples include the foreword, dedication, afterword, acknowledgments, author's note.
- Supplemental—elements that expand the reader's understanding of the content of the main text. Examples include endpapers, a glossary, a timeline (that's not included in the main text).
- Documentary—elements that identify external sources used in creating the work. Examples include a bibliography, source notes, image credits, suggestions for further reading.[39]

The PLF encourages readers to pay close attention to these various peritextual elements so that they will be better equipped to engage critically with both the main text and the peritext. It facilitates critical thinking and provides a structured framework readers can use in evaluating a book. In developing their nonfiction collections, librarians should look for books that provide not only engaging main texts, but engaging peritexts as well.

All nonfiction books will have some peritext, but some offer more—and richer—peritextual elements than others. A good example of a book where it pays to read the peritext is Neal Bascomb's *The Nazi Hunters: How a Team of Spies and Survivors Captured the World's Most Notorious Nazi* (2013). Bascomb's text relates the story of the thrilling manhunt that brought Adolf Eichmann to justice. The peritext adds to the story through the author's note (intratextual peritext) and the notes (documentary peritext) at the back of the book. In his author's note, Bascomb describes his meticulous research process but acknowledges that his "reconstruction of these events is no doubt imperfect" due to two factors: some of the information surrounding these events continues to remain secret and interviewees sometimes contradicted one another in their recollection of events.[40] He also says that in the notes section of the book he identifies several instances where "I've tried my best to reconcile conflicting accounts."[41] The author's note and the notes section highlight the challenges of weaving together a story when sources don't agree, and they invite critical engagement on the part of readers in interpreting these disparate sources for themselves. In other words, Bascomb both models and invites critical engagement. Readers who overlook these peritextual elements likely will miss this opportunity. Catherine Thimmesh provides equally rich peritextual elements in *Team Moon: How 400,000 People Landed Apollo 11 on the Moon* (2006). In the author's note, she doesn't say much about her research process; instead, she describes the challenges of writing about such a big project involving so many people: "Where to begin? With whom? Who goes in? Who has to come out?" She goes on to say, "The stories herein are but snapshots. Just a handful of players pulled from the bench of the greatest team ever."[42] Readers might think about what's lost and what's gained in providing only snapshots of these stories. As if to echo the notion of "snapshots," Thimmesh includes four pages of actual photographs of various members of the project team along with a quotation from each one, for a total of fourteen pictures and quotations altogether. These constitute an example of a supplemental peritextual element, and it enriches the main text by including the images and voices of some of the key players.

A final, important literacy in engaging with and evaluating multimodal texts is critical literacy. What do we mean by "critical literacy"? Various definitions have been offered over the years, but I'm especially drawn to Mitzi Lewison, Amy Seely Flint, and Katie Van Sluys's four dimensions of critical literacy, which they developed after reviewing numerous definitions of the term:

1. Disrupting the commonplace
2. Interrogating multiple viewpoints
3. Focusing on sociopolitical issues
4. Taking action and promoting social justice[43]

As for putting a critical literacy approach into action, Stephen Phelps suggests asking a series of questions when engaging with any text:

- What is the purpose of the text?
- How does the text try to position the reader?
- How does the text construct reality?
- Whose interests are or are not served by the ideas in the text?
- What worldviews are or are not represented?
- How are people marginalized by their culture, religion, or gender?[44]

The NCTE "Position Statement on the Role of Nonfiction Literature (K-12)" echoes the importance of nonfiction in fostering critical literacy. One use of nonfiction is "[t]o introduce a variety of perspectives, including those of traditionally marginalized or silenced groups."[45] The document goes on to suggest that teachers use multiple nonfiction books on the same topic in order to introduce multiple perspectives and to encourage students to "identify and interrogate sociocultural stereotypes and social narratives of the dominant or mainstream culture."

Fortunately, more and more nonfiction books are being published each year that help young people better understand diversity and help facilitate critical literacy development. Some of these books recover and celebrate the real-life stories of marginalized individuals or groups. Maryann Cocca-Leffler and Vivien Mildenberger's *Fighting for YES! The Story of Disability Rights Activist Judith Heumann* (2022) introduces children to the pioneering work of the woman who organized a sit-in that ultimately helped pave the way for passage of the Americans with Disabilities Act. Traci Sorrell and Frane Lessac's *We Are Still Here! Native American Truths Everyone Should Know* (2021) relays aspects of Native American history that are often omitted from mainstream history textbooks, for example, forced relocations, forced assimilation of Native children, tribal government, and land allotment. And *Lifting as We Climb: Black Women's Battle for the Ballot Box* (2020) by Evette Dionne, reclaims the heretofore overlooked role women of color played in the women's suffrage movement. It would be an instructive exercise in critical literacy for readers to compare this account of the suffrage movement with that of Winifred Conkling in *Votes for Women! American Suffragists and the Battle for the Ballot* (2018), a book aimed at a slightly older audience that presents a wider view of the topic while also depicting the racism within the movement.

Looking at nonfiction for children and young adults through a literacy lens not only allows us to see how these books can help facilitate the development of various literacies in young readers, but also provides a framework for us as librarians to evaluate nonfiction books that we're considering adding to our collections. We can ask of any given nonfiction book:

- How does this book promote text, visual, design, peritextual, and critical literacy?
- How does this book exemplify disciplinary thinking?
- How does this book encourage critical engagement?

Of course, no one book can do it all, so it is important to include a variety of nonfiction books in our collections, including a variety of books on the same topics. Ultimately, our goal should be for readers to comprehend what they read, connect it to what they already know, and critique what they've read by analyzing and questioning it. In the next chapter, we will consider the various nonfiction genres that are available to help us accomplish this goal.

NOTES

1. David Buckingham, "The Uselessness of Literacies," accessed February 10, 2024, https://davidbuckingham.net/blog/.

2. Abraham H. Maslow, *The Psychology of Science: A Reconnaissance* (New York: Harper & Row, 1966), 15-16.
3. "Literacy," Oxford English Dictionary, in *Oxford English Dictionary*, ed. Michael Proffitt (Oxford, U.K.: Oxford University Press, 2023).
4. UNESCO, "What You Need to Know About Literacy," accessed January 25, 2024, https://www.unesco.org/en/literacy/need-know.
5. Frank Serafini, *Reading the Visual: An Introduction to Teaching Multimodal Literacy* (New York: Teachers College Press, 2014), 19.
6. New London Group, "A Pedagogy of Multiliteracies: Designing Social Futures," *Harvard Educational Review* 66, no. 1 (1996): 60.
7. National Council of Teachers of English, "Definition of Literacy in a Digital Age," accessed February 9, 2024, https://ncte.org/statement/nctes-definition-literacy-digital-age/.
8. Ibid.
9. American Association of School Librarians, "Standards Framework for Learners," accessed February 9, 2024, https://standards.aasl.org/wp-content/uploads/2017/11/AASL-Standards-Framework-for-Learners-pamphlet.pdf.
10. Association of College and Research Libraries, "Framework for Information Literacy for Higher Education," accessed February 9, 2024, https://www.ala.org/acrl/standards/ilframework.
11. Thomas P. Mackey and Trudi E. Jacobson, *Metaliteracy: Reinventing Information Literacy to Empower Learners* (Chicago: Neal-Schuman, 2014), 1.
12. Ibid., 15, 24.
13. UNESCO, "What You Need to Know About Literacy."
14. Wikipedia, "Data Literacy," accessed February 11, 2024, https://en.wikipedia.org/wiki/Data_literacy.
15. Zhihui Fang and Suzanne Coatoam, "Disciplinary Literacy: What You Want to Know About It," *Journal of Adolescent & Adult Literacy* 56, no. 8 (2013): 628.
16. Serafini, *Reading the Visual: An Introduction to Teaching Multimodal Literacy*, 12-13.
17. Ibid., 15.
18. Frank Serafini, "Reading Multimodal Texts: Perceptual, Structural and Ideological Perspectives," *Children's Literature in Education* 41 (2010): 89.
19. Joe Sutliff Sanders, *A Literature of Questions: Nonfiction for the Critical Child* (Minneapolis: University of Minnesota Press, 2018), 7.
20. Ibid.
21. Kylene Beers and Robert E. Probst, *Reading Nonfiction: Notice & Note Stances, Signposts, and Strategies* (Portsmouth, NH: Heinemann, 2016), 19.
22. Myra Zarnowski, "Shaping Nonfiction: Making the Facts 'Dance Together'," *Journal of Children's Literature* 40, no. 2 (2014): 6.
23. Beers and Probst, *Reading Nonfiction: Notice & Note Stances, Signposts, and Strategies*, 117.
24. Susan Campbell Bartoletti, *They Called Themselves the K.K.K.: The Birth of an American Terrorist Group* (New York: Houghton Mifflin Harcourt, 2010), n.p.
25. B. A. Chauvin, "Visual or Media Literacy?," *Journal of Visual Literacy* 23, no. 2 (2003): 125.
26. Serafini, "Reading Multimodal Texts: Perceptual, Structural and Ideological Perspectives," 92, 96, 98.
27. Ibid., 89.

28. Serafini, *Reading the Visual: An Introduction to Teaching Multimodal Literacy*.
29. Zarnowski, "Shaping Nonfiction: Making the Facts 'Dance Together'," 9.
30. Sanders, *A Literature of Questions: Nonfiction for the Critical Child*, 135-36.
31. Ibid., 137.
32. Ibid.
33. Elizabeth Partridge and Lauren Tamaki, *Seen and Unseen: What Dorothea Lange, Toyo Miyatake, and Ansel Adams's Photographs Reveal About the Japanese American Incarceration* (San Francisco, CA: Chronicle Books, 2022).
34. Serafini, *Reading the Visual: An Introduction to Teaching Multimodal Literacy*, 52, 53.
35. Ariel Aberg-Riger, *America Redux: Visual Stories from Our Dynamic History* (New York: HarperCollins, 2023), 3.
36. Ibid., 4.
37. Gérard Genette, *Paratexts: Thresholds of Interpretation* (New York: Cambridge University Press, 1997), 4-5.
38. Melissa Gross and Don Latham, "The Peritextual Literacy Framework: Using the Functions of Peritext to Support Critical Thinking," *Library and Information Science Research* 39, no. 2 (2017).
39. Ibid., 119-20.
40. Neal Bascomb, *The Nazi Hunters: How a Team of Spies and Survivors Captured the World's Most Notorious Nazi* (New York: Scholastic Inc., 2013), 219.
41. Ibid.
42. Catherine Thimmesh, *Team Moon: How 400,000 People Landed Apollo 11 on the Moon* (New York: Houghton Mifflin, 2006), 64.
43. Mitzi Lewison, Amy Seely Flint, and Katie Van Sluys, "Taking on Critical Literacy: The Journey of Newcomers and Novices," *Language Arts* 78, no. 5 (2002): 382.
44. Stephen Phelps, "Critical Literacy: Using Nonfiction to Learn About Islam," *Journal of Adolescent & Adult Literacy* 54, no. 3 (2010): 194.
45. National Council of Teachers of English, "Position Statement on the Role of Nonfiction Literature (K-12)," accessed February 12, 2024, https://ncte.org/statement/role-of-nonfiction-literature-k-12/.

5

Nonfiction Genres

So far, in discussing how to evaluate and select nonfiction for children and young adults, we've considered how nonfiction can help address their developmental and information needs and can facilitate the development of various kinds of literacies. Another important aspect of nonfiction to consider is genre, or more accurately, the various subgenres found in nonfiction literature. According to the *Oxford Concise Dictionary of Literary Terms*, genre is defined as "a type, species, or class of composition. A literary genre is a recognizable and established category of written work employing such common conventions as will prevent readers from mistaking it for another kind."[1] It is important to remember, however, as Kimberly Reynolds points out in her discussion of genre *fiction*, "while writers may consciously be working within well-established genres, for most child readers these texts provide their first experiences of individual genres and so they will not find them familiar or predictable."[2] This is certainly true for younger readers although as children get older, they become familiar with various genres and often gravitate toward certain ones based on individual preferences. In the realm of fiction, for example, some children like fantasy more than realism while others may prefer contemporary adventure stories to historical fiction. The same is true with nonfiction genres: some children enjoy reading books about science while others find biographies more appealing. And, of course, there is overlap—both among genres and among reading interests. A child who enjoys a particular sport, basketball, for example, may want to read a history of basketball, biographies of famous basketball players, and even how-to books on becoming more skillful at basketball. Having a good understanding of nonfiction genres, like understanding children's and teens' developmental and information needs, can help librarians develop diverse collections and match readers with the right books. In the previous two chapters, we spent some time looking at self-help books and career advice; books dealing with health, fitness and nutrition, sex and sexuality; and advice and how-to books.

In this chapter we will focus on the big three, the genres more commonly associated with so-called literary nonfiction: biography and memoir, history, and science and technology. These are the books most frequently reviewed, and by far these are the books that receive the most awards.

In terms of evaluating the big three genres for collection development and readers' advisory purposes, certain criteria are more applicable to particular genres, but other criteria can be applied to nonfiction books in general. Marc Aronson advocates for nonfiction literature in which it is obvious that "an author [has] thought something through for him or herself and turned that into a new, an original, creative synthesis."[3] Aronson identifies five types of originality that one should look for in evaluating nonfiction for children and young adults:

- Conception ("how the author has thought about his or her subject")
- Organization ("how the author has juxtaposed the material he has found, to be both true to the subject and in tune with his or her readers")
- Voice ("finding a voice that is appropriate to a nonfiction topic but in tune with young people")
- Research strategies
- Design[4]

As an example of the use of an innovative research strategy, Aronson cites Susan Campbell Bartoletti's *Hitler Youth: Growing Up in Hitler's Shadow* (2005). He praises Campbell for constructing her book around interviews with former members of the Hitler Youth, with the effect of doing "more to combat a scourge by revealing its power than by merely condemning it."[5]

In addition, as Sandip Wilson reminds us, it is important to examine whether and how sources are documented in nonfiction books for children and young adults. Far from being a mere nicety, identifying sources helps authors demonstrate that their books are constructions, not simple transcriptions of facts. Wilson explains, "Sources show young readers that authors select information on their topic from all the information available to them, that sometimes lack of information is a topic authors address, and that selection makes a difference in the impression left on readers."[6] Authors sometimes discuss how they've interpreted their sources and when information is missing. Sometimes these discussions appear in the main text, but often they appear in the author's note or in the source notes.[7] Of course, not all books provide this information, and, when that's the case, "[w]hen sources are limited or absent, students cannot retrace the steps of investigation nor can they follow up on the information selected by the author. They do not have models for their own writing."[8] In contrast, the presence of sources "honor[s] young readers by giving them entry into processes of writing and providing avenues for further questioning and investigation regardless of how old they are."[9]

Wilson offers five key questions to ask when evaluating how a nonfiction book uses sources:

- What sources are used?
- Why are the sources used?
- What did the author have to learn in writing the book?
- What does the author say about the sources?
- What does the author want us to know about this topic?[10]

As one example, Wilson praises Diane McWhorter's *A Dream of Freedom: The Civil Rights Movement from 1954 to 1968* (2004) for its inclusion of many quotations and for McWhorter's explicit discussion of the kinds of sources she used, including interviews that she conducted, archival materials, and books and articles.[11]

A third element to consider when evaluating a nonfiction book is the extent to which it reflects inclusivity and cultural sensitivity. In doing so, we can apply Rudine Sims Bishop's concept of books' potential to be mirrors, windows, and sliding glass doors (discussed in chapter 3).[12] Another helpful tool is *10 Quick Ways to Analyze Children's Books for Racism and Sexism*, originally published as a pamphlet by the Council on Interracial Books for Children and now available online.[13] Although some of the council's recommendations may seem to apply more to fiction, they actually can all be applied to nonfiction as well, with a little tweaking. The council recommends checking the following with an eye toward detecting stereotypes and/or glaring omissions:

1. Check the Illustrations
2. Check the Story Line
3. Look at the Lifestyles
4. Weigh the Relationships Between People
5. Note the Heroes
6. Consider the Effects on a Child's Self Image
7. Consider the Author or Illustrator's Background
8. Check Out the Author's Perspective
9. Watch for Loaded Words
10. Look at the Copyright Date[14]

As a case in point, Denise Dávila and Sarah Elovich raise the issue of narrative authenticity in nonfiction books for children. They point out the problems of many of the books in National Geographic for Kids' Holidays Around the World series. The issue, according to Dávila and Elovich, is that the books are narrated from the viewpoint of a child who is a member of the culture being spotlighted while in reality many of the authors are adults who are not members of that culture.[15] To make matters worse, the narrators tend to speak in a collective

Nonfiction Genres

"we" and indicate that all members of their culture celebrate a holiday by doing certain things. This misleads children and essentializes members of the culture, suggesting that they all do these things. Dávila and Elovich point out this could easily be fixed by the authors writing in third person, to avoid appearing to be speaking on behalf of a culture, and using words like "some" or "many" instead of "all" and "everyone."[16] They offer key questions to consider in evaluating books that present cultural information:

- Does the narrative point-of-view correspond with the author's stated identity?
- Does the text include generalizations or essentializing statements about the group, employing terms such as all, every, none, never, always, and so on?
- How does the text recognize the diversity within any groups?
- Does the narration make neutral observations about the group or does it speak on behalf of the group?[17]

These evaluative criteria are important to consider regardless of the genre, but other criteria are more specific to certain genres—and that is where we now turn our attention. One note before we proceed: in chapter 6 we will be looking at formats, focusing on nonfiction picturebooks and graphic nonfiction. Most of my examples in the present chapter, therefore, will be chapter books, and I will save my discussion of picturebooks and graphic nonfiction for the next chapter, returning as appropriate to questions of genre.

BIOGRAPHY AND MEMOIR

It is tempting to think of biography as simply a skillfully arranged collection of facts about a person's life, but, of course, biography as an art form is more complicated than that. Hermione Lee, a well-respected writer of biographies for adults, says, "Any biographical narrative is an artificial construct." Moreover, biography reflects "the social and cultural politics of its time and place, so its assumptions change about what is major or minor, permitted or shocking, mainstream or alternative."[18] Milton Meltzer, a prolific writer of history and biography for adults and children, elaborates on the constructed aspect of writing biography: "[B]iography is not a compilation of the material you researched. It is a composition of that material. This gets us to the core of biography. It is only and always how one person sees another person."[19] Lee states the case more boldly: "All biography is an attempt to take possession of the subject . . . but some biographers are more possessed—or possessive—than others."[20] Young readers, however, will not necessarily recognize the constructed nature of biographies on their own, but with help they can come to discern the art and artifice behind the life story. Myra Zarnowski suggests three clues to identifying an author's unique perspective on the subject's life, and these are elements that we as librarians can also use not only with children, but also in evaluating biographies ourselves. One is to look for repetitions of the author's perspective throughout the book as evident in a thesis and repeated words and phrases. Another is to examine the author's note (if there is one) to see what the author has to say about their interest in and view of their subject. A third is to examine several biographies on the same subject written by different authors and compare the perspectives of each.[21] In addition, as Lee points out, the title and table of contents can reveal a lot about an author's approach to their subject.[22] The title of Steve Sheinkin's *The Notorious Benedict Arnold: A True Story of Adventure, Heroism & Treachery* (2010), for example, promises a swashbuckling tale while the title of Phillip Hoose's *Claudette Colvin: Twice Toward Justice* (2009) references the book's purpose of reclaiming an important figure of the Civil Rights Movement.

Not surprisingly, biography is a popular genre among children and young adults. As W. Bernard Lukenbill explains in his book *Biography in the Lives of Youth*, there are a number of reasons for the genre's popularity. It can help to transmit cultural information, promote greater self-awareness, and facilitate social and intellectual skills.[23] While at one time biography for youth had a more didactic purpose, offering models of obedience and hard work, nowadays biography "is more concerned with helping [youth] understand human experiences, social concerns, and history. At a more personal level, biography today is often used to help youth understand options and consequences of choices in terms of such areas as gender and social roles, relationships, and achievement."[24] Children and young adults alike enjoy reading about contemporary figures, such as entertainers and athletes, people not as well-known but who have done interesting things, and people who have overcome hardship.[25]

It's important for libraries to have a variety of biographies in their collections—including biographies on a variety of subjects and multiple biographies on single subjects. But how much variety is represented among what is available from publishers? A recent study, by Sunah Chung and Amina Chaudhri, of the Robert F. Sibert Informational Book Medal winners and honor books published between 2001 (the first year of the award) and 2019, found only 12 biographies of women—seven chapter books, four picturebooks, and one graphic novel. Three of these books are memoirs, and one is a collective biography (i.e., focuses on multiple individuals).[26] By comparison, 27 biographies of men were named as winners or honor books during this same time period. In another study, Adam Crawley examined picturebook biographies of individuals identified as LGBTQIA+ in other, adult publications. Of the 51 such picturebooks published between 2000 and 2019, he found that only five books were explicit about their subjects' sexuality, nine were implicit, and 37 excluded this element altogether.[27] Crawley notes that books have the potential to serve not only as mirrors and windows (citing Rudine Sims Bishop), but also as maps (citing Christopher Myers), "showing youth possibilities for their lives as well as the personal and professional journey taken by others."[28] A problem arises when biographers omit key information about their subjects:

> To intentionally conceal information about a person to make the text and the person more palatable to a wider audience is to re-present them, not to show the person as they are or were but rather to present them in an alternate way. Such alternate depictions are incomplete or inaccurate.[29]

Crawley's focus is on picturebooks, generally intended for younger readers, but one wonders to what extent this kind of erasure may also be occurring in chapter books for older readers.

Fortunately, there are many fine examples of biographies for children and young adults. Almost everyone who studies and writes about the genre mentions Russell Freedman's classic, *Lincoln: A Photobiography* (1987). In this book, Freedman weaves his narrative of Abraham Lincoln's life around numerous archival photographs. In addition, he includes several sections of back matter that provide supplemental information and encourage further exploration: "A Lincoln Sampler," which includes excerpts from some of the late President's speeches; "In Lincoln's Footsteps," a list of Lincoln-related places to visit such as his boyhood home and Ford's Theatre National Historic Site; "Books About Lincoln"; and "Acknowledgments and Picture Credits." While most biographies are not as profusely illustrated as this one (Steve Sheinkin's *The Notorious Benedict Arnold* [2010] contains only two), most do tend to focus on a single individual. Some notable examples include Candace Fleming's *The Rise and Fall of Charles Lindbergh* (2020), Elizabeth Partridge's *John Lennon: All I Want Is the Truth* (2005), and Ann Angels' *Janis Joplin: Rise Up Singing* (2010). Other biographies are dual biographies in that they depict the lives of two, usually closely related, people. Freedman, for example, focuses on Orville and Wilbur Wright in *The Wright Brothers: How They Invented the Airplane* (1991), Deborah Heiligman focuses her attention on a married couple in *Charles and Emma: The Darwins' Leap of Faith* (2009) and on two brothers in *Vincent and Theo: The Van Gogh Brothers* (2017). There are also collective biographies available, books that examine the lives of a group of individuals, usually connected in some way. Tanya Lee Stone's *Almost Astronauts: 13 Women Who Dared to Dream* (2009) looks at the lives of the first group of women to go through astronaut training in the United States. Candace Fleming's *The Enigma Girls: How Ten Teenagers Broke Ciphers, Kept Secrets, and Helped Win World War II* (2024) recovers the stories of the young women in Great Britain who were recruited to help crack coded Nazi messages during the war. *Latinitas: Celebrating 40 Big Dreamers* (2021) by Juliet Menéndez provides brief biographies that explore the early lives of 40 influential women from Latin America and the United States.

Fewer memoirs than biographies are published for children and young adults, but there are still some fine examples, especially by authors who write other genres for children and young adults. Before going any farther, it's worth considering the difference between memoir and autobiography. The terms are sometimes used interchangeably, but strictly speaking there are differences. An autobiography is generally defined as "the biography of a person narrated by that person: usually a written account of a person's life in their own words."[30] The assumption is that an autobiography covers the entire life up to the time of writing. A memoir is defined more narrowly as "a nonfiction narrative in which the author shares their memories from a specific time period or reflects upon a string of themed occurrences throughout their life."[31] An example of an autobiography is the young adult author Chris Crutcher's *King of the Mild Frontier: An Ill-Advised Autobiography* (2003). In the book Crutcher covers both his childhood and adulthood, up to the early 2000s. An example of a memoir is children's author Jack Gantos's *Hole in My Life* (2002), which focuses mostly on the time Gantos spent in prison for his involvement in a drug-running operation.

In any case, whether something is called an autobiography or a memoir is really less important for collection development purposes than understanding the characteristics of this kind of life writing. The psychologist Jerome Bruner describes autobiography as a way of "life-making," and, much like the process of writing biography, "recounting one's life is an interpretive feat."[32] Moreover, according to Bruner, "[T]he very telling of the self-story distorts what we have in mind to tell."[33] It would seem that no one is in a better position to recount a life than the person who is leading it, but memory can be selective, faulty, and more or less adept at self-reflection. As with a biographer, an autobiographer likely has an image in mind that they want to project. Bruner says that "a life is not 'how it was' but how it is interpreted and reinterpreted, told and retold."[34] Autobiography as a literary practice has developed somewhat differently for men and women. Jill Ker Conway, in *When Memory Speaks: Exploring the Art of Autobiography*, says that early on male autobiography was based on the epic hero's story: "Life is an odyssey, a journey through many trials and tests, which the hero must surmount alone through courage, endurance, cunning, and moral strength." With male Christian autobiography, the journey was moved from the external to the internal world, focusing on the process of conversion "with the author poised between sin and damnation, or belief and salvation."[35] For women, early autobiography was largely focused on one's relationship with God, meditation, and divine illumination. Then as society became more secular, women's autobiography began to reflect "the bourgeois preoccupation with romantic love, marriage, family and property."[36] No doubt, a trace of some of these early characteristics can be found in autobiography written today, including autobiography for children and young adults. Regardless of the author's gender and the approach they take, there is a kind of universal appeal to reading about someone else's life. Conway explains, "What makes the reading of autobiography so appealing is the chance it offers to see how this man or that woman whose public self interests us has negotiated the problem of self-awareness and has broken the internalized code a culture supplies about how life should be experienced."[37] To borrow Bishop's metaphor, we might say that autobiography provides not only a window into someone else's life, but also a mirror of our own, at least on a subconscious level.

In the case of famous individuals, there may be both biographies and autobiographies available, and some individuals write more than one autobiography—Maya Angelou wrote seven, beginning with *I Know Why the Caged Bird Sings* (1969). It can be interesting and instructive, when possible, to compare autobiographies and biographies. Laura May, Teri Holbrook, and Laura Meyers examined 14 biographies of Barack Obama and compared them with one another and with Obama's two (at the time) published autobiographies. Focusing on three key events in Obama's life, as reported in his autobiographies, they found that some of the biographies included these events while others omitted them. The ones that did include them framed them differently, and the way the narratives of these events were constructed differed as well.[38] Some of the biographies depicted Obama as a "lone hero" (even an epic hero, perhaps?), while others emphasized his working with grassroots community organizations.[39] May, Holbrook, and Meyers argue that these differences matter: "How Obama is storied in children's books is critical not only because the storying contributes to children's understandings of themselves within a cultural context, but because it also contributes to their notion of social and cultural change."[40]

Much recent autobiographical writing for children and young adults has been in the form of graphic memoirs, and we will discuss those in the next chapter. Many, though certainly not all, of the chapter book memoirs are by well-known writers of fiction for children and young adults. Lois Lowry, the author of the perennially popular Giver Quartet as well as other works, published her autobiography, *Looking Back: A Book of Memories*, in 1998 and then offered an expanded version in 2016. Filled with photographs, anecdotes, and reflections, the book provides insight into this highly regarded author's life and work. Jerry Spinelli, author of *Maniac Magee*, *Stargirl*, and countless other books for young adults, published his memoir, *Knots in My Yo-Yo String: The Autobiography of a Kid* (1998), the same year Lowry's original autobiography came out. Spinelli's account, as the subtitle suggests, focuses primarily on his childhood and adolescence. Similarly, Walter Dean Myers's *Bad Boy: A Memoir* (2001) recounts his experiences growing up in Harlem and his development as a reader and writer. In *The Scraps Book: Notes from a Colorful Life* (2014), author and illustrator Lois Ehlert includes illustrations and text that trace her development as an artist. Jacqueline Woodson's *Brown Girl Dreaming* (2014) recounts her growing up in South Carolina and New York in the 1960s and

1970s. Woodson's memoir consists of a series of poems, as does Nikki Grimes' *Ordinary Hazards: A Memoir* (2019), in which she relates the horrors of her difficult childhood.

Authors of children's and young adult fiction are by no means the only people who have written autobiographies for youth. *Turning 15 on the Road to Freedom: My Story of the 1965 Selma Voting Rights March* (2015) is Lynda Blackmon Lowery's account of her firsthand experiences as a young activist during the Civil Rights Movement. *Reaching for the Moon: The Autobiography of NASA Mathematician Katherine Johnson* (2019) tells of Johnson's pioneering work as one of the first African American women to be employed by NASA. Some autobiographies are originally written for an adult audience and then are adapted for younger readers. Such is the case with *The Boy Who Harnessed the Wind: Young Readers Edition* (2015). This is William Kamkwamba's account (co-authored by Bryan Mealer and illustrated by Anna Hymas) of how as a boy he helped find a solution to the drought that was ravaging his family's crops. The solution? To build a windmill that would generate electricity to power a pump to bring water to the family's farm. A more lighthearted but equally compelling story is told in Maya Van Wagenen's *Popular: A Memoir* (2014). Written when Van Wagenen was a young teenager, the book describes how during her eighth-grade year she attempted to implement advice from a 1950s popularity guide for girls in order to become popular. By turns funny and poignant, this real-life story is unique not only because of Van Wagenen's experiment but also because of her age: few memoirs for young adults are actually written by young adults.

HISTORY

The best history books for children and young adults, according to Myra Zarnowski, don't simply present facts, but also show how historians think and how history is done. Such books include four key components: "historical context, multiple perspectives, information about sources, and original interpretation."[41] As with biography, authors will sometimes provide insights into their own research and writing process in the author's note and/or the source notes. Such notes can be instrumental in showing how a particular author engaged in historical thinking while putting a book together. Zarnowski, a thoughtful and prolific scholar of nonfiction for children and young adults, praises Jim Murphy's *The Great Fire* (1995), *Blizzard!* (2000), and *An American Plague: The True and Terrifying Story of the Yellow Fever Epidemic of 1793* (2003) for achieving the four components of good historical writing. He provides historical context by including multisensory descriptions of the cataclysmic events he writes about: the great fire that destroyed much of Chicago in 1871, the fierce snowstorm that paralyzed the East Coast in 1888, and the yellow fever epidemic that decimated Philadelphia in 1793.[42] He offers multiple perspectives by incorporating the voices of people who witnessed the events firsthand.[43] He provides information about his sources—primary and secondary sources and various kinds of accounts (firsthand, etc.)—in all three books.[44] And he discusses his interpretation of the events in the final chapter of each of the books.[45] In another article, Zarnowski and Susan Turkel draw a comparison between historians and detectives: both collect evidence, make inferences, and develop a plausible story; at heart, both are engaged in problem-solving.[46] Of course, not all history books convey "history as mystery," but the best ones do. As Zarnowski and Turkel explain, "In contrast to presenting history as a finished and agreed upon story, presenting history as mystery introduces students to the thought processes that historians use as they evaluate evidence and construct historical accounts."[47]

Nonfiction history books for children and young adults can take as their focus virtually any subject—person, place, event, idea, or thing. In *Sugar Changed the World: A Story of Magic, Spice, Slavery, Freedom, and Science* (2010), Marc Aronson and Marina Budhos relate the dramatic history of what we now consider a basic commodity. In *The Good, the Bad, and the Barbie: A Doll's History and Her Impact on Us* (2010), Tanya Lee Stone recounts the development, marketing, and consumption of an iconic toy. Events can be specific, like the Tulsa Race Massacre, as recounted by Brandy Colbert in *Black Birds in the Sky: The Story and Legacy of the 1921 Tulsa Race Massacre* (2021), or they can be more wide-ranging and longer-term, like Elizabeth Partridge's *Boots on the Ground: America's War in Vietnam* (2018). Sometimes nonfiction history focuses on specific groups that made important contributions during a particular time and in a particular place. Such is the case with Sherri L. Smith and Elizabeth Wein's *American Wings: Chicago's Pioneering Black Aviators and the Race for Equality in the Sky* (2024), which tells the story of Black Americans, both women and men, who between World War I and World War II built an airfield outside of Chicago and set up a training school for pilots. Other group histories are much broader, covering a range of people over a long time period. Many books cover key events involving race relations in American history. For example, *Uprooted: The Japanese American Experience During World War II* (2016) by Albert Marrin describes the incarceration of over 100,000 Japanese Americans because they were considered a potential threat to national security. *More Than a Dream: The Radical March on Washington for Jobs and Freedom* (2023) by Yohuru Williams and Michael G. Long relates how a quarter of a million people, many of them Blacks and Latines, gathered on the National Mall in Washington, DC, in 1963 to demand their civil rights. A more wide-ranging history—approximately 400 years—is presented in Michael Bronski and Richie Chevat's *A Queer History of the United States for Young People* (2019).

Certain topics are of perennial interest to children and young adults. Sports books, including histories, are especially appealing to many young readers. *We Are the Ship: The Story of Negro League Baseball* (2008) by Kadir Nelson is a beautifully illustrated book about the Black pioneers who formed their own league in the years before America's pastime was integrated. *Hardcourt: Stories from 75 Years of the National Basketball Association* (2022) by Fred Bowen and James E. Ransome offers an exciting account of the important players, coaches, and teams of the NBA. Another topic of great interest to young people (and adults too) is histories of calamities, accidents, and disasters. In *Titanic: Voices from the Disaster* (2012), Deborah Hopkinson includes stories and firsthand accounts of witnesses to and survivors of the infamous maritime tragedy. Christina Soontornvat offers a breathtaking account of a remarkable rescue in *All Thirteen: The Incredible Cave Rescue of the Thai Boys' Soccer Team* (2020). Equally compelling are stories of true crime, and there is no shortage of these books for children and especially for young adults. *The Mona Lisa Vanishes: A Legendary Painter, Shocking Heist, and the Birth of a Global Celebrity* (2023) by Nicholas Day and Brett Helquist offers a thrilling account of a startling theft. *The 57 Bus: A True Story of Two Teenagers and the Crime That Changed Their Lives* (2017) by Dashika Slater tells the tragic and complicated story of a transgender teen who was set on fire by another teen.

Other books provide insights into culture and/or current issues. Susan Rubin Goldman's *The Quilts of Gee's Bend* (2017) relates the history of quilt-making among a group of women in southern Alabama, while Grace Lin's *Chinese Menu: The History, Myths, and Legends Behind Your Favorite Foods* (2023) includes both history and folklore associated with various popular Chinese foods. Current issues can be seen in a number of recent books. In *The 21: The True Story of the Youth Who Sued the U.S. Government Over Climate Change* (2023), Elizabeth Rusch shows how youth activism can have an impact on a global issue. *This Land Is Our Land: A History of American Immigration* (2016) by Linda Barrett Osborne looks at what's been a contentious issue in the United States since at least 1800. And *Call and Response: The Story of Black Lives Matter* (2021) by Veronica Chambers relates the story of a progressive social movement to tweens and teens.

SCIENCE AND TECHNOLOGY

As is the case with history books, the best science books depict science not as a finished product, merely a collection of facts, but rather as a process of solving problems.[48] Zarnowski and Turkel identify three key elements of nonfiction narratives about problem-solving; they focus on

- Identity—"a person who sees himself or herself as a creative thinker"
- Agency—"having the ability to impact a situation"
- Knowledge—"a person who knows relevant content and how to use it."[49]

They suggest asking the following questions when evaluating a problem-solver book:

- Who is doing the investigating?
- What is the problem?
- What is the process of investigation?
- What are the results? Are they convincing?[50]

Steve Jenkins criticizes the way science is often presented to children and young adults and offers a better alternative: "Far too often, science is taught as a collection of facts to be memorized rather than as a process. Understanding that science is a way of thinking rather than a set of data is at the crux of the issue."[51] Science nonfiction should encourage readers to ask questions and especially to question scientific conclusions.[52] Similarly, Zarnowski and Turkel criticize many science nonfiction books for being mostly collections of facts without providing context and illustrating problem-solving, collaboration, and the construction of knowledge.[53] Like historical nonfiction, good nonfiction writing reveals the mystery of science. As Zarnowski explains, "Nonfiction mysteries, especially those dealing with science, share the same compelling features as fictional mysteries: the puzzling situations, the process of seeking and solving, and the tension between the unknown and the possibility of knowing."[54] She suggests asking the following questions when evaluating a nonfiction science book:

- What is the mystery that scientists want to solve?
- What evidence have they gathered to solve the mystery? How?
- Did the scientists have any false starts? Did they toss out any assumptions?
- What did they learn?
- What else do they want to know?[55]

So how is science and how are scientists portrayed in nonfiction science books for children and young adults? Laura May and her colleagues undertook a study of 400 National Science Teachers Association Outstanding Trade Books for Students K-12 published between 2010 and 2017 in order "to determine how these books are organized and, broadly speaking, how they represent scientific knowledge."[56] They discovered that the books fell into two broad categories: the lived lives of scientists, books that "prioritize the how of science, focusing on how scientists create and establish knowledge," and accepted knowledge, books "written by a knowledgeable author seeking to communicate knowledge recognized as reliable by the relevant scientific community."[57] Approximately 38 percent of the books were categorized as "lived lives of scientists" while approximately 62 percent were categorized as "accepted knowledge."[58] In terms of organization (or modes of writing), they found that the lived lives of scientists books tended to use narrative and recounting whereas the accepted knowledge books tended to use expository writing. Books aimed at younger readers were more likely to use narrative than explanation or procedural text (how-to) and were usually about animals.[59] And it's not just a matter of how books depict science and scientific thinking; it's also a question of how they portray the professionals who work in science, technology, engineering, and mathematics (STEM). Aeriale Johnson and Clare Landrigan note that "[a]ll Black Indigenous People of Color (BIPOC) except Asian Americans are underrepresented across STEM occupations" and women continue to be underrepresented in engineering and computer science.[60] They argue that introducing young children to diverse nonfiction science books can help in closing those gaps: "Inclusive, multigenerational nonfiction science books can illustrate for children . . . that not only can their burgeoning scientific literacy help them '*do* science,' but that they can *be* scientists in ways that transform their communities" (emphasis in original).[61] But how inclusive are children's nonfiction science books? A study by Laura Beth Kelly of 28 nonfiction science picturebooks from the 2016 National Science Teachers Association's list of Outstanding Science Trade Books asked just that question. In representations of historical and living scientists, 77 percent were males and 67 percent were white. Among generic or child scientists represented, 52 percent were males and 74 percent were white.[62] As for the scientific fields represented, 71 percent of the scientists were in the life sciences, 18 percent in the earth and space sciences, and only 11 percent were in engineering, technology, and applied science.[63] Based on her analysis, Kelly concludes, "[T]he current children's book market, while offering valuable tools, does not adequately provide resources to teach the diversity of science and scientists."[64] We will say more about nonfiction science picturebooks in chapter 6, but now it's worth noting that diversity—both of the scientists and the science represented—is an important criterion to consider in evaluating all nonfiction science books for children and young adults.

Topics for nonfiction science and technology books are as diverse as the world we live in. A great resource covering a wide range of topics is *Indigenous Ingenuity: A Celebration of Traditional North American Knowledge* (2023) by Deidre Havrelock, Edward Kay, and Kalila Fuller, which introduces readers to the myriad contributions to science and technology made by Indigenous North Americans. Most science nonfiction, of course, isn't this wide ranging but instead focuses on a particular aspect of science or technology. A popular topic nowadays is the delicate ecosystems all around us. *Planet Ocean: Why We All Need a Healthy Ocean* (2021) by Patricia Newman and Annie Crawley is one good example; others are *Life on Surtsey: Iceland's Upstart Island* (2017) by Lorrie Griffin Burns and *Sea Otter Heroes: The Predators That Saved an Ecosystem* (2017) by Patricia Newman. Not surprisingly, there is a multitude of books looking at animals of all shapes and sizes and their status in the world. Some, such as Caitlin O'Connell, Donna M. Jackson, and Timothy Rodwell's *The Elephant Scientist* (2011) and Candace Fleming and Eric Rohmann's *Honeybee: The Busy Life of Apis Mellifera* (2020), focus primarily on the physical and behavioral traits of their subjects. Others, though, present species that are in some sort of danger, often because of human folly, and show the dedicated scientists who are trying to save them. In fact, the word "save" (or some variation) often appears in the title or subtitle. Two examples are Sy Montgomery and Nic Bishop's *Kakapo Rescue: Saving the World's Strangest Parrot* (2010) and *Chasing Cheetahs: The Race to Save Africa's Fastest Cats* (2014).

As Marcia Mardis points out, digging up the past and solving its mysteries is an engaging topic for a generation raised on the forensic science of the Crime Scene Investigation television shows.[65] *Bodies from the Ice: Melting Glaciers and the Recovery of the Past* (2008) by James M. Deem, *Written in Bone: Buried Lives of Jamestown and Colonial Maryland* (2009) by Sally M. Walker, and *Every Bone Tells a Story: Hominin Discoveries, Deductions, and Debates* (2010) by Jill Rubalcaba and Peter Robertshaw all show forensic archaeology in action. And Ian Lendler and C. M. Butzer's *The First Dinosaur: How Science Solved the Greatest Mystery on Earth* (2019) combines two perennially popular topics: forensics and dinosaurs. Another perennially popular theme is the "gross-out" factor, subject matter so disgusting it's mesmerizing. As one science teacher memorably puts it, "keep it gross, and they'll stay engrossed" (quoted in Mardis).[66] There is no shortage of books to satisfy this craving. A fine example is *Something Rotten: A Fresh Look at Roadkill* (2018) by Heather L. Montgomery and Kevin O'Malley. Gail Jarrow has some vivid offerings too, including *Blood and Germs: The Civil War Battle Against Wounds and Disease* (2020) and *American Murderer: The Parasite That Haunted the South* (2022).

Authors sometimes combine science writing with biography, especially for younger readers. *Isaac the Alchemist: Secrets of Isaac Newton, Reveal'd* (2017) by Mary Losure provides a look at Newton's early life, building machines and conducting experiments in alchemy. Joyce Sidman's *The Girl Who Drew Butterflies: How Maria Merian's Art Changed Science* (2018) combines science, art, and biography to recount the life of one of the first women who studied insects. And *Breaking the Mold: Changing the Face of Climate Science* (2023) by Dana Alison Levy is a collective biography of 16 scientists engaged in climate research.

Technology is a topic of interest to many children and young adults—technology of the past, present, and future. In *Crossing on Time: Steam Engines, Fast Ships, and a Journey to the New World* (2019), David Macaulay describes and illustrates the technological advances that allowed people to travel across the ocean in a much shorter amount of time. In *Team Moon: How 400,000 People Landed Apollo 11 on the Moon* (2006) and *How We Got to the Moon: The People, Technology, and Daring Feats of Science Behind Humanity's Greatest Adventure* (2020), Catherine Thimmesh and John Rocco, respectively describe the people and technology involved in traveling into outer space and landing someone on the moon. Of course, not every technology is seen as having an exclusively positive benefit. Steve Sheinkin, in *Bomb! The Race to Build—and Steal—the World's Most Dangerous Weapon* (2012), presents a thrilling tale of the people who developed the atomic bomb, but he doesn't shun a discussion of the ethical consequences of such an invention.

As we've seen, genre can be a highly useful way of examining and evaluating nonfiction books for children and young adults. Among the big three—biography and memoir, history, and science and technology—are many rich, engaging books for readers of all ages. In this chapter we have focused mostly on chapter books, which tend to be aimed at intermediate and young adult readers. In the chapter that follows, we will discuss format, focusing particularly on picturebooks, graphic nonfiction, e-books, and audiobooks, but we will continue to consider the big three genres as we look at noteworthy examples of highly visual books.

NOTES

1. Chris Baldick, "Genre," in *Oxford Concise Dictionary of Literary Terms* (New York: Oxford University Press, 2004), 104–05.
2. Kimberly Reynolds, *Children's Literature: A Very Short Introduction* (New York: Oxford University Press, 2011), 78.
3. Marc Aronson, "Originality in Nonfiction," *School Library Journal* 52, no. 1 (2006): 43.
4. Ibid.
5. Ibid.
6. Sandip Wilson, "Getting Down to Facts in Children's Nonfiction Literature: A Case for the Importance of Sources," *Journal of Children's Literature* 32, no. 1 (2006): 57.
7. Ibid., 58.
8. Ibid., 61.
9. Ibid., 62.
10. Ibid., 61.
11. Ibid., 60.
12. Rudine Sims Bishop, "Mirrors, Windows, and Sliding Glass Doors," *Perspectives: Choosing and Using Books for the Classroom* 6, no. 3 (1990): n.p.
13. Council on Interracial Books for Children, "10 Quick Ways to Analyze Children's Books for Racism and Sexism," accessed March 18, 2024, https://wowlit.org/links/evaluating-global-literature/10-quick-ways-to-analyze-childrens-books-for-racism-and-sexism/.
14. Ibid.
15. Denise Dávila and Sarah Elovich, "Evaluating the Narrative Authenticity of Informational Nonfiction for Children," in *Reading Teacher* (2022), 509.
16. Ibid., 508–9.
17. Ibid., 510.
18. Hermione Lee, *Biography: A Very Short Introduction* (New York: Oxford University Press, 2009), 122, 26.

19. Milton Meltzer, "Notes on Biography," *Children's Literature Association Quarterly* 10, no. 4 (1986): 173.
20. Lee, *Biography: A Very Short Introduction*, 135.
21. Myra Zarnowski, "'How One Person Sees Another Person': Focusing on the Author's Perspective in Picturebook Biographies," *Language Arts* 96, no. 3 (2019): 146–49.
22. Lee, *Biography: A Very Short Introduction*, 130.
23. W. Bernard Lukenbill, *Biography in the Lives of Youth: Culture, Information, and Society* (Westport, CT: Libraries Unlimited, 2006), 2.
24. Ibid., 3.
25. Ibid., 20.
26. Sunah Chung and Amina Chaudhri, "Biographies of Women in the Robert Sibert Award: A Critical Content Analysis," *Journal of Children's Literature* 47, no. 1 (2021): 65.
27. S. Adam Crawley, "Who's Out? Who's In? (Re)Presentations of LGB+ Individuals in Picturebook Biographies," *Taboo: The Journal of Culture & Education*, no. Winter (2020): 137, 40, 44.
28. Christopher Myers, qtd. in ibid., 129.
29. Ibid., 148.
30. "Autobiography," in Merriam-Webster.com (2024).
31. Rachel Meltzer, 2022, https://www.grammarly.com/blog/memoir-vs-autobiography/.
32. Jerome Bruner, "Life as Narrative," *Social Research* 71, no. 3 (2004): 692, 93.
33. Ibid., 693.
34. Ibid., 708.
35. Jill Ker Conway, *When Memory Speaks: Exploring the Art of Autobiography* (New York: Random House, 1998), 7.
36. Ibid., 11–12, 13.
37. Ibid., 17.
38. Laura A. May, Teri Holbrook, and Laura E. Meyers, "(Re)Storying Obama: An Examination of Recently Published Informational Texts," *Children's Literature in Education* 41, no. 4 (2010): 273, 81.
39. Ibid., 287.
40. Ibid.
41. Myra Zarnowski, "History Writing That's 'Good to Think With': *The Great Fire, Blizzard!* and *An American Plague*," *Children's Literature in Education* 40, no. 3 (2009): 251.
42. Ibid., 253–54.
43. Ibid., 254.
44. Ibid., 258.
45. Ibid., 259–60.
46. Myra Zarnowski and Susan Turkel, "How History as Mystery Reveals Historical Thinking: A Look at Two Accounts of Finding Typhoid Mary," *Language Arts* 94, no. 4 (2017): 234.
47. Ibid., 235.
48. Myra Zarnowski and Susan Turkel, "Nonfiction Literature That Highlights Inquiry: How Real People Solve Real Problems," *Journal of Children's Literature* 37, no. 1 (2011): 30.

49. Ibid.
50. Ibid., 36.
51. Steve Jenkins, "The Importance of Being Wrong," *The Horn Book Magazine* 87, no. 2 (2011): 67.
52. Ibid., 68.
53. Myra Zarnowski and Susan Turkel, "How Nonfiction Reveals the Nature of Science," *Children's Literature in Education* 44, no. 4 (2013): 298, 99.
54. Myra Zarnowski, "Reading for the Mystery in Nonfiction Science Books," *Journal of Children's Literature* 39, no. 2 (2013): 14.
55. Ibid., 18.
56. Laura May et al., "The Durable, Dynamic Nature of Genre and Science: A Purpose-Driven Typology of Science Trade Books," *Reading Research Quarterly* 55, no. 3 (2019): 400.
57. Ibid., 405, 09.
58. Ibid., 407, 10.
59. Ibid., 414, 15.
60. Aeriale N. Johnson and Clare Landrigan, "'I Wanna Learn More About That!' Providing Access to Scientific Literacy for All through Inclusive Nonfiction Science Texts," *Language Arts* 100, no. 4 (2023): 338.
61. Ibid., 339.
62. Laura Beth Kelly, "An Analysis of Award-Winning Science Trade Books for Children: Who Are the Scientists, and What Is Science?," *Journal of Research in Science Teaching* 55 (2018): 1199.
63. Ibid., 1204.
64. Ibid., 1188.
65. Marcia A. Mardis, "It's Not Just Whodunnit, but How: "The CSI Effect," Science Learning, and the School Library," *Knowledge Quest* 35, no. 1 (2006): 12.
66. Ibid., 16.

6

Formats

In the last chapter we considered how genre can be used to evaluate nonfiction for children and young adults, and most of the examples we discussed are nonfiction chapter books, that is, books that are divided into chapters with more text than illustrations. In this chapter we consider other formats, focusing particularly on picturebooks, graphic nonfiction, audiobooks, and e-books. We will revisit the big three nonfiction genres—biography and memoir, history, and science and technology—as we explore each of these formats. But first: what's the difference between genre and format? Genre, we may recall, is defined as "a recognizable and established category of written work employing such conventions as will prevent readers or audiences from mistaking it for another kind."[1] Format, on the other hand, is "the shape, size, and general makeup (as of something printed)."[2] The format of a chapter book looks different from that of a picture book, and both formats are different from that of graphic nonfiction. However, as we have seen (in the case of chapter books) and will see (in the case of picture books and graphic novels), the big three genres can be found across all three formats.

PICTURE BOOKS

In recent years, illustrations have proliferated in children's and young adult books, both fiction and nonfiction.[3] Kathy Short attributes this to advances in printing and production technology and to the fact that we're now living in a highly visual culture. She explains, "Books with strong visual images hold special appeal and meaning because children are completely immersed in a visual culture in which images are central to their experiences and interactions."[4] Strictly speaking, one can distinguish between illustrated books, in which the illustrations serve to enhance the text but are not essential to understanding the text, and picturebooks, in which "the words and images form an artistic whole."[5] (In fact, Maria Nikolajeva and Carole Scott advocate for spelling the term as one word, "picturebook," to convey the inseparable connection between words and pictures.[6]) This distinction, however, is becoming more blurred in today's children's books. In her survey of children's books published between 2013 and 2016, Short noticed that more middle grade novels include numerous illustrations, while more picturebooks are using panels, as is typical in comics and graphic novels.[7] These boundaries, I would argue, are even more blurred in nonfiction books for children and young adults. Evaluating picturebooks, regardless of genre, "require[s] evaluation of art, text, and how the two work together to create a unique art form."[8] The typical picturebook, as Kathleen Horning explains, is 32, 40, or 48 pages—usually some number divisible by eight.[9] They employ what Horning calls "patterned language": rhythm, rhyme, repetition, and questions.[10] And they can employ various media, including drawing, painting, printmaking, collage, and photography.[11] My own assessment of nonfiction picturebooks suggests a wider variability in these characteristics, depending on the age range of the intended readers. Nonfiction picturebooks aimed at younger readers are typically 32 or 48 pages, but plenty of books are 60 pages or more if they are intended for older readers. Patterned language is also more characteristic of picturebooks for younger readers, less so in those for older readers. The one constant is the rich variety of media that can be found across nonfiction picturebooks, regardless of the intended audience. Although at one time nonfiction picturebooks relied heavily on photographs, that is no longer true. And, in any case, drawings or diagrams—cross-sections, for instance—are more useful for conveying certain kinds of information than are photographs.[12]

When evaluating text, one should look for the patterned language discussed above if the book is intended for younger readers. With books for all ages, one should consider the writing style:

- Is the writing engaging?
- Is the language appropriate for the intended audience?
- Are there interactive elements?
- Are new terms defined?[13]

One should also consider how accurate and authoritative the book is. Look for such things as a source list, a description of the research process (possibly in an author's note), and supplemental materials (usually included in the backmatter).[14] In addition, if a book is a blend of fiction and nonfiction, as is usually the case where a fictional frame story is used to introduce factual concepts, is the hybrid nature of the book made clear?[15]

When evaluating illustrations, one need not be an art expert, but it is helpful to keep some basic visual concepts in mind. Sylvia Vardell provides an easy-to-understand list of elements to consider with any illustration: line (heavy, light); shape (angular, circular); color (or grey scale); texture (what does it look like it would feel like?), and composition (how are the parts arranged within the picture?).[16] Molly Bang, in *Picture This: How Pictures Work*, offers additional considerations. She outlines twelve principles, but the ones that seem to me most useful for our purposes are these: viewers pay more attention to images at the center of the page, light backgrounds feel safer than dark although there are exceptions, a large object feels stronger than a smaller one, and contrasts (in color, size, etc.) stand out.[17] All of these strategies can affect the way we read, or interpret, an image, and illustrators can use these techniques to direct our attention and interpretation. Sharon Ruth Gill reminds us that in evaluating the visual appeal of a picturebook, we should examine not only the illustrations within the main text, but also front and back covers, the endpapers, and the front and back matter.[18]

A key question to consider in evaluating picturebooks, whether fiction or nonfiction, is how successfully do the words and pictures work together to convey meaning? *The Cambridge Guide to Children's Books in English* puts it like this: "[P]icturebooks require that the pictures are as significant within the overall text as the words and that both should be physically close enough together for a reader to apprehend readily their mutual influence."[19] But how does this happen? Perry Nodelman in his classic study of children's picturebooks, *Words About Pictures*, points out that words and pictures, while very different kinds of vehicles for conveying information, have more in common than we may initially think. Words are typically associated with the lineal, sequential, and causal presentation of information, while pictures are associated with the non-lineal, simultaneous, and spatial presentation of information.[20] However, as he rightly points out, "We could not read words if we could not interpret the visual symbols that stand for them on paper; reading itself is an act of vision."[21] By the same token, pictures can have a lineal quality: "[T]he pictures in a picture book form a sequence—they can contribute to the act of storytelling because they do imply the cause-and-effect relationships of time."[22] Nodelman argues that "placing [words and pictures] into relationship with each other inevitably changes the meaning of both, so that good picture books as a whole are a richer experience than the simple sum of their parts."[23] Lawrence Sipe uses the term "synergy" to describe how words and pictures work together. By synergy, he means the "relationship in which the total effect depends not only on the union of text and illustrations but also on the perceived interactions or transactions between these two parts."[24] To put it another way, our reading of the text inspires a new reading of the pictures, and our reading of the pictures inspires a new reading of the text. "The resulting process," Sipe explains, "is a type of oscillation, as we adjust our interpretation of the pictures in terms of the words, and our interpretation of the words in terms of the pictures."[25] Courtney Shimek conducted an analysis of 2006–2016 Orbis Pictus books (winners and honor books) to see which ones relied more on text for their effect, which ones relied on images, and which ones relied on synergy between the two. She discovered several techniques authors and illustrators use to enhance synergy: two-page spreads, photographs with captions, a blending of words and pictures (through collage, for example), and a medium that reflects the content: "For example, in *Parrots Over Puerto Rico* by Susan L. Roth and Cindy Trumbore (2013), the use of collage emphasizes the feathered parrots and makes them appear to fly off the page."[26]

A specific type of picturebook that is becoming more prevalent is what Ted Kesler calls the "poetic nonfiction picture book," a kind of hybrid text that represents "the convergence of children's nonfiction and poetry in the form of picture books predominantly for readers in grades K through 8."[27] The poetic aspects of these books include musical language (such as rhythm, rhyme, and repetition), poetic devices (such as imagery and figurative language), and visual dimensions (such as line breaks and stanzas).[28] Based on his analysis of 76 picturebooks, Kesler developed a typology of six categories: collective poems (a collection of poems on a single topic), extended poem (one longer poem), rhyming verse, coupled poems (consisting of both poetry and expository writing), narrative or expository verse (prose presented in verse form), and lyric prose (narrative or expository writing making use of poetic elements).[29] The crucial point Kesler emphasizes is that these books should be evaluated on the basis of their quality as picturebooks, nonfiction, and poetry.[30] Drawing on Louise Rosenblatt's concept of the reader's stance, Kesler sees poetic nonfiction picturebooks as involving both an efferent stance and an aesthetic stance.[31] In other words, readers take something away from the work (what they learn), and they also enjoy the reading experience (what they feel).

Nonfiction picturebooks, like all nonfiction books, should also be evaluated on the extent to which they represent diversity. In the previous chapter, I discussed Laura Beth Kelly's content analysis of Outstanding Science Trade Books, in which she discovered that these books did not do a very good job of reflecting the diversity of scientists or science.[32] In a similar study, Margaret Vaughn and her colleagues undertook an analysis of Orbis Pictus winners and honor books (1990-2019), focusing on "who exerts agency, how, and for what purposes."[33] They found that these books tended to focus on white, European males and to depict their agency as occurring primarily in adulthood. Childhood agency was rarely evident.[34] The unfortunate effect of such representations, or lack thereof, is to erase diversity and to perpetuate the belief that children are passive.

As far as nonfiction genres are concerned, biography is a popular one in the picturebook format. Numerous picturebook biographies focus on figures from the American Civil Rights Movement. A classic is Doreen Rappaport and Bryan Collier's *Martin's Big Words: The Life of Dr. Martin Luther King* (2001), in which Rappaport weaves excerpts from Dr. King's speeches with her own narrative and Collier provides beautiful collage and watercolor illustrations.

Choosing Brave: How Mamie Till-Mobley and Emmett Till Sparked the Civil Rights Movement (2022) by Angela Joy and Janelle Washington tells the story of how the mother of Emmett Till, a 14-year-old boy who was lynched in Mississippi in 1955, used a horrific event to shine a spotlight on the need for social justice and civil rights. At 64 pages, this is a longer picturebook and is intended for readers eight to 12 years of age. In *When Marian Sang* (2002), Pam Muñoz Ryan and Brian Selznick portray the role Marian Anderson, an African American opera singer, played in focusing the nation's attention on civil rights. A more recent picturebook takes as its subject a figure from popular culture, Nichelle Nichols who played Lieutenant Uhuru on the original *Star Trek* television show. *To Boldly Go: How Nichelle Nichols and* Star Trek *Helped Advance Civil Rights* (2023) by Angela Dalton and Lauren Semmer relates Nichols's story as the first Black woman to play a character in a position of power on television.

Other picturebook biographies deal with people who achieved acclaim in the arts. Suzanne Slade and Cazbi Cabrera's *Exquisite: The Poetry and Life of Gwendolyn Brooks* (2020) introduces young readers to a poet of ordinary life who was also the first Black person to win the Pulitzer Prize. In *When Angels Sing: The Story of Rock Legend Carlos Santana* (2018), Michael Mahin and Jose Ramirez tell the story of the Mexican-American musician who combined various musical styles to produce angelic and innovative music. And in *Nina: A Story of Nina Simone* (2023), Traci Todd and Christian Robinson tell the story of the remarkable singer who used her popularity and rich voice to advocate for civil rights.

People who have made important contributions to science and technology are featured in picturebook biographies as well. Frequently, these are individuals who have fallen into obscurity, and the purpose of the biography is to reclaim their rightful place in history. It's also common for the titles or subtitles of these books to reveal the nature of the contributions. For example, *Secret Engineer: How Emily Roebling Built the Brooklyn Bridge* (2019) by Rachel Dougherty tells the story of the woman who took over for her engineer husband when he got sick during the building of the iconic bridge. *Ada Lovelace, Poet of Science: The First Computer Programmer* (2016) by Diane Stanley and Jessie Hartland showcases a visionary nineteenth-century woman who combined her love for math and machines with her vivid imagination to create computer programming.

Librarians have received attention as well in several picturebook biographies. *Planting Stories: The Life of Librarian and Storyteller Pura Belpré* (2019) by Anika Aldamuy Denise and Paolo Escobar recounts how Pura Belpré brought the folklore of her native Puerto Rico to story time at the New York Public Library. Similarly, *Go Forth and Tell: The Life of Augusta Baker, Librarian and Master Storyteller* (2024) by Breanna McDaniel and April Harrison relates the story of an influential storyteller and librarian, and the first Black person to serve as coordinator of children's services at the New York Public Library.

Memoir can be found in picturebook format as well although not to the same extent as biography. One fine example is *Coretta: The Autobiography of Mrs. Coretta Scott King* (2024) by Coretta Scott King (with Barbara Reynolds) and Ekua Holmes. In this beautifully illustrated book, Mrs. King tells her own story of how she fought for social justice alongside her husband, Martin Luther King Jr., and continued the fight after his assassination. Not surprisingly, several authors/illustrators have produced memoirs in picturebook format. Lois Ehlert looks back at her illustrious career in *The Scraps Book: Notes from a Colorful Life* (2014), while Ed Young revisits his childhood years in *The House Baba Built: An Artist's Childhood in China* (2011). Musicians, too, have contributed to the genre. In *Trombone Shorty* (2015), Troy "Trombone Shorty" Andrews (with Bryan Collier as illustrator) describes his childhood in New Orleans and his journey to becoming a world-famous trombone player. Roberta Flack (with Tonya Bolden and Hayden Goodman as illustrator), the successful rhythm-and-blues singer, describes her own musical journey in *The Green Piano: How Little Me Found Music* (2023).

Many nonfiction picturebooks focus on historical events and/or cultural history. Carole Boston Weatherford and Floyd Cooper do not shy away from a difficult topic in *Unspeakable: The Tulsa Race Massacre* (2021), and the same is true of Caren Stetson and Selina Alko in *Stars of the Night: The Courageous Children of the Czech Kindertransport* (2023), the story of Czechoslovakian children who were rescued from the Nazis and sent to live with foster families in England during World War II. Historical picturebooks sometimes focus on people and events that led to social change. Duncan Tonatiuh's *Separate Is Never Equal: Sylvia Mendez and Her Family's Fight for Desegregation* (2014) is the story of a family who successfully sued the state of California in the 1940s because their children, in spite of being American citizens, were forced to attend Mexican-only schools. Barry Wittenstein and Jessie Hartland's *The Day the River Caught Fire: How the Cuyahoga River Exploded and Ignited the Earth Day Movement* (2023) relates for young readers how an environmental disaster and the outrage that followed led to the creation of the Environmental Protection Agency. The cultural history of Indigenous peoples is celebrated in *We Are Still Here! Native American Truths Everyone Should Know* (2021) by Traci Sorell and Frané Lessac.

Science and technology are also featured in many nonfiction picturebooks. Animals, big and small, are a popular topic with children, and picturebooks reflect that. Some recent examples include *Jumper: A Day in the Life of the Backyard Jumping Spider* (2023) by Jessica Lanan, *Honeybee: The Busy Life of Apis Mellifera* (2020) by Candace Fleming and Eric Rohmann, *Summertime Sleepers: Animals That Estivate* (2021) by Melissa Stewart and Sarah S. Brannen, *Beware of the Crocodile* (2019) by Martin Jenkins and Satoshi Kitamura, and *Polar: Wildlife at the Ends of the Earth* (2023) by L. E. Carmichael and Byron Eggenschwiler. *We Go Way Back* (2023) by Idan Ben-Barak and Philip Bunting tackles no less a subject than life itself. Steven Jenkins, in *Eye to Eye: How Animals See the World* (2014), discusses the evolution of eyesight among various animals. Geography, along with its related flora and fauna, is a featured topic as well. Jason Chin illustrates and describes all three in his remarkable *Grand Canyon* (2017), while Nell Cross Beckerman and Kalen Chock explore a different kind of ecosystem in *Caves* (2022). The theme is even carried over into alphabet books, such as *¡Olinguito, de la A A La Z! Descubriendo El Bosque Nublado / Olinguito, from A to Z! Unveiling the Cloud Forest* (2016) by Lulu Delacre and *A Is for Australian Reefs* (2023) by Frané Lessac. Technological achievements receive attention also, in such books as *Moonshot: The Flight of Apollo 11* (expanded edition, 2019) by Brian Floca and *Jumbo: The Making of the Boeing 747* (2020) by Chris Gall.

GRAPHIC NONFICTION

In the last couple of decades, the number of graphic novels for children and young adults has grown exponentially. Strictly speaking, a graphic "novel" implies a work of fiction, and, indeed, there are many examples of graphic fiction for various audiences. Often, the term "graphic novel" gets used more broadly to encompass any book-length work in graphic (i.e., comics) format, even works of nonfiction such as history and memoir. I will use the term "graphic nonfiction" to refer to these nonfiction works, and in some cases I'll use a more specific term like "graphic biography" or "graphic memoir" to refer to particular nonfiction genres in graphic format. So perhaps we should start by considering what is meant by the term "comics." Scott McCloud, in *Understanding Comics: The Invisible Art*, quotes Will Eisner's simple yet elegant definition for comics: "sequential art."[35] McCloud offers his own, slightly more complex, definition: "[j]uxtaposed pictorial and other images in deliberate sequence, intended to convey information and/or to produce an aesthetic response in the viewer."[36] Comics and picturebooks obviously have many elements in common. In both formats, words and pictures must work together although in any given picture the words may carry more of the message or the pictures may—or they may be balanced.[37] In a memorable metaphor that echoes Sipe's concept of synergy in picturebooks, McCloud says, "In comics at its best, words and pictures are like partners in a dance and each one takes turns leading."[38]

There are also, of course, some key differences between comics and picturebooks, and this is where some comics-specific terminology will be helpful. Comics typically consist of a series of panels. A panel is a single picture, or scene, usually but not always surrounded by a border. In Western comics, the series of panels are read from left to right and top to bottom. In Japanese comics (called manga), the panels are read from right to left and top to bottom. The space between panels is called the gutter. The words within panels fall into three categories: speech balloons (which indicate what characters are saying), thought balloons (which indicate what characters are thinking), and captions (which provide the narration). Occasionally, a word or two will be included in a panel as a sound effect, such as "Wham!" or "Screech," in which case the words are typically incorporated as part of the picture. Other elements to consider are the same elements that apply to picturebooks: line, shape, color, texture, and composition. Also, as with picturebooks, the style of images may be more realistic or more abstract or somewhere in between. In the case of comics, more abstract usually means more cartoonish. For those wanting a more detailed discussion of comics and how they work, I highly recommend McCloud's *Understanding Comics*, which is written and drawn in comics form.

Understanding how comics work can be helpful in evaluating graphic nonfiction. As with picturebooks, one should consider the text, the pictures, the design, and how they work together. As with nonfiction in general, it is important to evaluate "engagement potential, quality, accuracy, authenticity, and attention to diversity."[39] And one should always consider graphic nonfiction's potential value to child and young adult readers. Barbara Guzzetti and Marcia Mardis say that graphic nonfiction offers several potential benefits to readers: they promote multimodal learning (which we discussed in chapter 4), appeal to many reluctant readers, can be helpful for English language learners, and are often more accessible than regular texts for readers with learning disabilities.[40] Guzzetti and Mardis, in two separate studies, found that graphic nonfiction could be used successfully with other texts (textbooks, primary texts) in English/language arts, social studies, and science classes.[41] With the science class, in particular, they found that the cartoons and graphics in the graphic nonfiction helped "by providing context for abstract ideas"; the textbook, by comparison, contained almost too many visuals per page, more than students could reasonably process.[42]

In spite of their perceived benefits, graphic nonfiction and graphic novels are not without their critics. The complaints usually run along the lines of one or more of the following: reading comics is not really reading because, after all, they're mostly pictures; comics are mostly fluff, consisting of only funny stories or superhero adventures; and comics are too, well, graphic in their depictions of sex and violence.[43] Proponents of the format (Frank Serafini, for example) point to the benefits of engaging with multimodal texts, namely, reading graphic formats facilitates the development of multiple (or multimodal) literacies: reading words, pictures, and design, and reading each element in terms of the others.[44] Moreover, the content can be as complex as the format. Art Spiegelman's *Maus I* (1986) and *Maus II* (1992) are a case in point. Spiegelman chose to use anthropomorphic animals to tell the story of his father's experiences in a Nazi concentration camp: the Jews are mice, the Germans are cats, the French are frogs, the Poles are pigs, and so on. These groundbreaking books combine memoir, biography, and history to relate a compelling story of persecution, resilience, and survival. Together these volumes were the first graphic work to win a Pulitzer Prize. Other examples of graphic nonfiction with complex content are the works of Don Brown, such as *Drowned City: Hurricane Katrina and New Orleans* (2015) and *In the Shadow of the Fallen Towers: The Seconds, Minutes, Hours, Days, Weeks, Months, and Years after the 9/11 Attacks* (2021).

A particular type of graphic nonfiction is actually a blend of fiction and nonfiction presented in graphic format. We've discussed these so-called hybrid books previously in discussing nonfiction chapter books and picturebooks, and we've noted that while some people are critical of mixing fact and fiction, others find these kinds of books to be an effective way of engaging young readers. Sara Kersten-Parrish and Ashley Dallacqua, for example, argue that "[i]n graphic nonfiction, in which illustrated elements are made up, this helps enhance the nonfictional content, creating a point of engagement for students; an investment in the story creates an environment where they are interested in discovering the truth."[45] They recommend three graphic nonfiction series in particular that they feel successfully marry fictional narratives with factual information. The Science Comics series features different authors and illustrators, and each of the volumes has a different fictional frame. Maris Wicks's *Coral Reefs: Cities of the Ocean* (2016), for example, is narrated by a yellow and orange goby fish.[46] Nathan Hale's Hazardous Tales is a series of graphic books focused on American history. Narrated by the Nathan Hale who was a Revolutionary War spy, the various volumes relate stories of the Revolutionary War, the Underground Railroad, World War I, and so forth.[47] And the Secret Coders series by Gene Luen Yang and Mike Holmes showcases a group of middle school friends who solve mysteries and introduce the concepts of binary numbers and coding to readers.[48] To that list I would add the Max Axiom: Super Scientist series, in which Max explores all kinds of scientific phenomena, including electricity, food chains, viruses, volcanoes, earthquakes, and chemical reactions.

All of the nonfiction genres can be found in graphic format. As with picturebooks, biography and memoir are quite popular. Single-subject biographies present the lives of subjects, some well known, others less so, including scientists, explorers, artists, and social activists. Arthur Flowers and Manu Chitrakar offer their take on the life and legacy of Martin Luther King Jr. in *I See the Promised Land: A Life of Martin Luther King Jr.* (2010). Jim Ottaviani, working with various illustrators, has authored several volumes on important scientists: the Nobel Prize–winning physicist Richard Feynman in *Feynman* (with Leland Myrick; 2011), the cosmologist and disability rights activist Stephen Hawking in *Hawking* (with Leland Mayrick; 2019), and the mathematician and World War II codebreaker Alan Turing in *The Imitation Game: Alan Turing Decoded* (with Leland Purvis; 2016). In *Photographic: The Life of Graciela Iturbide* (2018), Isabel Quintero and Zeke Peña chronicle the life of the internationally famous photographer through lyrical text and compelling black-and-white illustrations. Dual and collective biographies are available in graphic format as well. Joseph Lambert portrays the lives of Helen Keller, who lost her sight and hearing at an early age, and her tutor, Annie Sullivan, in *Annie Sullivan and the Trial of Helen Keller* (2008), part of the Center for Cartoon Studies graphic biography series and winner of a Will Eisner Comic Industry Award. In *Lewis & Clark* (2011), Nick Bertozzi depicts the exciting, difficult journey of explorers Meriweather Lewis and William Clark from St. Louis, Missouri, to the Pacific Ocean in the early 1800s. Jim Ottaviani and Maris Wicks focus on the lives of pioneering women in *Primates: The Fearless Science of Jane Goodall, Dian Fossey, and Biruté Galdikas* (2013) and *Astronauts: Women on the Final Frontier* (2020). Pénélope Bagieu addresses a similar subject in *Brazen: Rebel Ladies Who Rocked the World* (2018), depicting the contributions of women both well known and not so well known.

Some of the most innovative work is being done in graphic memoir. Indeed, as librarian and comics enthusiast Bonnie Brzozowski says, "Memoir is the giant of graphic nonfiction."[49] A wildly popular giant of graphic novels and graphic nonfiction is Raina Telgemeier, and she has produced three memoirs focused on her adolescence: *Smile* (2010), about an accident she had and a subsequent series of dental surgeries; *Sisters* (2014), about her fraught relationship with her younger sister; and *Guts* (2019), about her struggles with anxiety. Jarrett J. Krosoczka, author and illustrator of the Lunch Lady series, has published two graphic memoirs: *Hey, Kiddo: How I Lost My Mother, Found My Father, and Dealt with Family Addiction* (2018) and *Sunshine: How One Camp Taught Me About Life, Death, and Hope* (2023). In the former, Krosoczka describes how as a child he gradually came to realize his mother was addicted to drugs; in the latter, he relates his experiences as a young adult working as a counselor at a camp for children with cancer. And, as mentioned in the previous chapter, Cece Bell's *El Deafo* (2014) describes Bell's childhood, adolescence, and shifting friendships after losing her hearing at the age of four.

Some graphic memoirs focus on identity issues related to being part of different cultures. In *¡Ay, Mijah!: My Bilingual Summer in Mexico* (2023), Christine Suggs recounts a trip to Mexico to visit grandparents and other family. This book would pair nicely with Pedro Martín's *Mexikid* (2023), in which Martín recounts a family trip to Mexico in the 1970s. *Family Style: Memories of an American from Vietnam* (2023) is Thien Pham's account of how as a young boy he and his family immigrated to the United States shortly after the end of the Vietnam War. And *Monstrous: A Transracial Adoption Story* (2023) is Sarah Myer's heartfelt memoir of growing up as an adopted Korean child in a white family living in a community with few other Asian residents.

As should be evident by now, authors don't shy away from exploring difficult topics in their memoirs, and, as might be expected, because of the mature themes, these books are intended for young adults rather than children. In *Akim Aliu: Dreamer* (illustrated by Karen De la Vega and Marcus Williams;

2023), the professional hockey player Akim Aliu (with Greg Anderson Elysée) describes the isolation, poverty, and racial violence he experienced growing up. In *A Game for Swallows: To Die, To Leave, To Return* (2012), Zeina Abirached recounts an incident growing up in a violent and divided Beirut: when one day her parents didn't return as expected, neighbors came together to help Zeina and her brother survive the day. And in *Persepolis: The Story of a Childhood* (2003), Marjane Satrapi recounts growing up in Tehran during the Islamic Revolution; in *Persepolis 2: The Story of a Return* (2005), she describes going to Vienna for school but returning to Iran after graduation.

A subgenre of graphic memoir that has received special attention, and not always in a positive way, is LGBTQIA+ memoir. Many of these books are intended for adults, but feature adolescent characters and are, of course, read by teens, and for that reason are frequently challenged in libraries. *Gender Queer: A Memoir* (2019) is Maia Kobabe's coming-of-age story of being non-binary and asexual. *Honor Girl: A Graphic Memoir* (2017), another frequently challenged title, is Maggie Thrash's account of how as a 15-year-old she fell in love with an older girl who was a counselor at her camp. And in *Fun Home: A Family Tragicomic* (2007), Alison Bechdel relates her coming-of-age and coming out along with her awareness that her father was a closeted gay man with a predilection for teenaged boys.

History, a close cousin to biography and memoir, is also well-represented in graphic nonfiction. A book that would pair well with Art Spiegelman's two-volume *Maus* (1986, 1992) is Don Brown's *Run and Hide: How Jewish Youth Escaped the Holocaust* (2023), the powerful story of the different ways a few Jewish children managed to survive the Nazis. Brown is known for his historical nonfiction in graphic format and his incorporation of authentic voices from the event he is writing about. In *Drowned City: Hurricane Katrina and New Orleans* (2015), he describes the devastating effects the storm had on the city. A similar book is Josh Neufeld's *A.D.: New Orleans After the Deluge* (2009), which offers the true stories of seven people who survived the storm.

Other graphic histories focus on the courage and heroism of individuals or groups. In *Alia's Mission: Saving the Books of Iraq* (2004), Mark Alan Stamaty relates the story of Alia Muhammad Baker, the librarian who saved 30,000 books from the Central Library in Basra during the Iraq War. *March, Book One* (2013), *Book Two* (2014), and *Book Three* (2016) comprise John Lewis's account of his activism during the Civil Rights Movement. Part memoir and part history, the series (co-authored by Andrew Aydin and illustrated by Nate Powell) includes many famous and not-so-famous figures and events from the 1950s and 1960s.

Some graphic nonfiction presents the history of a people or a place. Larry Gonick focuses his attention on the United States in *The Cartoon History of the United States* (1991) and goes even bigger in the three-volume *The Cartoon History of the Universe* (1990, 1994, 2002) and the two-volume *The Cartoon History* of the Modern World (2006, 2009). *District Comics: An Unconventional History of Washington, DC* (2012) is an edited volume (by Matt Dembicki) that offers a sweeping history of our nation's capital. And, aimed at older readers, *Queer: A Graphic History* (2016), by Meg-John Barker and Jules Scheele, traces the history of queer thought and activism.

For readers interested in true crime, there's no better graphic storyteller than Rick Geary. His Treasury of Victorian Murder includes volumes on *Jack the Ripper* (1995), *The Borden Tragedy* (1997), and *The Murder of Abraham Lincoln* (2005). His Treasury of XXth Century Murder offer volumes on *The Lindbergh Child* (2008), about the kidnapping and murder of Charles and Anne Morrow Lindbergh's one-year-old son, and *The Lives of Sacco and Vanzetti* (2011), about the anarchists who were convicted of murder on somewhat sketchy evidence.

The graphic format also includes books on science and technology. In addition to the science and technology series mentioned earlier, there are a number of stand-alone volumes on a myriad of topics. In *Trinity: A Graphic History of the First Atomic Bomb* (2012), for example, Jonathan Fetter-Vorm offers a part historical and part scientific account of the Manhattan Project, which led to the development of the atomic bomb. A good companion book to this one is Steven Sheinkin's *Bomb! The Race to Build—and Steal—the World's Most Dangerous Weapon* (2012), which is now available in a graphic adaptation (2023), illustrated by Nick Bertozzi. Biology professor Jay Hosler has written and illustrated a number of volumes, combining humorous fictional framing devices with sound scientific information. Some examples include *Clan Apis* (2000), an action story that also provides information about bee behavior and anatomy; *Optical Allusions* (2014), about a brain who loses his boss's eyeball; and *Evolution: The Story of Life on Earth* (illustrated by Kevin Cannon and Zander Cannon; 2011), in which an alien scientist is tasked with explaining evolution to the leader of his planet. And Dan Nott's *Hidden Systems: Water, Electricity, the Internet, and the Secrets Behind the Systems We Use Every Day* (2023) explores how these various systems came to be—and at what cost. It is worth remembering that science-related graphic nonfiction also includes graphic biographies of scientists, as discussed above, and those biographies typically include not just information about the person, but also accessible scientific information as well.

AUDIOBOOKS AND E-BOOKS

Two other formats that deserve our attention are audiobooks and e-books (aka digital books). Many of today's nonfiction books for children and young adults are available in both print and e-book versions. Because now everything is "born digital," it is relatively easy for publishers to make e-books available along with the print versions although typically buying one format does not give you access to the other. Libraries, of course, don't typically purchase individual e-book titles but instead offer access to e-books through one (or more) vendors. Bernadette Lear and Andrea Pritt conducted a study of seven vendors (two aimed at academic libraries and five at school and public libraries) to assess which ones provided access to the e-book versions of over 1,600 award-winning books for PreK–12 published between 2014 and 2018.[50] Approximately 44 percent of the books were nonfiction.[51] They found that, while no single vendor offered all of the titles, Follett, Mackin, and Overdrive provided access to between 75 and 80 percent of the titles.[52] The good news? Diverse books (i.e., pertaining to people of color, women, LGBTQIA+ individuals, and people with disabilities) were well-represented across the vendors.[53] The not-so-good news? Nonfiction titles (on all topics, not just diverse books) were poorly represented in the preschool and young adult categories.[54] For librarians, the take-away from all of this is that, while nonfiction e-books may be available in vendors' e-book platforms, they are not uniformly available across age ranges.

E-books do offer some advantages over print books as well as some disadvantages. The advantages include portability (if you have a tablet, e-reader, or smart phone), storage (the books don't take up room on a shelf), and, in some cases, special features (such as highlighting, note-taking, and hyperlinks).[55] The disadvantages are the need to be connected to wi-fi in order to download a book, eyestrain from prolonged screen reading, and the lack of tactile pleasures associated with holding a physical book.[56] In addition to those is the challenge of being able to clearly see illustrations on a small screen, which can be a particular issue with highly visual formats like picturebooks and graphic nonfiction. Regardless, it's always nice for readers to have the option of a physical book or an e-book. But that raises the question: which do young readers prefer? An international survey including families in the United States and the UK found that, while young people read across a variety of platforms—print books, tablets, e-readers, smart phones, and laptops—70 percent strongly prefer or tend to prefer reading print books.[57] What's more, 60 percent say they like to share books they've read with their friends.[58] As with a print book, it's easy to recommend an e-book to a friend, but unlike a print book, it's much harder to lend a friend your copy.

As noted above, it's fairly easy nowadays for publishers of print books to make e-book versions available also, and many of them do. With audiobooks, however, it's a different story. The production process involves scheduling and recording narration, adding sound effects and background music (if being used), arranging sound files, and comparing the finished version with the written text.[59] The narration may consist of a single narrator or a cast with a narrator and characters.[60] Maria Cahill and Jennifer Moore, who have done some interesting and important work on audiobooks for children and teens, explain that in recent years "there have been significant increases in the number of children and young adult audiobooks sold, suggesting an increase in adolescents' and children's engagement with audiobooks."[61] Indeed, the Audio

Formats

Publishers Association reports a sales increase of children's and young adult audiobooks of between 8 and 8.5 percent for each year from 2018 to 2022.[62]

So what's the appeal? Gene Wolfson explains that, for educators, using audiobooks with adolescents can offer several potential benefits: "Audiobooks can model reading, teach critical listening, build on prior knowledge, improve vocabulary, encourage oral language usage, and increase comprehension."[63] In addition, they can allow students with special needs, such as learning disabilities, to experience books like the other students in the class.[64] And, according to some research studies, audiobooks can improve recreational reading, improve reading scores, and improve the literacy skills of English language learners.[65] However, in a more recent literature review of research on the use of audiobooks with adolescents, Moore and Cahill discovered that the results are mixed. For adolescents learning a second language, comprehension has been shown to improve, but the demographics of the adolescents in the studies were different from those of most second-language learners in US schools.[66] For both adolescents with learning disabilities and typically developing adolescents, there was no evidence that comprehension increased, and, in fact, in some cases it decreased.[67] Moore and Cahill point out, however, that, while there may be little instructional value in using audiobooks with adolescents, there are still potential benefits, including the fact that audiobooks can facilitate the social aspect of reading (for example, through group listening), provide enjoyment, and get an adolescent hooked on reading (or listening). Their conclusion is that "[m]ovies, audiobooks, and printed books provide different experiences that are enjoyed in different manners."[68]

In terms of evaluating audiobooks for children and young adults, we would do well to consider the criteria the Odyssey Award committee uses. The Odyssey Award, which is given each year to the producer of the best audiobook for children and/or young adults in the United States, focuses on three criteria: narration (expression, dynamics, clarity, pacing, etc.), sound quality (no background noise), and background music and sound effects (appropriate for the mood).[69] We might also note that, as Cahill and Moore point out, "[w]hile print book reviews tend to focus on the quality of the writing and plot, audiobook reviews focus on the quality of the narration and production elements."[70] Fortunately, most of the review sources discussed in chapter 3 include reviews of audiobooks. Still, there's nothing quite like listening yourself. In evaluating nonfiction audiobooks for children and young adults, then, it's important to consider the same criteria used in evaluating nonfiction texts—engagement, accuracy, diversity, documentation—and also to consider the quality of the narration as well as the sound effects and background music (if used). Another important thing to consider with the audiobook version of highly visual texts—and most of today's nonfiction is highly visual—is how the audiobook compensates for the lack of visual materials. Are these described in some way? Is the spoken text supplemented with more descriptions and/or explanations?

Is listening to the audiobook a reasonably equivalent experience to reading the print or e-book versions?

Most of the Odyssey Award winners and honor books have been fiction, but several nonfiction titles are represented, specifically in the categories of biography, memoir, and history. Sometimes an audiobook is released at the same time as the print version of the book; sometimes there's a delay of several years. Two recent examples are Cece Bell's graphic memoir, *El Deafo*, an Odyssey Award winner; the book was published in 2014, but the audiobook was not released until 2023. In contrast, Pedro Martín's graphic memoir *Mexikid*, an Odyssey honor title, was released as an audiobook the same year it was published in book form, 2023. Both *El Deafo* and *Mexikid* are narrated by a full cast. Two audiobook biographies have been named Odyssey honor titles since the award's inception in 2008. *Emmanuel's Dream: The True Story of Emmanuel Ofosu Yeboah* (2021) tells the story of a Ghanian boy with a deformed leg who learned to play soccer and later became an avid cyclist. Based on a picturebook biography, the audiobook is written by Laurie Ann Thompson and narrated by Adjoa Andoh. *Esquivel! Space-Age Sound Artist* (2018), also a picturebook biography, is the story of Juan Garcia Esquivel, a Mexican immigrant who invented space-age lounge music. The book is written by Susan Wood and narrated by Brian Amador. History is represented as well among the Odyssey titles. *We Are the Ship: The Story of Negro League Baseball*, Kadir Nelson's 2008 picturebook, was released as an audiobook narrated by Dion Graham the following year. More recently, Grace Lin's nonfiction chapter book *Chinese Menu: The History, Myths, and Legends Behind Your Favorite Foods*, published in 2023, was released the same year as the audiobook narrated by Lisa Ling. And *Stamped: Racism, Antiracism, and You* (2020), Jason Reynolds and Ibram X. Kendi's history of racism and antiracism in America, is available as an audiobook (also 2020), narrated by Reynolds with an introduction by Kendi. Thus far, no science or technology titles have been named Odyssey winners or honor books.

In this chapter we have looked at children's and young adult nonfiction in various formats—specifically, picturebooks, graphic nonfiction, e-books, and audiobooks—and discussed how to evaluate each of these. In the chapter that follows, we will consider ways of promoting nonfiction resources to children and young adults, focusing on how these resources can help meet their information needs, literacy development needs, and reading interests and preferences.

NOTES

1. Chris Baldick, "Genre," in *Oxford Concise Dictionary of Literary Terms* (New York: Oxford University Press, 2004).
2. "Format," in Merriam-Webster.com (2024).

3. Kathy G. Short, "What's Trending in Children's Literature and Why It Matters," *Language Arts* 95, no. 5 (2018): 287.
4. Ibid., 289.
5. Carrie Hintz and Eric L. Tribunella, *Reading Children's Literature: A Critical Introduction* (Boston, MA: Bedford/St. Martin's, 2013), 160.
6. Cited in ibid.
7. Short, "What's Trending in Children's Literature and Why It Matters," 290.
8. Kathleen T. Horning, *From Cover to Cover: Evaluating and Reviewing Children's Books*, Rev. ed. (New York: HarperCollins, 2010), 85.
9. Ibid., 95.
10. Ibid., 89.
11. Ibid., 105.
12. Rebecca J. Lukens, *A Critical Handbook of Children's Literature*, fifth ed. (New York: HarperCollins, 1995), 281.
13. Sharon Ruth Gill, "What Teachers Need to Know About the 'New' Nonfiction," *The Reading Teacher* 63, no. 4 (2009): 262.
14. Ibid.
15. Ibid.
16. Sylvia M. Vardell, *Children's Literature in Action: A Librarian's Guide* (Westport, CT: Libraries Unlimited, 2008), 54.
17. Molly Bang, *Picture This: How Pictures Work, Revised and Expanded 25th Anniversary Edition* (San Francisco, CA: Chronicle Books, 2016 [1991]), 76, 84, 90, 100.
18. Gill, "What Teachers Need to Know About the 'New' Nonfiction," 262.
19. Victor Watson, ed. *The Cambridge Guide to Children's Books in English* (Cambridge, UK: Cambridge University Press, 2001), 557.
20. Perry Nodelman, *Words About Pictures: The Narrative Art of Children's Picture Books* (Athens, GA: The University of Georgia Press, 1988), 198.
21. Ibid., 199.
22. Ibid.
23. Ibid.
24. Lawrence R. Sipe, "How Picture Books Work: A Semiotically Framed Theory of Text-Picture Relationships," *Children's Literature in Education* 29, no. 2 (1998): 98-99.
25. Ibid., 102-3.
26. Courtney Shimek, "Sites of Synergy: Strategies for Readers Navigating Nonfiction Picture Books," *The Reading Teacher* 72, no. 4 (2018): 519-21.
27. Ted Kesler, "Evoking the World of Poetic Nonfiction Picture Books," *Children's Literature in Education* 43, no. 4 (2012): 340.
28. Ibid.
29. Ibid., 343.
30. Ibid., 347-48.
31. Ibid., 351.
32. Laura Beth Kelly, "An Analysis of Award-Winning Science Trade Books for Children: Who Are the Scientists, and What Is Science?," *Journal of Research in Science Teaching* 55 (2018): 1188.
33. Margaret Vaughn et al., "Examining Agency in Children's Nonfiction Picture Books," *Children's Literature in Education* 53, no. 1 (2022): 33.
34. Ibid.

35. Scott McCloud, *Understanding Comics: The Invisible Art* (New York: HarperCollins, 1993), 5.
36. Ibid., 9.
37. Ibid., 153–55.
38. Ibid., 156.
39. Karla J. Moller, "Integrating Graphic Nonfiction into Classroom Reading and Content Area Instruction: A Critical Literacy Focus on Selection Issues," *Journal of Children's Literature* 41, no. 2 (2015): 53.
40. Barbara J. Guzzetti and Marcia A. Mardis, "From Dickens to 9/11: Exploring Graphic Nonfiction to Support the Secondary-School Curriculum," *The Journal of Research on Libraries and Young Adults* (2014): n.p.
41. Ibid.; "The Potential of Graphic Nonfiction for Teaching and Learning Earth Science," *School Libraries Worldwide* 23, no. 1 (2017): 27.
42. Ibid.
43. Robin Brenner, "Comics and Graphic Novels," in *Handbook of Research on Children's and Young Adult Literature*, ed. Shelby Anne Wolf (New York: Routledge, 2011), 258, 62.
44. Frank Serafini, *Reading the Visual: An Introduction to Teaching Multimodal Literacy* (New York: Teachers College Press, 2014), 2–3.
45. Sara Kersten-Parrish and Ashley K. Dallacqua, "Three Graphic Nonfiction Series That Excite and Educate," *The Reading Teacher* 71, no. 5 (2018): 627.
46. Ibid., 628.
47. Ibid., 629–30.
48. Ibid., 630–32.
49. Bonnie Brzozowski, "Drawing on Reality," *Library Journal* (Feb. 1, 2012): 32.
50. Bernadette A. Lear and Andrea L. Pritt, "'We Need Diverse E-Books:' Availability of Award-Winning Children's and Young Adult Titles in Today's E-Book Platforms," *Collection Management* 46, no. 3–4 (2021): 223.
51. Ibid., 233.
52. Ibid., 235.
53. Ibid., 242–43.
54. Ibid., 233.
55. Page Publishing, "Ebooks Vs. Print Books: Pros and Cons," accessed April 11, 2024, https://pagepublishing.com/ebooks-vs-print-books-pros-and-cons/.
56. Ibid.
57. David Kleeman, "Books and Reading Are Powerful with Kids, but Content Discovery Is Challenging," *Publishing Research Quarterly* 32 (2016): 38, 40–41.
58. Ibid., 42.
59. Maria Cahill and Jennifer Richey, "What Sound Does an Odyssey Make? Content Analysis of Award-Winning Audiobooks," *Library Quarterly* 85, no. 4 (2015): 372–73.
60. Ibid., 372.
61. Maria Cahill and Jennifer Moore, "A Sound History: Audiobooks Are Music to Children's Ears," *Children and Libraries*, no. Spring (2017): 26.
62. Audio Publishers Association, "Apa 5-Year Industry Date," accessed April 11, 2024, https://www.audiopub.org/apa-5-year-data.
63. Gene Wolfson, "Using Audiobooks to Meet the Needs of Adolescent Readers," *American Secondary Education* 36, no. 2 (2008): 106.

64. Ibid., 107.
65. Ibid., 109.
66. Jennifer Moore and Maria Cahill, "Audiobooks: Legitimate 'Reading' Material for Adolescents?," *School Library Research* 19 (2016): 8, 9.
67. Ibid., 8.
68. Ibid., 9–10.
69. Cahill and Richey, "What Sound Does an Odyssey Make? Content Analysis of Award-Winning Audiobooks," 373.
70. Cahill and Moore, "A Sound History: Audiobooks Are Music to Children's Ears," 27.

7

Promoting Nonfiction

As we've seen, nonfiction for children and young adults offers many benefits across different genres and different formats. And, as we've also seen, not all nonfiction is created equal; there are specific criteria to consider in choosing the best nonfiction to add to your collection. However, the finest nonfiction collection will be of little value if no one uses it. In this chapter we will consider what librarians can do to effectively promote nonfiction to children and young adults, including services, which are typically sought and offered on an as-needed basis; programs, which are planned and promoted in advance; and evaluation of services and programs. What follows is not intended to be a comprehensive overview of services and programming for children and young adults. Instead, it is a look at some commonly used strategies with a special emphasis on how nonfiction can be included. Old pros (and young pros too!) will likely recognize things they're already doing but may also be inspired to try things they haven't tried before. Newcomers to the field hopefully will find some new ideas.

But before plunging in, we should consider a couple of key elements in developing programs and services for youth: the role of libraries in promoting formal and informal learning and the value of using participatory design. Frances Jacobson Harris cites the MacArthur Foundation's Digital Media and Learning Project in describing young people's engagement with digital media. Specifically, there are three different "genres of participation," or types of engagement: that which is friendship driven (called "hanging out"), that which is interest driven (called "geeking out"), and that which bridges the two (called "messing around").[1] Although the MacArthur Project was focused on the use of digital media, there's a lesson for libraries here in developing programs for tweens and teens: don't forget what *they're* interested in, and don't neglect the social factor. Even younger children will be more motivated by something they find interesting and the opportunity to experience it with other children. In a similar vein, Mega Subramaniam argues that "[i]t is imperative that teen services librarians understand [teens'] interests by intentionally talking to teens about their interests, listening to them, facilitating non-dominant teens to voice their opinions, and reflecting on their roles as they engage in these conversations with teens."[2] In other words, librarians should involve teens in participatory design so that they are not just recipients, but also co-designers of library services and programs for teens. Subramaniam offers specific participatory design techniques that librarians can use with teens, which I will not go into here. Suffice it to say that getting teens involved through various kinds of brainstorming and problem-solving activities can help facilitate the development of services and programs that teens will actually want to participate in. The same is also true for tweens. In fact, in designing the International Digital Library for Children, an interdisciplinary team at the University of Maryland involved children as young as seven years old.[3] With younger children, participatory design might be more of a challenge, but even with this group, it's not a bad idea to get some input from the children, as well as their parents, caregivers, and teachers.

SERVICES

Services to children and young adults are related to the common kinds of questions they ask and typically include ready reference, research based, and readers' advisory.[4] Ready reference questions can usually be answered with short facts.[5] Online resources, including encyclopedias and dictionaries, are often used in answering these kinds of questions, but nonfiction books can be useful too, especially the ones that are intended to be introductions to or overviews of certain topics. DK's Eyewitness series is one example that comes to mind. Brian Cosgrove's *DK Eyewitness Weather* (2007), for instance, allows one to dip in to learn about different kinds of clouds, how tornadoes are formed, and the science of forecasting the weather. This is a book that certainly can be read from cover to cover, but it can also be consulted as a source for quick facts. Research-based questions tend to be more in-depth than ready-reference questions and usually require multiple sources.[6] A student working on a class assignment who has chosen or been given the topic of weather could make more extensive use of *DK Eyewitness Weather*, as well as consulting other weather-related sources. Encyclopedias can provide a good overview of such a topic, but additional resources that are more in-depth are usually required to successfully complete the assignment.

Meghan Harper, in *Reference Sources and Services for Youth*, says that with research-based questions librarians often need to conduct a reference interview, and she suggests using a combination of open and closed questions. Open questions might include "How will you use the information?," "Where have you already looked?," and "What do you already know about your topic?"[7] Closed questions might include "When is the assignment/project due?" and "What formats do you want—articles, books, websites?"[8] Again, the important thing to remember is that nonfiction books (along with other kinds of resources) might be exactly the right thing to recommend. For one thing, it's not unusual, especially in the secondary grades, for teachers to require a certain number of books, a certain number of articles, and a certain number of web resources for a research project. For another, books that are clearly organized and well indexed allow young researchers to consult certain sections rather than feeling like they have to read the whole thing—an important consideration when the project is due in a couple of days!

Readers' advisory, the third type of reference question, is usually geared toward what to read for pleasure.[9] Of course, there's nothing wrong with students finding pleasure in something they are required to read for an assignment. While a textbook can be dry and an encyclopedia somewhat pedestrian, high-quality literary nonfiction can bring a subject to life and inspire joy and engagement in readers. But we should not forget about recommending nonfiction even when the patron is purely interested in reading for pleasure, and that's where readers' advisory comes into play. Heather Booth explains that "[r]eaders' advisory is more than just passing on suggestions of good books. It is a skill that is part science and part art, with a healthy dash of mind reading."[10] The science comes in knowing the various genres and categories of books, the art in being able to describe books so that their potential interest (or not) is clear, and the mind reading in intuiting what a patron is really looking for.[11] Booth goes on to say, "The simplest way I have found to explain readers' advisory to those unfamiliar with the concept is to liken it to reference work for recreational reading."[12] She suggests that in conducting a readers' advisory interview, librarians listen actively, repeat things to make sure they understand what they're being told, ask open-ended questions, and be objective rather than judgmental.[13] Logan Shea says that readers' advisory is especially important for middle grade readers, that is, readers ages eight to 12 years, because children in this age group are going through many changes—forming strong friendships, becoming more independent, and developing an understanding of multiple perspectives—as well as experiencing multiple stressors—"peer pressure, growing academic challenges, and body changes."[14] Shea provides multiple strategies for doing readers' advisory with this age group: talk to them about their interests and needs; offer multiple options and formats; consider their physical, emotional, and cultural needs; offer passive programming, which can actually increase engagement and make middle graders feel more comfortable with library staff; and be enthusiastic.[15]

In doing readers' advisory, you might start with questions like "Do you read a lot or not so much?," "Are you looking for a specific book that you know of?," "Can you think of a book that you've liked recently?," and "Have you read anything recently that you really hated?"[16] In gauging a reader's interests, a librarian can, of course, ask about which topics someone likes and which they dislike, but, going further, they can also ask about such things as pacing, character, story line, and frame.[17] These appeal factors, as Booth calls them, might seem more related to fiction, but they can easily be adapted for nonfiction. A young patron who likes fast-paced books might enjoy Steve Sheinkin's *Bomb! The Race to Build—and Steal—the World's Most Dangerous Weapon* (2012) or James Swanson's *Chasing Lincoln's Killer* (2009). These books have a strong story line, as is the case with most well-written historical nonfiction. A young reader interested in strong characters may find biographies appealing—picturebook biographies for younger readers, chapter book biographies for older ones. Frame refers to such things as setting, background, and subplots.[18] Some readers, for example, enjoy reading about a particular historical period (such as the Civil Rights Movement of the 1950s and 1960s) or a particular subgenre (such as accounts of real-life disasters). I would add another important appeal factor, especially for nonfiction, and that's illustrations. Most literary nonfiction nowadays contains various kinds of illustrations, and these can help elucidate a topic as well as provide pleasure in and of themselves. And, of course, illustrations are a vital part of the appeal of graphic nonfiction.

Book displays can also promote books based on different appeal factors. Displays can be organized according to genre (all nonfiction or a mix of nonfiction and fiction), format (all graphic nonfiction or a mix of graphic nonfiction and graphic fiction), or theme (women's history, for example, or climate change).[19] Another way to highlight high-quality nonfiction is to organize a book display around recent nonfiction award winners and honors books—the Orbis Pictus Award, the Robert F. Sibert Medal, and the YALSA Excellence in Nonfiction Award. Regardless of what organizing principle you use, Booth says that books chosen for displays should have appealing covers because, after all, the purpose of the display is to attract potential readers' attention.[20] Fortunately, many nonfiction book covers are designed to grab the readers' attention. A striking example (forgive the pun) is the cover of Nic Bishop's *Snakes* (2012), which shows a green snake, its jaws open wide, extending out toward the viewer. In fact, all of Bishop's books, including the ones he's done with Sy Montgomery, feature his astonishing photographs on the covers. Book displays, when carefully curated, can serve as a kind of passive readers' advisory, enticing young people to check out books they perhaps wouldn't have known about otherwise. It's a good idea, by the way, to have a handout or a bookmark nearby with a list of the books in the display, or if you want to get fancy, provide a QR code that young patrons can scan to access a list of the books online.

PROGRAMS

There are a variety of book-related programs that can be offered to children and young adults, including story times, booktalks and book trailers, book discussion groups, summer reading programs, after-school programs, and visits from authors, illustrators, or local experts. All of these can, and should, include nonfiction along with the more typical fiction titles. Before looking at the specifics, we should stop to consider the bigger picture of developing and presenting programs. First of all, what do we mean by "programming" in the library context? Patrick Jones, Michele Gorman, and Tricia Suellentrop define a program as "a library-sponsored activity that takes place outside of the context of reference services and is designed to inform, entertain, or enrich users, as well as promote use of the library and its collection."[21] As for developing successful programs, Melissa Gross, Cindy Mediavilla, and Virginia Walter recommend using a five-step process:

1. Gather information about the target population;
2. Determine the outcomes you want to achieve for your target population and consider how you will know if you've achieved those outcomes;
3. Develop programs and services for your target population, again considering how you will evaluate the outcomes;
4. Evaluate the programs and services; and
5. Share the results/impact of your programs and services with stakeholders.[22]

We will return to the topic of evaluation later in this chapter, but for now it's important to keep in mind that in developing any program you should have a clear sense of what you want to achieve and ways of determining whether you met your goals. And, as noted earlier, developing programs should always involve, if at all possible, input from the target population. In the case of very young children, getting input from parents and caregivers and/or teachers is a good idea.

Storytimes are a popular activity in many libraries, and they often involve more than just reading or telling a story to young children. Given the short attention span of this age group, the program is usually filled out with additional activities such as singing, movement, and crafts. The story, though, whether read or told, is still a key part of the program. Unfortunately, as Jacqueline Kociubuk explains, "A recent study found that across all storytime age groups, informational books were being shared at a much lower rate than any other genre, both in number shared per storytime and the time spent interacting with them."[23] This is too bad because even young children benefit from exposure to informational books: these books help support content-area knowledge, build vocabulary, enhance visual skills, and make it more likely that a child will be academically successful in the years to come.[24] Books with a narrative are especially effective since young children (like older ones) find stories interesting and engaging.[25] In incorporating nonfiction into story times, librarians should look for books with appealing visuals and strong narratives. For example, Melissa Stewart and Candace R. Bergum's *Under the Snow* (2009) is an engaging look at animals in their habitats on a snowy day. Read-alouds are great for some nonfiction books, but, as Abby Johnson points out, "Don't be afraid to paraphrase if the book you want to share is too wordy for this age group. If a book contains too much text to read aloud, talk about the pictures and share some simple facts."[26]

For older children and teens, booktalks and book trailers are time-honored ways to promote books, more often fiction, but nonfiction as well. A booktalk, according to Jones, Gorman, and Suellentrop, "is a paperback blurb as performance. . . . It is not a summary; it is a sales pitch."[27] Joni Richards Bodart, a well-known expert on booktalking, offers four rules for ensuring successful booktalks, and I quote them in full:

1. Don't talk about a book you haven't read.
2. Don't talk about a book you don't like.
3. Don't tell the ending.
4. Do your own thing.[28]

How long should a booktalk be? Bodart says no more than three minutes per book, and half that time might be just fine: "You want your talks to be as long as necessary but as short as possible."[29] She also suggests four different ways to approach a booktalk. You can provide a plot summary (but don't give away too much and certainly not the ending!). You can offer an anecdote or excerpt from the book, a "teaser" if you will. You can describe a character in some detail; you can even take on the role of a character and speak as if you are that person. Or you can focus on the mood of a book or even of a particular scene.[30] While these approaches may seem oriented more toward fiction, they can easily be adapted for nonfiction. For example, historical nonfiction lends itself nicely to plot summary, while biography and memoir offer opportunities for a focus on character. Any kind of nonfiction might have memorable scenes, and you can certainly share an excerpt from any nonfiction book. Be creative and mix and match. As Jane Charles says, nonfiction can be an especially compelling choice for booktalking: "The more shocking, bizarre, absurd, silly, spooky, frightening, gross, and alarming, the better. People of all ages love learning about and sharing astonishing stories that actually happened."[31]

A key aspect of delivering a great booktalk is to have a successful hook—an opening that will grab the audience's attention. Jones, Gorman, and Suellentrop suggest several possible strategies: you can open by focusing on a character, asking a question, describing a dramatic action, describing a shared experience ("I'm sure we've all . . ."), or stating something shocking or surprising.[32] All of these strategies can work when booktalking nonfiction as well as fiction. In booktalking Gail Jarrow's *American Murderer: The Parasite That Haunted the South* (2022), you might start with an astonishing fact: In the 1800s, people in the South were getting sick as if their blood was being sucked by invisible vampires—but no one could figure out why. This sets the stage for a brief overview of this book about hookworms and how they were discovered. A great way to end would be by showing the cover of the book, which features a close-up of a hookworm with its ravenous mouth wide open.

Tweens and teens can also get in on the act. With a few pointers, they can develop and deliver their own booktalks to their peers. Bodart advocates for using student booktalks in the classroom because "booktalks by students can serve to integrate literature into all parts of the curriculum, to substitute for book reports, and to help students analyze books. Having students critique each other's work teaches them not only how to critique but also how to accept criticism."[33] She suggests that students choose a book not widely known, read it, write the talk, and practice giving it so that it sounds natural rather than memorized.[34] And I would add: encourage students to choose at least some nonfiction books to share with their peers, as nonfiction helps promote critical thinking and is something emphasized by the Common Core State Standards as well as many individual state's standards.

A similar marketing tool is the book trailer. Whereas a booktalk is given live and in person, a book trailer is recorded and posted online, on the library's website, or on sites such as YouTube. A book trailer can be essentially a recorded booktalk with someone standing or sitting, talking, and showing the covers of the books, or it can be a series of images with music with voice-over. If you're creating your own book trailer and planning to use music and/or images, it's important to make sure you're not violating copyright restrictions. A crash course in copyright and fair use is beyond the scope of this discussion; however, helpful resources can be found by searching online for "royalty free images" and "royalty free music." Many publishers, and for that matter a number of authors, produce their own book trailers, and you can point young patrons to those. Scholastic, for instance, has a YouTube playlist devoted to book trailers[35] and so does Penguin Teen.[36] Many of these are fiction titles, but not all. Tweens and teens can also create their own nonfiction book trailers under the guidance of a librarian. This can be an effective strategy for getting them to read nonfiction books, use technology to create something, and learn about copyright and fair use in the bargain. And, while the classroom provides a more structured environment in which to have students practice booktalking, it can also be done in a school or public library setting as part of an after-school book club, for example, or in conjunction with a summer reading program, both of which I'll discuss later in this chapter.

If you feel that booktalks might be a bit too old school for today's tweens and teens, Vanessa Irvin offers a new take on an old idea: the BEMT framework. BEMT stands for "Booktalking to Engage Millennial Teens" (although the technique would work equally well with tweens). Noting the degree to which today's young people are involved in multitasking, texting, and social media, Irvin argues that "[b]ook-review-length booktalks are no longer a convincing sell. The times call for strategies that reflect the creativity, clarity, brevity, and speed that today's teens employ when interacting socially and online."[37] She recommends short, impactful talks and offers six possible strategies:

1. Book tweets—"one-or-two-line hooks"
2. Wrap back—connecting the talk back to the title
3. Open end—beginning and ending the talk with a question
4. Graphic form—passing a book around so that the audience can see the illustrations
5. Snap'n read—giving a quick snapshot of the book and reading a short passage
6. Power-full points—using slides with visuals when presenting a talk to a large group.[38]

These strategies, I believe, can be used with any nonfiction book, but they would work particularly well with science nonfiction, which often doesn't contain a strong storyline but does include memorable illustrations. For example, in giving a booktalk to tweens on Mary Kay Carson and Tom Uhlman's *The Tornado Scientist: Seeing Inside Severe Storms* (2019), a librarian could use a combination of the graphic form (passing the book around so that the audience could see the illustrations) and snap'n read (reading a short, exciting passage about the work of the tornado scientist, Robin Tanamachi).

Book clubs are another book-focused program that can be offered by public and school libraries. I'm using the term "book club" in a generic sense to include a variety of programs, including book discussion groups, after-school programs, and summer reading programs. Before looking at specifics, I'll offer three guiding principles: (1) book clubs can and should include nonfiction as well as fiction and other genres; (2) whatever the approach, it's a good idea to set up a book club so that participants don't have to attend every meeting and are welcome to attend a meeting even if they haven't read the book; and (3) the target audience should be allowed to have input into which books are featured. Beyond that, there are a number of options. Clubs can meet weekly, biweekly, or monthly, depending on the interest and availability of participants. Booktalks, given by the librarian or given by the participants, can be an effective way to introduce potential books for the group to read and discuss.[39] And the group can all read the same book and discuss it, or participants can read different books and then share them with one another.[40]

The ways of structuring a book club are virtually limitless, so I'll just highlight a few possibilities. One way is to use book pairings, in which two related nonfiction books are read and discussed, perhaps over two consecutive meetings. Biographies work well with this approach as there are often multiple biographies on famous individuals. Participants can read two biographies on the same individual and compare how the authors (and, in the case of picture- book biographies, illustrators) present their subject. This was the approach used by May,

Holbrook, and Meyers in examining children's biographies of Barack Obama (discussed in chapter 5).[41] They looked at 14 biographies, but the framework they used could easily be adapted for a book club to use in comparing two biographies of any individual. The same can be done with historical events. There are a number of nonfiction books for children and young adults dealing with the Holocaust, for example. In some cases, history and biography work well together. A good book to pair with Swanson's *Chasing Lincoln's Killer* (2009) is James Cross Giblin's *Good Brother, Bad Brother: The Story of Edwin Booth and John Wilkes Booth* (2005). With some topics there are both nonfiction books and fiction books that pair well. Laurie Halse Anderson's fictional account of the yellow fever epidemic, *Fever 1793* (2000), pairs nicely with Jim Murphy's nonfiction account, *An American Plague* (2003). Similarly, Brandy Colbert's nonfiction book on the 1921 Tulsa Race Massacre, *Black Birds in the Sky* (2021), can be paired with Randi Pink's fiction book that focuses on the same event, *Angel of Greenwood* (2021).

Theme is a popular way of organizing a book club, and the theme can change (or not) every few months. Moreover, a book club can include other kinds of activities as well. Monica Gingerich, a school librarian, worked with the AP English teacher in her school to establish a literary club for grades six through 12 the goal of which "is to cultivate readers, writers, speakers, and listeners to promote literacy as a tool of community building and activism."[42] The group makes use of books (mostly passages from books), articles, and podcasts, and engages in discussions, hands-on activities, and service-learning projects.[43] Participants can read about and discuss current issues and then explore what they can do in their community to help address these issues. Reneé Lyons, for example, advocates for using nonfiction books to foster an awareness of and inspire activism around environmental issues. She suggests using such books as Sy Montgomery and Nic Bishop's *Kakapo Rescue: Saving the World's Strangest Parrot* (2010) and Phillip Hoose's *The Race to Save the Lord God Bird* (2004).[44] Another take on this approach is offered by Kafi Kumasi, who developed the Circle of Voices after-school book club aimed at engaging youth of color in the library.[45] The book club is organized around Kumasi's cultural inquiry framework (which she adapted from Daniel Callison's work on information inquiry). Explaining that "[i]nquiry-based instruction teaches students *how* to think rather than *what* to think," Kumasi encourages participants to:

1. Question—identify problems in their community;
2. Explore—discover what the community knows and what they want to know;
3. Assimilate—confirm or refute received knowledge about the topic of focus;

4. Infer—derive conclusions about what community members would say about my findings;
5. Reflect—consider how my conclusions may benefit other people in the community.[46]

Although Kumasi does not specify which books her club has read, a librarian interested in replicating her program might consult the booklists on the Social Justice Books website.[47] These lists, on a variety of social justice issues, include both fiction and nonfiction. Book clubs can also involve, in addition to reading books, creative activities, such as writing and drawing, and these creative works can be published by the library in print and/or online in order "to promote teen voices that are otherwise muffled in traditional publishing and media outlets."[48] Writing can include all kinds of genres: fiction (including fanfiction), poetry, graphic narratives, and nonfiction, such as journalistic articles and reviews of books, movies, television shows, and music.[49]

Yet another approach is to organize a book club based on looking at the peritext of books to facilitate pre-reading, reading, and post-reading. Melissa Gross and her research team (including myself) held monthly Peritext Book Club meetings after school in a middle school library. Students used the Peritextual Literacy Framework (discussed in chapter 4) to examine the six kinds of peritext in nonfiction STEAM books: bibliographic, promotional, intratextual, navigational, supplemental, and documentary.[50] As a pre-reading activity, students examined a particular kind of peritext in each of five books:

- Chip Kidd's *Go: A Kidd's Guide to Graphic Design* (2013)—bibliographic and promotional
- Stephen Kramer and Dennis Kunkel's *Hidden Worlds: Looking Through a Scientist's Microscope* (2001)—intratextual
- Paul B. Janeczko and Jenna LaReau's *Top Secret: A Handbook of Codes and Ciphers* (2006)—navigational
- Donna Latham and Andrew Christensen's *Skyscrapers: Investigate the Feats of Engineering with 25 Projects* (2013)—supplemental
- Catherine Thimmesh's *Team Moon: How 400,000 People Landed Apollo 11 on the Moon* (2006)—documentary.[51]

Students discussed the peritextual elements in the books, participated in games focused on knowledge of peritextual concepts, and used presentation software to create a peritext presentation for younger students.[52] Pre- and post- surveys indicated students understood how examining peritext could be an aid to determining whether to read a book, how to navigate a book, and how to assess a book's credibility.[53] Peritextual concepts can be used with younger readers as well by, for example, looking at the covers of books such as picture book biographies or science books like the Scientists in the Field series.

Speaking of STEAM texts, there are a number of ways of introducing young readers to nonfiction STEAM (or STEM) books. Annette Shtivelband, Lauren Riendeau, and Robert Jakubowski emphasize the importance of starting when children are young: "[B]y the time youth reach fourth grade, a third of all students have lost interest in science; and by eighth grade nearly half of students have deemed science and technology irrelevant to their future career paths."[54] They recommend librarians make use of the hands-on activities available on the STARnet website.[55] While the site doesn't feature science or technology books, one could easily use books in conjunction with these activities. The activities on engineering, for example, would go along nicely with Latham and Christensen's *Skyscrapers: Investigate the Feats of Engineering with 25 Projects* (2013), the ones on space exploration with Brian Floca's *Moonshot: The Flight of Apollo 11* (2019; expanded edition). Mary-Kate Sableski agrees that it's important to introduce children to STEM topics while they're young, and she argues that public library programming in particular can help address the "documented dearth of representation across women and minorities in STEM fields" by "fostering an early interest in science, technology, engineering, and math in all children, regardless of their background or access to STEM curriculum in school."[56] Her strategy is to use picture books—some fiction, some nonfiction—for read-alouds, vocabulary enrichment, and discussion in conjunction with hands-on activities.[57] Three nonfiction titles she recommends are Elizabeth Rusch and Susan Swan's *Volcano Rising* (2013), about what happens when a volcano erupts; George Ella Lyon and Katherine Tillotson's *All the Water in the World* (2011), a combination of poetry and prose about the water cycle; and Gwendolyn Hooks and Colin Bootman's *Tiny Stitches: The Life of Medical Pioneer Vivien Thomas* (2016), the story of a young black man who helped develop a procedure used in the first open-heart surgery on a child.[58]

STEAM-related picture book biographies can be used to illustrate STEAM thinking skills: problem solving, design thinking, and higher-order concepts.[59] As Kristin Morgan and Jamie Anderson Collett explain, "[T]he value of learning about people who have achieved something extraordinary is immeasurable. Children need to find heroes and role models who can inspire and motivate them."[60] They offer pairings of books and activities across the various STEAM categories. For example, a librarian can pass around a shark tooth while introducing children to Jess Keating and Marta Álvarez Miguéns' *Shark Lady: The True Story of How Eugenie Clark Became the Ocean's Most Fearless Scientist* (2017). Laurie Wallmark and Katy Wu's *Grace Hopper: Queen of Computer Code* (2017) can be paired with an activity using a programmable robot. And an activity involving photographs and collage can be paired with Javaka Steptoe's *Radiant Child: The Story of Young Artist Jean-Michel Basquiat* (2016).[61] Sylvia Vardell advocates using picture books that combine poetry and science because "[p]oetry's brevity, conceptual focus, and rich vocabulary make it a natural teaching tool for connecting with science."[62] Among the titles she recommends are Joyce Sidman and Rick Allen's *Dark Emperor and Other Poems of the Night* (2010), Jane Yolen and Jason Stemple's *Bug Off! Creepy, Crawly Poems* (2012), and Douglas Florian's *Comets, Stars, the Moon, and Mars: Space Poems and Paintings* (2007). By using poetry-and-science picture books, librarians "can encourage children to think like a poet *and* a scientist in observing the world and how things work, using all of their senses, and gathering 'big words' as they read, write, and learn."[63] Vardell and the poet Janet Wong suggest specific strategies that librarians can use in sharing poetry-and-science books with children: notice side bars and the additional information they provide, pay attention to back matter for supplemental information, look closely at the photographs or illustrations that accompany poems, and pair poetry-and-science books with other nonfiction books on the same topic.[64] Vardell and Wong, by the way, have edited a poetry-and-science anthology, *The Poetry of Science: The Poetry Friday Anthology for Science for Kids* (2015).

There are plenty of STEAM-related books for older children and young adults that dovetail nicely with hands-on activities. In one of her "Focus on STEM" *Booklist* columns, Anastasia Yuen highlights several recent nonfiction books on food that can be used to introduce children and young adults to cultural and culinary history with a healthy dose of science thrown in. Some of the titles include Marc Aronson and Paul Freedman's *Bite by Bite: American History through Feasts, Foods, and Side Dishes* (2024), Grace Lin's *Chinese Menu: The History, Myths, and Legends Behind Your Favorite Foods* (2023), and Alliah L. Agostini and Taffy Elrod's *The Juneteenth Cookbook: Recipes and Activities for Kids and Families to Celebrate* (2024).[65] Such books practically beg for group interaction, like sharing stories around food traditions, creating a group cookbook, and even preparing some simple dishes. STEM or STEAM programs like these can involve children only or may include families as well. Brooks Mitchell, Claire Ratcliffe, and Keliann LaConte say that "[f]or learning to occur, people must experience a scenario, context, or investigation that calls for them to interact and process concepts, facts, and ideas in a meaningful way."[66] Families can work together in the library to investigate STEAM-related problems, and, in doing so, they may (or may not) consult books—although they are more likely to do so if the librarian has already pulled some relevant books ahead of time and made them readily available. As Mitchell, Ratcliffe, and LaConte note, librarians need not be STEAM experts, but they should be prepared to use certain strategies to facilitate successful interactions: asking questions in such a way that people aren't afraid of making mistakes, using open-ended questions, making sure everyone is heard, and using shared storytelling, in which each person contributes their own perspective or experience.[67]

Nonfiction can also be incorporated into summer reading programs. Many public libraries offer summer reading programs as a way to combat the so-called summer slide or summer loss that some students experience while out of school. In other words, the reading skills they've developed during the academic year tend to erode over the summer unless they're motivated to read. This effect is even more pronounced in children who come from economically disadvantaged backgrounds.[68] Susan Roman and Carole Fiore in an IMLS-funded study of 367 rising fourth graders discovered that participating in a summer reading program helped students maintain and, in some cases, even increase their reading skills.[69] The takeaways from their study, according to Roman and Fiore, are that public libraries should partner with schools, the definition of reading should be expanded to include more than just "literature," and libraries should emphasize the social aspects of reading.[70] To this last point, Ann Hotta has structured book clubs for fourth and fifth graders in her public library so that the social aspect of reading is the main point: "We don't aim to improve reading comprehension; we don't even require kids to read the book (although that is encouraged!). We simply want kids to experience reading as a fun social activity."[71] To ensure everyone feels included and facilitate the social aspect of the club, Hotta uses open-ended questions that can have more than one answer, and she encourages each participant to give everyone a chance to talk and to connect comments and questions to other participants' comments.[72] Summer reading clubs are usually intended to promote independent reading and often provide incentives for reading X number of books, incentives such as coupons to local eateries, passes to movies or other activities, and free books and T-shirts. One study, however, found that teens who participated in a summer reading club in Columbus, Ohio, were less motivated by extrinsic factors and more by intrinsic factors like pleasure, engagement, and knowledge.[73] The authors of the study, much like Roman and Fiore and Hotta, recommend setting up summer reading clubs so as to facilitate discussion and social interaction rather than focusing solely on extrinsic rewards and to provide "choices and options for reading multiple genres, lengths, and types of reading material."[74] Those options, of course, should include the various genres of nonfiction. Circling back to our previous discussion, I would point out, as Shaulskiy and her colleagues do, that readers' advisory and book displays are two ways of making teens (and tweens, I would add) aware of the options that are available.[75]

Yet another way to promote nonfiction is through author and illustrator visits. These can be quite effective in generating interest among children and young adults, as they will enjoy meeting creators they know and being exposed to the work of those they may be less familiar with. Most people, children and teens included, enjoy getting a glimpse into the creative process, and they may even be inspired to try their own hand at writing or drawing (if they're not already doing so). Having an author or illustrator visit your library can be costly although some, especially many nonfiction authors and illustrators, are more affordable than you may think. As a way of sharing the cost, schools and public libraries can partner with each other and with other community organizations, and those fortunate enough to have an active Friends group may find funding there. Don't forget about local authors and illustrators. There may be people in your community or your state who are just beginning to break into publishing for children and young adults, and they would welcome the opportunity to promote their work. Also, don't forget about local experts. They may not be authors or illustrators, but they often have fascinating stories to tell about their work. This can be an especially effective strategy with nonfiction, as there's almost always at least one nonfiction book in your collection that would pair with a local community member's expertise (like Black, Latine, or Native American history, for example). These visits can be stand-alone events, or they can be scheduled as part of an existing book club or summer reading program.

As a final word, I will stress the importance of being intentional in thinking about how nonfiction can be incorporated into both existing and new programs. Many public libraries now sponsor comics events, where participants can come in costume (cosplay), participate in discussions and activities, attend presentations by comics authors and illustrators, and get free comics-related merchandise. Such events offer an excellent opportunity to highlight the vast array of graphic nonfiction available, including biography and memoir, history, and science. Participants and librarians can even dress as their favorite *nonfiction* characters! Librarians who have makerspaces in their libraries can mount nonfiction book displays focusing on different kinds of technology, design, and hands-on activities. Increasingly, libraries are offering programs related to, well, programming—specifically, computer programming. As Marijke Visser explains, "Coding is one CT [computational thinking] literacy tool used by libraries to ensure that all youth, especially those with the greatest need, are prepared for college and life."[76] Computational thinking has to do with the "thought processes used to formulate problems and their solutions."[77] Librarians that are offering coding programs to tweens and teens can also highlight nonfiction books on the topic—Rachel Ignotofsky's *The History of the Computer* (2022), for example, or Karen Blumenthal's *Steve Jobs: The Man Who Thought Different* (2012).

The point is, be creative in thinking about how to incorporate nonfiction. As I was once told by a waiter, "If we don't have it on the menu, just ask. We're only limited by your imagination." Indeed.

EVALUATION

A vital step in designing and delivering services and programs is one that is sometimes overlooked, or considered as an afterthought at best, and that's evaluation. How will you know what impact you're having, if you don't have some way(s) of measuring the intended outcomes? As noted earlier, evaluation should be a part of the planning process in developing programs and services: as you determine the outcomes of those programs and services, you should also be thinking about how you will measure those outcomes.[78] Gross, Mediavilla, and Walter offer six possible ways of assessing outcomes:

- Outputs—consider such things as program attendance and circulation statistics;
- Surveys—these are easy to administer, but the data is limited by the closed responses;
- Interviews—these provide richer data but take longer to conduct;
- Focus groups—usually consist of six to ten people, last about an hour, and work well with teens but not as well with younger patrons;
- Observations—notice what's working and what's not;
- Tests—can be used to measure changes in knowledge.[79]

It's important, they stress, to use more than one form of evaluation so that you can triangulate the data—in other words, compare the data to see whether your findings are corroborated or not. If not, then you may need to rethink your evaluation strategies.[80] With very young children, you may need to gather data from parents and caregivers. With slightly older children, you'll want to keep the evaluation simple, but even four-year-olds can tell you what they liked and what they didn't like about a book or an activity. As a rule, as children get older and become more capable of reflection, they're increasingly able to give you more specific information about what's working for them and what's not. Still, it's worth keeping in mind that a long, detailed evaluation is likely to seem burdensome at the end of an otherwise pleasurable and informative program. The key is to strike a balance.

Two key elements to consider in evaluating programs and services are diversity and accessibility. In evaluating attendance, you need to go beyond mere head counts. Who are the people attending your programs and making use of your services? Do they reflect the diversity of the community you serve? Are there any barriers, physical or otherwise, for anyone in your target audience who wants to attend your programs or use your services? If so, what can be done to remove these barriers? Strategies might include offering programs with no registration required, evening and weekend programs, sensory story times, virtual programs, programs friendly to different kinds of neurodiversity, and take-home kits with activities.[81] The big question, of course, is how do you collect data from people you never see? It's easier in school libraries because you have a captive audience, so to speak, but in public libraries this can be much more challenging. One way to hear from the people who aren't coming to your programs or taking advantage of your services is to go where they are—schools, community centers, churches—and ask them about their needs and interests. In other words, revisit your community analysis, which is the first step in outcome-based planning. What's more, this kind of outreach also provides opportunities for you to advertise your programs and services to your target audiences.

Finally, don't forget to share your successes (and challenges) with other stakeholders. Directors, library boards, parents and caregivers, principals and teachers, and community leaders need to know what your library is accomplishing in meeting the needs of children and young adults—and what more you might be able to accomplish with additional resources. And this is where the words of program participants and service recipients (anonymized, of course) can be powerful tools in telling your library's story.

NOTES

1. Frances Jacobson Harris, "Gimme Shelter: Informal and Formal Learning Environments in Library Land," *The Journal of Research on Libraries and Young Adults* 2, no. 1 (2011), https://www.yalsa.ala.org/jrlya/2011/11/gimme-shelter-informal-and-formal-learning-environments-in-library-land/.
2. Mega Subramaniam, "Designing the Library of the Future for and with Teens: Librarians as the 'Connector' in Connected Learning," *The Journal of Research on Libraries and Young Adults* 7, no. 2 (2016), https://www.yalsa.ala.org/jrlya/2016/06/designing-the-library-of-the-future-for-and-with-teens-librarians-as-the-connector-in-connected-learning/.
3. Allison Druin, "What Children Can Teach Us: Developing Digital Libraries for Children with Children," *Library Quarterly* 75, no. 1 (2005): 25.
4. Meghan Harper, *Reference Sources and Services for Youth* (New York: Neal-Schuman, 2011), 81.
5. Ibid.
6. Ibid.
7. Ibid.
8. Ibid., 81–82.
9. Ibid., 81.
10. Heather Booth, *Serving Teens through Readers' Advisory* (Chicago: American Library Association, 2007), 19.
11. Ibid.
12. Ibid., 20.
13. Ibid., 23.
14. Logan Shea, "Finding What's Right: Readers' Advisory for Middle Grades," *Children and Libraries* 21, no. 3 (2023), https://journals.ala.org/index.php/cal/article/view/8106, 13.
15. Ibid., 14.
16. Booth, *Serving Teens through Readers' Advisory*, 54.
17. Ibid., 59.
18. Ibid.
19. Ibid., 120.
20. Ibid.

21. Patrick Jones, Michele Gorman, and Tricia Suellentrop, *Connecting Young Adults and Libraries: A How-to-Do-It Manual for Librarians*, third ed. (New York: Neal-Schuman, 2004), 219.
22. Melissa Gross, Cindy Mediavilla, and Virginia A. Walter, *5 Steps of Outcome-Based Planning & Evaluation for Youth Services* (Chicago: ALA Editions, 2022), 26–30.
23. Jacqueline Kociubuk, "Branching Out: Promoting Genre Diversity in Storytime," *Children and Libraries* 19, no. 3 (2021): 11.
24. Ibid., 11–12.
25. Ibid., 12.
26. Abby Johnson, "Nonfiction Programming," *American Libraries* (May 2013), https://americanlibrariesmagazine.org/2013/05/28/nonfiction-programming/.
27. Jones, Gorman, and Suellentrop, *Connecting Young Adults and Libraries: A How-to-Do-It Manual for Librarians*, 167.
28. Joni Richards Bodart, "Booktalking Tips from a Pro," in *The Whole Library Handbook: Teen Services*, ed. Heather Booth and Karen Jensen (Chicago: ALA Editions, 2014), 111.
29. Ibid., 114.
30. Ibid., 113.
31. Jane V. Charles, "Get Real! Booktalking Nonfiction for Teen Read Week," *Young Adult Library Services* 4 (Fall 2005): 12.
32. Jones, Gorman, and Suellentrop, *Connecting Young Adults and Libraries: A How-to-Do-It Manual for Librarians*, 175.
33. Joni Bodart, "Student Booktalks Can Motivate Readers," *Book Report* 13, no. 5 (1995): n.p.
34. Ibid.
35. Scholastic, "Book Trailers," accessed May 15, 2024, https://www.youtube.com/playlist?list=PLOA3EC21903A84659.
36. Penguin Teen, "Book Trailers," accessed May 15, 2024, https://www.youtube.com/playlist?list=PL52482DB99ABC834E.
37. Vanessa Irvin, "Book Tweets and Happy Reads: Booktalking to Engage Millenial Teens," *The Journal of Research on Libraries and Young Adults* 16 (November 2015), https://www.yalsa.ala.org/jrlya/2015/11/book-tweets-and-snappy-reads-booktalking-to-engage-millennial-teens/, 2.
38. Ibid.
39. Jones, Gorman, and Suellentrop, *Connecting Young Adults and Libraries: A How-to-Do-It Manual for Librarians*, 228.
40. Ibid., 227.
41. Laura A. May, Teri Holbrook, and Laura E. Meyers, "(Re)Storying Obama: An Examination of Recently Published Informational Texts," *Children's Literature in Education* 41, no. 4 (2010).
42. Monica Gingerich, "Literary Activism: A New Type of Book Club," *Young Adult Library Services* 19, no. 2 (2021), http://yalsjournal.ala.org/publication/?m=53337&i=709838&p=1&ver=html5, 38.
43. Ibid., 39.
44. Reneé Lyons, "Creating Environmental Stewards: Nonfiction Prompting a Sustained Planet," *Children and Libraries* 17, no. 2 (2019), https://journals.ala.org/index.php/cal/article/view/7021, 15, 18.

45. Kafi Kumasi, "Cultural Inquiry: A Framework for Engaging Youth of Color in the Library," *The Journal of Research on Libraries and Young Adults* 1, no. 1 (2010), https://www.yalsa.ala.org/jrlya/2010/11/cultural-inquiry-a-framework-for-engaging-youth-of-color-in-the-library/, n.p.
46. Ibid., n.p.; emphasis in original.
47. Teaching for Change, "Social Justice Books," accessed May 17, 2024, https://socialjusticebooks.org/booklists/.
48. Stephanie Katz, "Publishing Teen Writers: Amplify Teen Voices through Library Publications," *Young Adult Library Services* 19, no. 2 (2021), http://yalsjournal.ala.org/publication/?m=53337&i=709838&p=1&ver=html5, 32.
49. Ibid., 33–34.
50. Melissa Gross and Don Latham, "The Peritextual Literacy Framework: Using the Functions of Peritext to Support Critical Thinking," *Library and Information Science Research* 39, no. 2 (2017): 119–20.
51. Melissa Gross et al., "The Peritext Book Club: Reading to Foster Critical Thinking About Steam Texts," *School Library Research* 19 (2016), https://www.ala.org/sites/default/files/aasl/content/aaslpubsandjournals/slr/vol19/SLR_Peritext%20Book%20Club_V19.pdf, 4–5.
52. Ibid., 5.
53. Ibid., 14.
54. Annette Shtivelband, Lauren Riendeau, and Robert Jakubowski, "Building Upon the Stem Movement: Programming Recommendations for Library Professionals," *Children and Libraries* 15, no. 4 (2017), https://journals.ala.org/index.php/cal/article/view/6510, 23–24.
55. STARnet, "Starnet," accessed May 17, 2024, https://clearinghouse.starnetlibraries.org/32-collections.
56. Mary-Kate Sableski, "Stretching Stem: Using Picturebooks to Connect Stem and Literacy," *Children and Libraries* 17, no. 3 (2019), https://journals.ala.org/index.php/cal/article/view/7111, 23.
57. Ibid.
58. Ibid., 24, 26.
59. Kristin Morgan and Jamie Anderson Collett, "Steam Success: Utilizing Picturebook Biographies," *Children and Libraries* 16 (2018), https://journals.ala.org/index.php/cal/article/view/6795, 14–15.
60. Ibid., 14.
61. Ibid., 15–16.
62. Sylvia M. Vardell, "Connecting Science and Poetry," *Book Links* (November 2013): 16.
63. Ibid., 17; emphasis in original.
64. Sylvia Vardell and Janet Wong, "The Symbiosis of Science and Poetry," *Children and Libraries* 13, no. 1 (2015), https://journals.ala.org/index.php/cal/article/view/5620, 17.
65. Anastasia Suen, "Focus on Stem: Family Recipes," accessed May 17, 2024, https://www.booklistonline.com/Focus-on-STEM-Family-Recipes-Suen-Anastasia/pid=9796228?_zs=5G01k1&_zl=AwQc9.
66. Brooks Mitchell, Claire Radcliffe, and Kelliann LaConte, "Steam Learning in Public Libraries: A 'Guide on the Side' Approach for Inclusive Learning," *Children and*

Libraries 18, no. 3 (2020), https://journals.ala.org/index.php/cal/article/view/7432, 7.
67. Ibid., 8-9.
68. Susan Roman and Carole D. Fiore, "Do Public Library Summer Reading Programs Close the Achievement Gap? The Dominican Study," *Children and Libraries* 8 (2010): 28.
69. Ibid., 30.
70. Ibid., 31.
71. Ann Hotta, "Meaning Makers: Leading Book Discussions That Actually Work," ibid. 19, no. 4 (2021): 20.
72. Ibid., 20-21.
73. Stephanie Levitt Shaulskiy et al., "Motivantional Attributes of Children and Teenagers Who Participate in Summer Reading Clubs," *The Journal of Research on Libraries and Young Adults* 4 (May 2014), https://www.yalsa.ala.org/jrlya/2014/05/motivational-attributes-of-children-and-teenagers-who-participate-in-summer-reading-clubs/, n.p.
74. Ibid.
75. Ibid.
76. Marijke Visser, "Libraries Ready to Code: Past, Present, and Future," *Young Adult Library Services* 17 (Winter 2019), https://yalsa.ala.org/blog/wp-content/uploads/2019/11/YALS_Winter-2019-Final.pdf, 14.
77. Ibid., 15.
78. Gross, Mediavilla, and Walter, *5 Steps of Outcome-Based Planning & Evaluation for Youth Services*, 27-28.
79. Ibid., 80-82, 84.
80. Ibid., 82-83.
81. Kate Grafelman and Sarah Barriage, "No Finish Line: Creating Inclusiveness in Children's Programs," *Children and Libraries* 20, no. 3 (2022), https://journals.ala.org/index.php/cal/article/view/7906, 6-7.

8

The Freedom to Read Nonfiction

Nonfiction for children and young adults is alive and well—in fact, we are arguably in a golden age of nonfiction books with innovative, high-quality works being published in a variety of genres and formats and a number of awards now available to recognize the best of these offerings. All a librarian has to do, it would seem, is stay well-informed and be proactive in sharing these books with young readers. Of course, things are never that simple, for with great success comes greater scrutiny, and indeed there are challenges—both external and internal—in developing and promoting nonfiction collections. In this final chapter, we will look at those challenges as well as the opportunities surrounding nonfiction for children and young adults.

CENSORSHIP

According to the American Library Association's Office for Intellectual Freedom, a record 4,240 unique titles were targeted for censorship in 2023, representing a 65 percent increase over the previous year.[1] It is worth noting, by the way, that an estimated 70 to 80 percent of challenges are never reported.[2] Both public and school libraries receive challenges, and nonfiction is not exempt. Of the books on the "Top Ten Most Challenged Books" list in 2023, four are nonfiction intended for young adults (ages 14+). In order these are: (1) *Gender Queer: A Memoir* (2019) by Maia Kobabe, (2) *All Boys Aren't Blue: A Memoir-Manifesto* (2020) by George M. Johnson, (3) *This Book Is Gay* (2021, second edition) by Juno Dawson, and (9) *Let's Talk About It: The Teen's Guide to Sex, Relationships, and Being a Human* (2021) by Erika Moen and Matthew Nolan. The reasons given for the challenges were LGBTQIA+ content, sexual explicitness, and, in the case of the latter two, sex education.[3] Over the last ten years, the number of nonfiction titles appearing on the "Top Ten" list have ranged from one (2016, 2018, 2020) to three (2015, 2017, 2022) to four

(2014, 2019, 2021, 2023), and most of these are books intended for children or, more frequently, young adults.[4] Some titles, of course, appear year after year. *Gender Queer*, *All Boys Aren't Blue*, and *This Book Is Gay* have been on the "Top Ten" list for the past three years (2021–2023).

Challenges can be brought by parents, other adults (including teachers, administrators, and politicians), and groups of various kinds (religious, political, etc.); they can be brought by conservatives and by liberals[5]—and by anyone in between. The reasons for challenges are myriad, but the most common are profanity, sexual content, depictions of substance abuse, violence, anti-religious themes, and controversial ideas.[6] Amy McClure groups reasons for book challenges into three broad categories:

- Moral—a sense of right and wrong as defined by religious and societal teachings
- Psychological—a concern for the "mental and emotional well-being of the child"
- Sociological—a desire to protect a particular group (from sexism or racism, for example).[7]

These concerns often stem from adults' belief that children need to be protected from disturbing content or controversial ideas. The result of a challenge may be that nothing changes—the challenged book is left in place. Or it may be restricted so that a child or teen wanting to check it out would need their parent's or guardian's permission. Or it may be removed from the collection altogether. Restrictions and removals obviously can limit potential readers' access to materials, but, as Sylvia Vardell notes, there is "[o]ne irony: often banned books become the most sought after. There is nothing more irresistible to kids than something a grown up has said you can't have."[8] And children are not the only ones who notice. As Kenneth Kidd says, "[T]he repetition of certain books in banned books lists year after year itself has a canonizing effect; these seem the classics of banned literature."[9] And he adds, the quickest way to kill a book is not by censoring it, but by ignoring it.[10]

Given the surge in book challenges, what's a librarian to do? A full discussion of censorship and anticensorship are beyond the scope of this book, and in any case there are a number of resources available for those wanting to know more and perhaps needing more guidance. A good place to start is with the American Library Association's Office for Intellectual Freedom (OIF) web page.[11] That said, I will echo Rosemary Chance's thoughtful advice. First, it's important to be informed: be familiar with the resources available from the OIF, including their *Intellectual Freedom Manual* and also be aware of which books are considered controversial.[12] I would add: also be familiar with state laws and local regulations pertaining to libraries and controversial materials. Second, be prepared by having a detailed written collection development policy that's been approved by your school or library board and also have a written procedure in place for dealing with challenges.[13] Third, understand the types of challenges, casual vs. formal. With the former, it may be a matter of simply talking with someone and allowing them to voice their concerns. With the latter, you'll need to follow the written procedure you have in place.[14] Fourth, be proactive in educating students, parents, teachers, and administrators about intellectual freedom. This can be done through Banned Books Week activities, displays, and programs such as a parent-student book club.[15]

SELECTION

In 1953, Lester Asheim published what would become a famous article distinguishing between censorship and selection of library materials. "Not Censorship But Selection" was originally published in *Wilson Library Bulletin* and is now available on the American Library Association's website.[16] Asheim's article asks the provocative question "Is there really a difference between censorship and selection?" In a statement that's as relevant today as it was then, Asheim writes, "Our concern here, of course, is not with cases where the librarian is merely carrying out an obligation placed upon him by law. Where the decision is not his to make, we can hardly hold him responsible for that decision."[17] As he points out, there are three instances where a book might be censored, or made unavailable: when a government bans the book, when a person or group forces a book to be removed, and when a librarian decides not to purchase a book.[18] It is this third case I want to look at in more detail. Due to space and budgetary constraints no library (except perhaps the Library of Congress) can have every book in its collection.[19] How, then, does a librarian decide what to include and what to exclude? As Asheim points out, some librarians might exclude a book in order to avoid "anticipated pressures" from would-be censors.[20] In other cases, self-censorship may occur because of a librarian's own biases.[21] And, to be fair, librarians aren't the only ones who engage in self-censorship. Authors, editors, and publishers sometimes decide a topic is too controversial for children or young adults, and they don't write or publish a book because they are not willing to risk the repercussions that may occur in the marketplace.[22] But is this really a case of censorship, or is it a matter of careful selection? Or is it a matter of one's perspective? As Asheim wryly observes, one is tempted to say, "*I* select but *he* censors."[23]

Selection, according to Carrie Hintz and Eric Tribunella, is defined as "the process of choosing to include or omit certain books from classrooms, curricula, and libraries."[24] Overall, Asheim sees the selection process as positive and focused on protecting readers' rights whereas censorship is negative and focused on protecting readers themselves from supposedly harmful reading materials.[25] The selection process for any given library should be clearly spelled out in the library's collection development document, and the document should be reviewed on a regular basis and revised as needed. It's always important for librarians to know the user community they are serving and to get input from members of that community—through advisory boards, book discussion groups, and surveys. In terms of nonfiction for children and young adults, it's important to be aware of what's available and how it relates to the needs of the user community, and then be conscientious about regularly adding nonfiction to the collection. Here a more subtle kind of exclusion can occur: it's easy to give nonfiction less attention than fiction because there may seem to be more of a demand for fiction. After all, there are few nonfiction blockbusters (like Harry Potter or The Hunger Games series). Moreover, some (maybe many) librarians prefer fiction to nonfiction, and this bias is reflected in their library's collection. However, it's important to recognize that nonfiction for children and young adults can help meet their information and developmental needs and facilitate various literacies. In addition, it can be entertaining, engaging, and enlightening. While some young readers will seek out nonfiction on their own, many others need the impetus of librarians promoting nonfiction through readers' advisory and library programs. Being truly inclusive means including nonfiction in the library's regular repertoire, aiming for balance and variety among genres, formats, and topics as well as striving for diversity among the individuals and groups represented.

NOTES

1. American Library Association, "Top 10 Most Challenged Books of 2023," accessed April 15, 2024, https://www.ala.org/advocacy/bbooks/frequentlychallengedbooks/top10.
2. Michael Cart, *Young Adult Literature: From Romance to Realism*, fourth ed. (Chicago: ALA Neal-Schuman, 2022), 175.
3. American Library Association, "Top 10 Most Challenged Books of 2023."
4. "Top 10 Most Challenged Books and Frequently Challenged Books Archive," accessed June 11, 2024, https://www.ala.org/bbooks/frequentlychallengedbooks/top10/archive.
5. Carrie Hintz and Eric L. Tribunella, *Reading Children's Literature: A Critical Introduction* (Boston: Bedford/St. Martin's, 2013), 439.
6. Rosemary Chance, *Young Adult Literature in Action: A Librarian's Guide* (Westport, CT: Libraries Unlimited, 2008), 144.
7. Amy McClure, "Censorship," *Children's Literature Association Quarterly* 8, no. 1 (1983): 22.
8. Sylvia M. Vardell, *Children's Literature in Action: A Librarian's Guide* (Westport, CT: Libraries Unlimited, 2008), 151.
9. Kenneth Kidd, "'Not Censorship but Selection': Censorship and/as Prizing," *Children's Literature in Education* 40 (2009): 210.
10. Ibid., 214.
11. American Library Association, "Office for Intellectual Freedom," accessed June 11, 2024, https://www.ala.org/aboutala/offices/oif.

12. Chance, *Young Adult Literature in Action*, 137-39.
13. Ibid., 140.
14. Ibid., 140-42.
15. Ibid., 142-43.
16. Lester Asheim, "Not Censorship but Selection," accessed June 11, 2024, https://www.ala.org/advocacy/intfreedom/NotCensorshipButSelection.
17. Ibid., n.p.
18. Ibid.
19. Ibid.
20. Ibid.
21. Vardell, *Children's Literature in Action*, 151.
22. Hintz and Tribunella, *Reading Children's Literature*, 441-42.
23. Asheim, "Not Censorship but Selection" n.p.; emphasis in original.
24. Hintz and Tribunella, *Reading Children's Literature*, 431.
25. Asheim, "Not Censorship but Selection."

Appendix A

Awards for Children's and Young Adult Nonfiction

CHILDREN'S AND YOUNG ADULT NONFICTION AWARDS

Children's Book Guild Nonfiction Award

- Authors and author-illustrators who have created outstanding nonfiction for children
- Children's Book Guild of Washington, DC
- https://www.childrensbookguild.org/nonfiction-award

Orbis Pictus Award

- Excellence in nonfiction writing for children
- National Council of Teachers of English
- https://ncte.org/awards/orbis-pictus-award-nonfiction-for-children/

Robert F. Sibert Informational Book Medal

- Outstanding nonfiction for children up to age 14
- Association for Library Service to Children
- https://www.ala.org/alsc/awardsgrants/bookmedia/sibert

YALSA Award for Excellence in Nonfiction for Young Adults

- Outstanding nonfiction for young adults, ages 12 to 18
- Young Adult Library Services Association
- https://www.ala.org/yalsa/nonfiction

GENRE/SUBJECT-SPECIFIC AWARDS

Mathical Book Prize

- Outstanding fiction and nonfiction books "that inspire children of all ages to see math in the world around them"
- Simons Laufer Mathematical Sciences Institute with the National Council of Teachers of English, the National Council of Teachers of Mathematics, and the Children's Book Council
- https://www.mathicalbooks.org/

Norman A. Sugarman Children's Biography Award

- Outstanding biography for children grades K-8
- Cleveland Public Library
- https://cpl.org/aboutthelibrary/subjectscollections/youth-services/norman-a-sugarman-childrens-biography-award/

Notable Social Studies Trade Books for Young People

- Outstanding social studies books for young people grades K-12
- National Council for the Social Studies with the Children's Book Council
- https://www.socialstudies.org/notable-trade-books

Outstanding Science Trade Books for Students K–12

- Outstanding science books for young people grades K-12
- National Science Teaching Association
- https://www.nsta.org/outstanding-science-trade-books-students-k-12

CHILDREN'S AND YOUNG ADULT LITERATURE AWARDS WITH NONFICTION CATEGORIES

The Boston Globe–Horn Book Awards

- Awards in three categories: Picture Book, Fiction and Poetry, and Nonfiction
- *The Boston Globe* and *The Horn Book*
- https://www.hbook.com/page/boston-globe-horn-book-awards-landing-page

The Golden Kite Awards

- Awards in several categories, including Nonfiction Text for Younger Readers and Nonfiction Text for Older Readers

- Society of Children's Book Writers and Illustrators
- https://www.scbwi.org/awards-and-grants/for-pal-published/golden-kite-awards

NONFICTION-ELIGIBLE CHILDREN'S AND YOUNG ADULT LITERATURE AWARDS

Charlotte Zolotow Award

- Best children's picture book
- Cooperative Children's Book Center (School of Education, University of Wisconsin–Madison)
- https://ccbc.education.wisc.edu/literature-resources/charlotte-zolotow-award/

John Newbery Medal

- Best work of literature for children up to age 14
- Association for Library Service to Children
- https://www.ala.org/alsc/awardsgrants/bookmedia/newbery

Michael L. Printz Award

- Best book for young adults ages 12 to 18
- Young Adult Library Services Association
- https://www.ala.org/yalsa/printz

National Book Awards

- Best literature published in the United States; has a category for Young People's Literature
- National Book Foundation
- https://www.nationalbook.org/national-book-awards/

Randolph Caldecott Medal

- Best picture book for children up to age 14
- Association for Library Service to Children
- https://www.ala.org/alsc/awardsgrants/bookmedia/caldecott

NONFICTION-ELIGIBLE CHILDREN'S AND YOUNG ADULT LITERATURE AWARDS WITH A SPECIAL FOCUS

American Indian Youth Literature Award

- Outstanding books for children and young adults by and about Native American and Indigenous peoples of North America
- American Indian Library Association
- https://ailanet.org/activities/american-indian-youth-literature-award/

Américas Award

- Outstanding books for children and young adults that portray Latin America, the Caribbean, or Latine cultures in the United States
- Consortium of Latin American Studies Programs
- https://claspprograms.org/americas-award/about-the-award/

Arab American Book Award

- Outstanding books for children and young adults by or about Arab Americans
- Arab American National Museum
- https://arabamericanmuseum.org/book-awards/

Asian/Pacific American Librarians Association Awards

- Outstanding books for children and young adults by and about Asian/Pacific Islander American people
- Asian/Pacific American Librarians Association
- https://www.apalaweb.org/awards/literature-awards/

Coretta Scott King Book Awards

- Outstanding African American authors and illustrators of books for children and young adults
- ALA's Coretta Scott King Book Awards Round Table
- https://www.ala.org/awards/books-media/coretta-scott-king-book-awards

Jane Addams Children's Book Award

- Outstanding books for children that promote peace, social justice, global community, and equity
- Jane Addams Peace Association
- https://www.janeaddamschildrensbookaward.org/book-award/

Pura Belpré Award

- Outstanding Latine authors and illustrators of books for children and young adults
- Association for Library Service to Children, Young Adult Library Services Association, and REFORMA
- https://www.ala.org/alsc/awardsgrants/bookmedia/belpre

Mike Morgan and Larry Romans Children's and Young Adult Literature Award

- Outstanding LGBTQIA+ books for children and young adults; part of the Stonewall Book Awards
- ALA's Rainbow Round Table
- https://www.ala.org/awards/books-media/stonewall-book-awards-mike-morgan-larry-romans-childrens-young-adult-literature

Rise: A Feminist Book Project for Ages 0–18

- Outstanding books with feminist content for children and young adults
- ALA's Social Responsibilities Round Table and Feminist Task Force
- https://risefeministbooks.wordpress.com/

Sydney Taylor Book Award

- Outstanding books for children and young adults that portray the Jewish experience
- Association of Jewish Libraries
- https://jewishlibraries.org/sydney_taylor_book_award/

Walter Dean Myers Award

- Outstanding books for children and young adults by *and* about diverse individuals
- We Need Diverse Books
- https://diversebooks.org/programs/walter-awards/

U.S. AWARDS FOR INTERNATIONAL BOOKS FOR CHILDREN AND YOUNG ADULTS

Mildred L. Batchelder Award

- Outstanding books originating outside of the United States, originally published in a language other than English, and then translated into English

- Association for Library Service to Children
- https://www.ala.org/alsc/awardsgrants/bookmedia/batchelder

Outstanding International Books List

- Outstanding books originally published in another country and then published or distributed in the United States
- United States Board on Books for Young People (USBBY)
- https://www.usbby.org/outstanding-international-books-list.html

Appendix B

Review Resources

PERIODICALS

Booklist
   https://www.booklistonline.com/Default.aspx

The Bulletin of the Center for Children's Books
   https://bccb.ischool.illinois.edu/

The Horn Book Guide
   https://www.hornbookguide.com/site/

The Horn Book Magazine
   https://www.hbook.com/

Kirkus Reviews
   https://kirkusreviews.com/

The New York Times Book Review—Children's Books
   https://www.nytimes.com/column/childrens-books

Publishers Weekly
   https://www.publishersweekly.com/

School Library Journal
   https://www.slj.com/

DATABASES

Book Review Digest Plus

https://www.ebsco.com/products/research-databases/book-review-digest-plus

Children's Literature Comprehensive Database

https://www.clcd.com/

Literature Resource Center

https://www.gale.com/c/literature-resource-center

NoveList

https://www.ebsco.com/novelist

WEB RESOURCES

Amazon

https://www.amazon.com/

Book Riot

https://bookriot.com/

The Children's Book Review

https://www.thechildrensbookreview.com/

Children's Literature

https://www.childrenslit.com/

Common Sense Media

https://www.commonsensemedia.org/

Cooperative Children's Book Center

https://ccbc.education.wisc.edu/

Diverse BookFinder

https://diversebookfinder.org/

Goodreads

https://www.goodreads.com/

Social Justice Books
    https://socialjusticebooks.org/sources/
Through the Looking Glass Children's Book Reviews
    https://lookingglassreview.com/books/
We Need Diverse Books
    https://diversebooks.org/

Appendix C

Literacies and Standards

American Association of School Librarians, *AASL Standards Framework for Learners*

    https://standards.aasl.org/wp-content/uploads/2017/11/AASL-Standards-Framework-for-Learners-pamphlet.pdf

Association of College and Research Libraries, *Framework for Information Literacy for Higher Education*

    https://www.ala.org/acrl/standards/ilframework

Common Core State Standards Initiative, *Common Core State Standards*

    https://www.thecorestandards.org/

International Literacy Association, *Resources*

    https://www.literacyworldwide.org/get-resources

National Association for Media Literacy Education, *Why Is Media Literacy Important?*

    https://namle.org/why-media-literacy/

National Council of Teachers of English, *Definition of Literacy in a Digital Age*

    https://ncte.org/statement/nctes-definition-literacy-digital-age/

National Council of Teachers of English, *Key Aspects of Critical Literacy: An Excerpt*

    https://ncte.org/blog/2019/07/critical-literacy/

National Council of Teachers of English, *Position Statement on the Role of Nonfiction Literature (K–12)*

    https://ncte.org/statement/role-of-nonfiction-literature-k-12/

NGSS, *Next Generation Science Standards*

    https://www.nextgenscience.org/

Public Library Association and Association for Library Service to Children, *Every Child Ready to Read @ your library*

    http://everychildreadytoread.org/

Reading Rockets, *Early Literacy Development*

    https://www.readingrockets.org/topics/early-literacy-development

UNESCO, *What You Need to Know About Literacy*

    https://www.unesco.org/en/literacy/need-know

Visual Literacy Today, *What Is Visual Literacy?*

    https://visualliteracytoday.org/what-is-visual-literacy/

Appendix D

Nonfiction Books Cited

CHAPTER BOOKS

Aberg-Riger, Ariel. *America Redux: Visual Stories from Our Dynamic History.* New York: Balzer + Bray, 2023.

Agostini, Alliah L., and Tiffany Elrod. *The Juneteenth Cookbook: Recipes and Activities for Kids and Families to Celebrate.* New York: becker&mayer! kids, 2024.

Angel, Ann. *Janis Joplin: Rise up Singing.* New York: Harry N. Abrams, 2010.

Angelou, Maya. *I Know Why the Caged Bird Sings.* New York: Random House, 1969.

Aronson, Marc. *Sir Walter Ralegh and the Quest for El Dorado.* New York: Clarion Books, 2000.

Aronson, Marc, and Marina Budhos. *Sugar Changed the World: A Story of Magic, Spice, Slavery, Freedom, and Science.* New York: Clarion Books, 2010.

Aronson, Marc, and Paul Freedman. *Bite by Bite: American History through Feasts, Foods, and Side Dishes.* New York: Atheneum Books for Young Readers, 2024.

Bartoletti, Susan Campbell. *Hitler Youth: Growing up in Hitler's Shadow.* New York: Scholastic, 2005.

———. *They Called Themselves the K.K.K.: The Birth of an American Terrorist Group.* New York: Clarion Books, 2010.

Bascomb, Neal. *The Nazi Hunters: How a Team of Spies and Survivors Captured the World's Most Notorious Nazi.* New York: Arthur A. Levine Books, 2013.

Blumenthal, Karen. *Steve Jobs: The Man Who Thought Different.* New York: Feiwel & Friends, 2012.

Bowen, Fred, and James E. Ransome. *Hardcourt: Stories from 75 Years of the National Basketball Association.* New York: Margert K. McElderry Books, 2022.

Bronski, Michael, and Richie Chevat. *A Queer History of the United States for Young People.* Boston: Beacon Press, 2019.

Burns, Lorrie Griffin. *Life on Surtsey: Iceland's Upstart Island*. New York: Clarion Books, 2017.

Carson, Mary Kay, and Tom Uhlman. *The Tornado Scientist: Seeing Inside Severe Storms*. New York: Clarion, 2019.

Chambers, Veronica. *Call and Response: The Story of Black Lives Matter*. New York: Versify, 2021.

Colbert, Brandy. *Black Birds in the Sky: The Story and Legacy of the 1921 Tulsa Race Massacre*. New York: Balzer + Bray, 2021.

Conkling, Winifred. *Votes for Women! American Suffragists and the Battle for the Ballot*. New York: Algonquin Young Readers, 2018.

Cosgrove, Brian. *DK Eyewitness Weather*. New York: DK Children, 2007.

Covey, Sean. *The 7 Habits of Highly Effective Teens*. New York: Simon & Schuster, 2014.

Crutcher, Chris. *King of the Mild Frontier: An Ill-Advised Autobiography*. New York: Greenwillow Books, 2003.

Dawson, Juno. *This Book Is Gay*. Second ed. Naperville, IL: Sourcebooks Fire, 2021.

Day, Nicholas, and Brett Helquist. *The Mona Lisa Vanishes: A Legendary Painter, Shocking Heist, and the Birth of a Global Celebrity*. New York: Random House Studio, 2023.

Deem, James M. *Bodies from the Ice: Melting Glaciers and the Recovery of the Past*. New York: Clarion Books, 2008.

Dionne, Evette. *Lifting as We Climb: Black Women's Battle for the Ballot Box*. New York: Viking Books for Young Readers, 2020.

DK Publishing. *Careers: The Ultimate Guide to Planning Your Future*. New York: DK Publishing, 2022.

Doeden, Matt. *What Are Satire and Parody?* Minneapolis, MN: Lerner Publications, 2019.

———. *What Are Hoaxes and Lies?* Minneapolis, MN: Lerner Publications, 2019.

———. *What Is Propaganda?* Minneapolis, MN: Lerner Publications, 2019.

Doerfler, Jill, and Matthew J. Martinez. *Deb Haaland: First Native American Cabinet Secretary*. Minneapolis, MN: Lerner Publications, 2022.

Ehlert, Lois. *The Scraps Book: Notes from a Colorful Life*. San Diego, CA: Beach Lane Books, 2014.

Fleming, Candace. *The Rise and Fall of Charles Lindbergh*. New York: Schwartz & Wade, 2020.

———. *The Enigma Girls: How Ten Teenagers Broke Ciphers, Kept Secrets, and Helped Win World War II*. New York: Scholastic Focus, 2024.

Freedman, Russell. *Lincoln: A Photobiography*. New York: Clarion Books, 1987.

———. *The Wright Brothers: How They Invented the Airplane*. New York: Holiday House, 1991.

Fritz, Jean. *The Great Little Madison*. New York: G. P. Putnam's Sons, 1989.

Gantos, Jack. *Hole in My Life*. New York: Farrar, Straus and Giroux, 2002.

Giblin, James Cross. *Good Brother, Bad Brother: The Story of Edwin Booth and John Wilkes Booth*. New York: Clarion Books, 2005.

Goldman, Susan Rubin. *The Quilts of Gee's Bend.* New York: Abrams Books for Young Readers, 2017.

Goldstein, Margaret J. *What Are Conspiracy Theories?* Minneapolis, MN: Lerner Publications, 2019.

Grant, John. *Debunk It! Fake News Edition: How to Stay Sane in a World of Misinformation.* Minneapolis, MN: Zest Books, 2019.

Grimes, Nikki. *Ordinary Hazards: A Memoir.* New York: Wordsong, 2019.

Harris, Robie H., and Michael Emberley. *It's Perfectly Normal: Changing Bodies, Growing Up, Sex, Gender, and Sexual Health.* Somerville, MA: Candlewick Press, 2021.

Harrison, Vashti. *Little Dreamers: Visionary Women around the World.* New York: Little, Brown Books for Young Readers, 2018.

Havrelock, Deidre, Edward Kay, and Kalila Fuller. *Indigenous Ingenuity: A Celebration of Traditional North American Knowledge.* New York: Christy Ottaviano Books, 2023.

Heiligman, Deborah. *Charles and Emma: The Darwins' Leap of Faith.* New York: Henry Holt and Company, 2009.

———. *Vincent and Theo: The Van Gogh Brothers.* New York: Henry Holt and Company, 2017.

Hoose, Phillip. *The Race to Save the Lord God Bird.* New York: Farrar, Straus and Giroux, 2004.

———. *Claudette Colvin: Twice toward Justice.* New York: Farrar, Straus and Giroux, 2009.

Hopkinson, Deborah. *Titanic: Voices from the Disaster.* New York: Scholastic, 2012.

Ignotofsky, Rachel. *The History of the Computer.* Berkeley, CA: Ten Speed Press, 2022.

Janeczko, Paul B., and Jenna LaReau. *Top Secret: A Handbook of Codes and Ciphers.* Somerville, MA: Candlewick, 2004.

Jarrow, Gail. *Blood and Germs: The Civil War Battle against Wounds and Disease.* New York: Calkins Creek, 2020.

———. *Ambushed: The Assassination Plot against President Garfield.* New York: Calkins Creek, 2021.

———. *American Murderer: The Parasite That Haunted the South.* New York: Calkins Creek, 2022.

Johnson, George M. *All Boys Aren't Blue: A Memoir-Manifesto.* New York: Farrar, Straus and Giroux, 2020.

Johnson, Katherine. *Reaching for the Moon: The Autobiography of Nasa Mathematician Katherine Johnson.* New York: Atheneum Books for Young Readers, 2019.

Kamkwamba, William, Bryan Mealer, and Anna Hymas. *The Boy Who Harnessed the Wind: Young Readers Edition.* New York: Dial Books for Young Readers, 2015.

Kennedy-Moore, Eileen, and Christine McLaughlin. *Growing Friendships: A Kids' Guide to Making and Keeping Friends.* New York: Aladdin/Beyond Words, 2017.

Kidd, Chip. *Go: A Kidd's Guide to Graphic Design.* New York: Workman Publishing, 2013.

Kramer, Stephen, and Dennis Kunkel. *Hidden Worlds: Looking through a Scientist's Microscope.* Boston: HMH Books for Young Readers, 2001.

Latham, Donna, and Andrew Christensen. *Skyscrapers: Investigate the Feats of Engineering with 25 Projects.* White River Junction, VT: Nomad Press, 2013.

Lauber, Patricia. *Volcano: The Eruption and Healing of Mount St. Helens.* New York: Simon & Schuster Books for Young Readers, 1986.

Lendler, Ian, and C. M. Butzer. *The First Dinosaur: How Science Solved the Greatest Mystery on Earth.* New York: Margaret K. MeElderry Books, 2019.

Levi, Lia, Jess Mason, and Sylvia Notini. *Just a Girl: A True Story of World War II.* New York: HarperCollins, 2022.

Levy, Dana Alison. *Breaking the Mold: Changing the Face of Climate Science.* New York: Holiday House, 2023.

Lin, Grace. *Chinese Menu: The History, Myths, and Legends Behind Your Favorite Foods.* New York: Little, Brown Books for Young Readers, 2023.

Losure, Mary. *Isaac the Alchemist: Secrets of Isaac Newton, Reveal'd.* Somerville, MA: Candlewick, 2017.

Lowery, Linda Blackmon. *Turning 15 on the Road to Freedom: My Story of the 1965 Selma Voting Rights March.* New York: Dial Books, 2015.

Lowry, Lois. *Looking Back: A Book of Memories.* Revised and expanded ed. New York: Clarion Books, 2016.

Macaulay, David. *The Way We Work.* New York: Clarion Books, 2008.

———. *Crossing on Time: Steam Engines, Fast Ships, and a Journey to the New World.* New York: Roaring Brook Press, 2019.

Macy, Sue. *Wheels of Change: How Women Rode the Bicycle to Freedom (with a Few Flat Tires Along the Way).* Washington, DC: National Geographic Kids, 2011.

Marrin, Albert. *Uprooted: The Japanese American Experience during World War II.* New York: Knopf Books for Young Readers, 2016.

McWhorter, Diane. *A Dream of Freedom: The Civil Rights Movement 1954–1968.* New York: Scholastic, 2004.

Menéndez, Juliet. *Latinitas: Celebrating 40 Big Dreamers.* New York: Henry Holt and Company, 2021.

Miller, Michael. *Fake News: Separating Truth from Fiction.* Minneapolis, MN: Twenty-First Century Books, 2019.

Montgomery, Heather L., and Kevin O'Malley. *Something Rotten: A Fresh Look at Roadkill.* New York: Bloomsbury Children's Books, 2018.

Montgomery, Sy, and Nic Bishop. *Saving the Ghost of the Mountain: An Expedition among Snow Leopards in Mongolia.* New York: Clarion Books, 2009.

———. *Kakapo Rescue: Saving the World's Strangest Parrot.* New York: Clarion Books, 2010.

———. *Chasing Cheetahs: The Race to Save Africa's Fastest Cats.* New York: Clarion Books, 2014.

Murphy, Jim. *The Great Fire.* New York: Scholastic, 1995.

———. *Blizzard!* New York: Scholastic, 2000.
———. *An American Plague: The True and Terrifying Story of the Yellow Fever Epidemic of 1793.* New York: Clarion Books, 2003.
Myers, Walter Dean. *Bad Boy: A Memoir.* New York: Amistad Books for Young Readers, 2001.
National Geographic Kids. *National Geographic Kids Look and Learn: Count!* Washington, DC: National Geographic Society, 2011. Board book.
Nelson, Kadir. *We Are the Ship: The Story of Negro League Baseball.* New York: Little, Brown Books for Young Readers, 2008.
Newman, Catherine. *What Can I Say? A Kid's Guide to Super-Useful Social Skills to Help You Get Along and Express Yourself.* New York: Storey Publishing, 2022.
Newman, Patricia. *Sea Otter Heroes: The Predators That Save an Ecosystem.* Minneapolis, MN: Millbrook Press, 2017.
Newman, Patricia, and Annie Crawley. *Planet Ocean: Why We All Need a Healthy Ocean.* Minneapolis, MN: Millbrook Press, 2021.
O'Connell, Caitlin, Donna M. Jackson, and Timothy Rodwell. *The Elephant Scientist.* New York: Clarion Books, 2011.
Osborne, Linda Barrett. *This Land Is Our Land: A History of American Immigration.* New York: Abrams Books for Young Readers, 2016.
Partridge, Elizabeth. *John Lennon: All I Want Is the Truth.* New York: Viking Books for Young Readers, 2005.
———. *Boots on the Ground: America's War in Vietnam.* New York: Viking Books for Young Readers, 2018.
Partridge, Elizabeth, and Lauren Tamaki. *Seen and Unseen: What Dorothea Lange, Toyo Miyatake, and Ansel Adams's Photographs Reveal About the Japanese American Incarceration.* San Francisco, CA: Chronicle Books, 2022.
Patricelli, Leslie. *Potty.* Somerville, MA: Candlewick Press, 2010. Board book.
Peare, Catherine Owen. *Mary Mcleod Bethune.* New York: Vanguard Press, 1951.
Rocco, John. *How We Got to the Moon: The People, Technology, and Daring Feats of Science Behind Humanity's Greatest Adventure.* New York: Crown Books for Young Readers, 2020.
Rubalcaba, Jill, and Peter Robertshaw. *Every Bone Tells a Story: Hominim Discoveries, Deductions, and Debates.* Watertown, MA: Charlesbridge, 2010.
Rusch, Elizabeth. *The 21: The True Story of the Youth Who Sued the U.S. Government over Climate Change.* New York: Greenwillow Books, 2023.
Sandler, Martin W. *Shipwrecked! Diving for Hidden Time Capsules on the Ocean Floor.* New York: Astra Young Readers, 2023.
Sheinkin, Steve. *Bomb! The Race to Build—and Steal—the World's Most Dangerous Weapon.* New York: Roaring Brook Press, 2012.
———. *The Notorious Benedict Arnold: A True Story of Adventure, Heroism & Treachery.* New York: Flash Point, 2013.
Sidman, Joyce. *The Girl Who Drew Butterflies: How Maria Merian's Art Changed Science.* New York: Clarion Books, 2018.
Slater, Dashika. *The 57 Bus: A True Story of Two Teens and the Crime That Changed Their Lives.* New York: Farrar, Straus and Giroux, 2017.

Smith, Sherri L., and Elizabeth Wein. *American Wings: Chicago's Pioneering Black Aviators and the Race for Equality in the Sky.* New York: G. P. Putnam's Sons Books for Young Readers, 2024.

Soontornvat, Christina. *All Thirteen: The Incredible Cave Rescue of the Thai Boys' Soccer Team.* Somverville, MA: Candlewick, 2020.

Spinelli, Jerry. *Knots in My Yo-Yo String: The Autobiography of a Kid.* New York: Knopf, 1998.

Stevenson, Robin. *Pride: Celebrating Diversity & Community.* Victoria, BC: Orca Book Publishers, 2016.

Stone, Tanya Lee. *Almost Astronauts: 13 Women Who Dared to Dream.* Somerville, MA: Candlewick, 2009.

———. *The Good, the Bad, and the Barbie: A Doll's History and Her Impact on Us.* New York: Viking Books for Young Readers, 2010.

Swanson, James L. *Chasing Lincoln's Killer.* New York: Scholastic, 2009.

Takei, George, Justin Eisinger, Steven Scott, and Harmony Becker. *They Called Us Enemy.* Marietta, GA: Top Shelf Productions, 2019.

Tamarin, Alfred H., and Shirley Glubok. *Voyaging to Cathay: Americans in the China Trade.* New York: Viking Juvenile, 1976.

Thimmesh, Catherine. *Team Moon: How 400,000 People Landed Apollo 11 on the Moon.* New York: Clarion Books, 2006.

Thimmesh, Catherine, and Melissa Sweet. *Girls Think of Everything: Stories of Ingenious Inventions by Women.* New York: Clarion Books, 2018.

Van Wagenen, Maya. *Popular: A Memoir.* New York: Dutton Books for Young Readers, 2014.

Vardell, Sylvia, and Janet Wong. *The Poetry of Science: The Poetry Friday Anthology for Science for Kids.* Princeton, NJ: Pomelo Books, 2015.

Walker, Sally M. *Written in Bone: Buried Lives of Jamestown and Colonial Maryland.* Minneapolis, MN: Carolrhoda Books, 2009.

Williams, Yohuru, and Michael G. Long. *More Than a Dream: The Radical March on Washington for Jobs and Freedom.* New York: Farrar, Straus and Giroux, 2023.

Woodson, Jacqueline. *Brown Girl Dreaming.* New York: Nancy Paulsen Books, 2014.

Yates, Elizabeth. *Amos Fortune, Free Man.* London, UK: Puffin Books, 1989.

Zoboi, Ibi. *Star Child: A Biographical Constellation of Octavia Estelle Butler.* New York: Dutton Books for Young Readers, 2022.

PICTURE BOOKS

Andrews, Troy, and Bryan Collier. *Trombone Shorty.* New York: Abrams Books for Young Readers, 2015.

Beckerman, Nell Cross, and Kalen Chock. *Caves.* London, UK: Orchard Books, 2022.

Ben-Barak, Idan, and Philip Bunting. *We Go Way Back: A Book About Life on Earth and How It All Began.* New York: Roaring Brook Press, 2023.

Bishop, Nic. *Spiders*. New York: Scholastic Nonfiction, 2007.

———. *Snakes*. New York: Scholastic, 2012.

Carmichael, L. E., and Byron Eggenschwiler. *Polar: Wildlife at the Ends of the Earth*. Toronto, CA: Kids Can Press, 2023.

Chin, Jason. *Grand Canyon*. New York: Roaring Brook Press, 2017.

———. *Your Place in the Universe*. New York: Neal Porter Books, 2020.

———. *The Universe in You: A Microscopic Journey*. New York: Neal Porter Books, 2022.

Cocca-Leffler, Maryann, and Vivien Mildenberger. *Fighting for Yes! The Story of Disability Rights Activist Judith Heumann*. New York: Abrams Books for Young Readers, 2022.

Cole, Joanna, and Bruce Degen. *The Magic School Bus at the Waterworks*. New York: Scholastic, 1986.

———. The Magic School Bus. New York: Scholastic Press, 1986-2020.

Dalton, Angela, and Lauren Semmer. *To Boldly Go: How Nichelle Nichols and Star Trek Helped Advance Civil Rights*. New York: HarperCollins, 2023.

Delacre, Lulu. *¡Olinguito, De La a a La Z! Descubriendo El Bosque Nublado / Olinguito, from a to Z! Unveiling the Cloud Forest*. New York: Lee & Low Books, 2016.

Denise, Anika Aldamuy, and Paolo Escobar. *Planting Stories: The Life of Librarian and Storyteller Pura Belpré*. New York: HarperCollins, 2019.

Denise, Anika Aldamuy, and Loris Lora. *Phenomenal AOC: The Roots and Rise of Alexandria Ocasio-Cortez*. New York: HarperCollins, 2022.

Dougherty, Rachel. *Secret Engineer: How Emily Roebling Built the Brooklyn Bridge*. New York: Roaring Brook Press, 2019.

Engle, Margarita, and Rafael López. *Drum Dream Girl: How One Girl's Courage Changed Music*. New York: Clarion Books, 2015.

Finley, Julia, and Daniel Rieley. *The Girl Who Thought in Pictures: The Story of Dr. Temple Grandin*. Seattle, WA: The Innovation Press, 2017.

Flack, Roberta, Tonya Bolden, and Hayden Goodman. *The Green Piano: How Little Me Found Music*. New York: Anne Schwartz Books, 2023.

Fleming, Candace, and Eric Rohmann. *Honeybee: The Busy Life of Apis Mellifera*. New York: Neal Porter Books, 2020.

Floca, Brian. *Moonshot: The Flight of Apollo 11*. New York: Atheneum, 2019.

Florian, Douglas. *Comets, Stars, the Moon, and Mars: Space Poems and Paintings*. New York: Clarion Books, 2007.

Gall, Chris. *Jumbo: The Making of the Boeing 747*. New York: Roaring Brook Press, 2020.

Hooks, Gwendolyn, and Colin Bootman. *Tiny Stitches: The Life of Medical Pioneer Vivien Thomas*. New York: Lee & Low, 2016.

Jandu, Allison. *Let's Go to the Potty! A Potty Training Book for Toddlers*. New York: Callisto Kids, 2021.

Jenkins, Martin, and Satoshi Kitamura. *Beware of the Crocodile*. Somerville, MA: Candlewick, 2019.

Jenkins, Steven. *Eye to Eye: How Animals See the World*. New York: Clarion Books, 2014.

Johnson, Stephen T. *Alphabet City*. New York: Viking Books for Young Readers, 1995.

Joy, Angela, and Janelle Washington. *Choosing Brave: How Mamie Till-Mobley and Emmett Till Sparked the Civil Rights Movement*. New York: Roaring Brook Press, 2022.

Keating, Jess, and Marta Álvarez Miguéns. *Shark Lady: The True Story of How Eugenie Clark Became the Ocean's Most Fearless Scientist*. Naperville, IL: Sourcebooks Explore, 2017.

King, Coretta Scott, Barbara Reynolds, and Ekua Holmes. *Coretta: The Autobiography of Mrs. Coretta Scott King*. New York: Godwin Books, 2024.

Lacovara, Janis, Anthony Pinto, and Carlos Varejão. *Brothers and Sisters: The Book for Siblings Who Don't Get Along*. San Diego, CA: Puppy Dogs & Ice Cream, 2022.

Lanan, Jessica. *Jumper: A Day in the Life of the Backyard Jumping Spider*. New York: Roaring Brook Press, 2023.

Lenski, Lois. *Mr. Small Series*. New York: Random House Books for Young Readers, 1934-1962.

Lessac, Frané. *A Is for Australian Reefs*. Somerville, MA: Candlewick, 2023.

Leung, Julie, and Chris Sasaki. *Paper Son: The Inspiring Story of Tyrus Wong, Immigrant and Artist*. New York: Schwartz & Wade, 2019.

Lyon, George Ella, and Katherine Tillotson. *All the Water in the World*. New York: Atheneum/Richard Jackson Books, 2011.

Macaulay, David, and Sheila Keenan. *Toilet: How It Works*. New York: Macmillan, 2013.

Macy, Sue, and Stacy Innerst. *The Book Rescuer: How a Mensch from Massachusetts Saved Yiddish Literature for Generations to Come*. New York: Simon & Schuster/Paul Wiseman Books, 2019.

Mahin, Michael, and Jose Ramirez. *When Angels Sing: The Story of Rock Legend Carlos Santana*. New York: Atheneum Books for Young Readers, 2018.

Maillard, Kevin Noble, and Juana Martinez-Neal. *Fry Bread: A Native American Family Story*. New York: Roaring Brook Press, 2019.

McClung, Robert. *Peeper, First Voice of Spring*. New York: Morrow, 1977.

McDaniel, Breanna, and April Harrison. *Go Forth and Tell: The Life of Augusta Baker, Librarian and Master Storyteller*. New York: Dial Books, 2024.

Nettleton, Pamela Hill, and Becky Shipe. *Look, Listen, Taste, Touch, and Smell: Learning About Your Five Senses*. Bloomington, MN: Picture Window Books, 2004.

Paeff, Colleen, and Nancy Carpenter. *The Great Stink: How Joseph Bazalgette Solved London's Poop Pollution Problem*. New York: Margaret K. McElderry Books, 2021.

Pitman, Gayle E., and Kristyna Litten. *This Day in June*. Washington, DC: Magination Press, 2014.

Rappaport, Doreen, and Bryan Collier. *Martin's Big Words: The Life of Dr. Martin Luther King*. New York: Little, Brown Books for Young Readers, 2001.

Roth, Susan L., and Cindy Trumbore. *Parrots over Puerto Rico*. New York: Lee & Low Books, 2013.

Rusch, Elizabeth, and Susan Swan. *Volcano Rising.* Watertown, MA: Charlesbridge, 2013.

Ryan, Pam Muñoz, and Brian Selznick. *When Marian Sang.* New York: Scholastic, 2002.

Sidman, Joyce, and Rick Allen. *Dark Emperor and Other Poems of the Night.* New York: Clarion Books, 2010.

Simon, Seymour. *Saturn.* New York: HarperCollins, 1985.

———. *Jupiter.* New York: William Morrow & Co., 1985.

Slade, Suzanne, and Cazbi Cabrera. *Exquisite: The Poetry and Life of Gwendolyn Brooks.* New York: Harry N. Abrams, 2020.

Sorrell, Traci, and Natasha Donovan. *Classified: The Secret Career of Mary Golda Ross, Cherokee Space Engineer.* Minneapolis, MN: Millbrook Press, 2021.

Sorrell, Traci, and Frane Lessac. *We Are Still Here! Native American Truths Everyone Should Know.* Watertown, MA: Charlesbridge, 2021.

Stanley, Diane, and Jessie Hartland. *Ada Lovelace, Poet of Science: The First Computer Programmer.* New York: Simon & Schuster, 2016.

Steptoe, Javaka. *Radiant Child: The Story of Young Artist Jean-Michel Basquiat.* New York: Little, Brown Books for Young Readers, 2016.

Stetson, Caren, and Selina Alko. *Stars of the Night: The Courageous Children of the Czech Kindertransport.* Minneapolis, MN: Carolrhoda Books, 2023.

Stewart, Melissa, and Candace R. Bergum. *Under the Snow.* New York: Holiday House, 2009.

Stewart, Melissa, and Sarah S. Brannen. *Summertime Sleepers: Animals That Estivate.* Watertown, MA: Charlesbridge, 2021.

Tlaib, Rashida, Adam Tlaib, Miranda Paul, and Olivia Aserr. *Mama in Congress: Rashida Tlaib's Journey to Washington.* New York: Clarion Books, 2022.

Todd, Traci N., and Christian Robinson. *Nina: A Story of Nina Simone.* New York: G. P. Putnam's Sons, 2023.

Todd, Traci N., and Shannon Wright. *Holding Her Own: The Exceptional Life of Jackie Ormes.* London: Orchard Books, 2023.

Tonatiuh, Duncan. *Separate Is Never Equal: Sylvia Mendez and Her Family's Fight for Desegregation.* New York: Harry N. Abrams, 2014.

———. *Funny Bones: Posada and His Day of the Dead Calaveras.* New York: Harry N. Abrams, 2015.

Wallmark, Laurie, and Katy Wu. *Grace Hopper: Queen of Computer Code.* New York: Union Square Kids, 2017.

Weatherford, Carole Boston, and Floyd Cooper. *Unspeakable: The Tulsa Race Massacre.* Minneapolis, MN: Carolrhoda Books, 2021.

Wittenstein, Harry, and Jessie Hartland. *The Day the River Caught Fire: How the Cuyahoga River Exploded and Ignited the Earth Day Movement.* New York: Simon & Schuster, 2023.

Yolen, Jane, and Jason Semple. *Bug Off! Creepy, Crawly Poems.* New York: Wordsong, 2012.

Young, Ed. *The House Baba Built: An Artist's Childhood in China.* New York: Little, Brown Books for Young Readers, 2011.

GRAPHIC FORMAT

Abirached, Zeina. *A Game for Swallows: To Die, to Leave, to Return*. Minneapolis, MN: Graphic Universe, 2012.

Aliu, Akim, Greg Anderson Elysée, Karen De la Vega, and Marcus Williams. *Akim Aliu: Dreamer*. New York: Graphix, 2023.

Bagieu, Pénélope. *Brazen: Rebel Ladies Who Rocked the World*. New York: First Second, 2018.

Barker, Meg-John, and Jules Scheele. *Queer: A Graphic History*. London, UK: Icon Books, 2016.

Bechdel, Alison. *Fun Home: A Family Tragicomic*. Boston: Mariner Books, 2007.

Bell, Cece. *El Deafo*. New York: Harry N. Abrams, 2014.

Bertozzi, Nick. *Lewis & Clark*. New York: First Second, 2011.

Brown, Don. *Drowned City: Hurricane Katrina and New Orleans*. New York: Clarion Books, 2015.

———. *In the Shadow of the Fallen Towers: The Seconds, Minutes, Hours, Days, Weeks, Months, and Years after the 9/11 Attacks*. New York: Clarion Books, 2021.

———. *Run and Hide: How Jewish Youth Escaped the Holocaust*. New York: Clarion Books, 2023.

Conyngham, Richard. *All Rise: Resistance and Rebellion in South Africa 1910–1948: A Graphic History*. Minneapolis, MN: Catalyst Press, 2022.

Dembicki, Matt, ed. *District Comics: An Unconventional History of Washington, DC*. Chicago, IL: Chicago Review Press—Fulcrum, 2012.

Fetter-Vorm, Jonathan. *Trinity: A Graphic History of the First Atomic Bomb*. New York: Hill and Wang, 2012.

Flowers, Arthur, and Manu Chitrakar. *I See the Promised Land: A Life of Martin Luther King Jr.* Chennai, India: Tara Books, 2010.

Geary, Rick. *Jack the Ripper: A Journal of the Whitechapel Murders 1888–1889*. New York: NBM Publishing, 1995.

———. *The Borden Tragedy: A Memoir of the Infamous Double Murder at Fall River, Mass., 1892*. New York: NBM Publishing, 1997.

———. *The Murder of Abraham Lincoln*. New York: NBM Publishing, 2005.

———. *The Lindbergh Child*. New York: NBM Publishing, 2008.

———. *The Lives of Sacco and Vanzetti*. New York: NBM Publishing, 2011.

Gonick, Larry. *The Cartoon History of the Universe Volumes 1–7: From the Big Bang to Alexander the Great*. New York: Crown, 1990.

———. *The Cartoon History of the United States*. New York: William Morrow, 1991.

———. *The Cartoon History of the Universe Volumes 8–13: From the Springtime of China to the Fall of Rome*. New York: Three Rivers Press, 1994.

———. *The Cartoon History of the Universe: From the Rise of Arabia to the Renaissance*. New York: W. W. Norton, 2002.

———. *The Cartoon History of the Modern World: From Columbus to the U.S. Constitution*. New York: William Morrow, 2006.

———. *The Cartoon History of the Modern World: From the Bastille to Baghdad.* New York: William Morrow, 2009.
Hale, Nathan. *Nathan Hale's Hazardous Tales.* New York: Amulet, 2012-.
Hosler, Jay. *Clan Apis.* Columbus, OH: Active Synapse, 2000.
———. *Optical Allusions.* Columbus, OH: Active Synapse, 2014.
Hosler, Jay, Kevin Cannon, and Zander Cannon. *Evolution: The Story of Life on Earth.* New York: Hill and Wang, 2011.
Kobabe, Maia. *Gender Queer: A Memoir.* Portland, OR: Oni Press, 2019.
Krosoczka, Jarrett J. *Hey, Kiddo: How I Lost My Mother, Found My Father, and Dealt with Family Addiction.* New York: Graphix, 2018.
———. *Sunshine: How One Camp Taught Me About Life, Death, and Hope.* New York: Graphix, 2023.
Lambert, Joseph. *Annie Sullivan and the Trial of Helen Keller.* New York: Little, Brown Ink, 2018.
Lewis, John, Andrew Aydin, and Nate Powell. *March: Book One.* Marietta, GA: Top Shelf Productions, 2013.
———. *March: Book Two.* Marietta, GA: Top Shelf Productions, 2015.
———. *March: Book Three.* Marietta, GA: Top Shelf Productions, 2016.
Martín, Pedro. *Mexikid: A Graphic Memoir.* New York: Dial Books, 2023.
Moen, Erika, and Matthew Nolan. *Let's Talk About It: The Teen's Guide to Sex, Relationships, and Being a Human.* New York: Random House Graphics, 2021.
Myer, Sarah. *Monstrous: A Transracial Adoption Story.* New York: First Second, 2023.
Neufeld, Josh. *A.D.: New Orleans after the Deluge.* New York: Pantheon, 2009.
Nott, Dan. *Hidden Systems: Water, Electricity, the Internet, and the Secrets Behind the Systems We Use Every Day.* New York: Random House Graphic, 2023.
Ottaviani, Jim, and Leland Myrick. *Feynman.* New York: First Second, 2011.
———. *Hawking.* New York: First Second, 2019.
Ottaviani, Jim, and Leland Purvis. *The Imitation Game: Alan Turing Decoded.* New York: Abrams ComicArts, 2016.
Ottaviani, Jim, and Maris Wicks. *Primates: The Fearless Science of Jane Goodall, Dian Fossey, and Biruté Galdikas.* New York: First Second, 2013.
———. *Astronauts: Women on the Final Frontier.* New York: First Second, 2020.
Pham, Thien. *Family Style: Memories of an American from Vietnam.* New York: First Second, 2023.
Quintero, Isabel, and Zeke Peña. *Photographic: The Life of Graciela Iturbide.* Los Angeles, CA: Getty, 2018.
Santat, Dan. *A First Time for Everything.* New York: First Second, 2023.
Satrapi, Marjane. *Persepolis: The Story of a Childhood.* New York: Pantheon, 2003.
———. *Persepolis 2: The Story of a Return.* New York: Pantheon, 2005.
Science Comics. *Science Comics.* New York: First Second, 2016-.
Sheinkin, Steve, and Nick Bertozzi. *Bomb (Graphic Novel): The Race to Build—and Steal—the World's Most Dangerous Weapon.* New York: Roaring Brook Press, 2023.

Spiegelman, Art. *Maus I: A Survivor's Tale: My Father Bleeds History*. New York: Pantheon, 1986.

———. *Maus II: A Survivor's Tale: And Here My Troubles Began*. New York: Pantheon, 1991.

Stamaty, Mark Alan. *Alia's Mission: Saving the Books of Iraq*. New York: Knopf Books for Young Readers, 2004.

Suggs, Christine. *¡Ay, Mija! My Bilingual Summer in Mexico*. New York: Little, Brown Ink, 2023.

Telgemeier, Raina. *Smile*. New York: Graphix, 2010.

———. *Sisters*. New York: Graphix, 2014.

———. *Guts*. New York: Graphix, 2019.

Thrash, Maggie. *Honor Girl: A Graphic Memoir*. Somerville, MA: Candlewick, 2017.

Wicks, Maris. *Coral Reefs: Cities of the Ocean*. New York: First Second, 2016.

Yang, Gene Luen, and Mike Holmes. *Secret Coders*. New York: First Second, 2015–.

AUDIOBOOKS

Bell, Cece. *El Deafo*. New York: Listening Library/Penguin Random House Audio, 2023.

Lin, Grace. *Chinese Menu: The History, Myths, and Legends Behind Your Favorite Foods*. New York: Little, Brown Young Readers, 2023.

Martín, Pedro. *Mexikid: A Graphic Memoir*. New York: Listening Library/Penguin Random House Audio, 2023.

Nelson, Kadir. *We Are the Ship: The Story of Negro League Baseball*. Grand Haven, MI: Brilliance Audio, 2009.

Reynolds, Jason, and Ibram X. Kendi. *Stamped: Racism, Antiracism, and You*. New York: Little, Brown Young Readers, 2020.

Thompson, Laurie Ann. *Emmanuel's Dream: The True Story of Emmanuel Ofosu Yeboah*. New York: Listening Library, 2021.

Wood, Susan. *Esquivel! Space-Age Sound Artist*. Pine Plains, NY: Live Oak Media, 2018.

Bibliography

Adkins, Denice, and Bobbie Bushman. "A Special Needs Approach: A Study of How Libraries Can Start Programs for Children with Disabilities." *Children and Libraries* 13, no. 3 (2015): 28-33.

Agosto, Denise E., and Sandra Hughes-Hassell. "People, Places, and Questions: An Investigation of the Everyday Life Information-Seeking Behaviors of Urban Young Adults." *Library and Information Science Research* 27 (2005): 141-63.

Amazon. "Amazon." https://www.amazon.com/.

American Association of School Librarians. "Standards Framework for Learners." American Association of School Librarians, https://standards.aasl.org/wp-content/uploads/2017/11/AASL-Standards-Framework-for-Learners-pamphlet.pdf.

American Library Association. "Booklist." https://www.booklistonline.com/Default.aspx.

———. "Top 10 Most Challenged Books of 2023." https://www.ala.org/advocacy/bbooks/frequentlychallengedbooks/top10.

———. "Office for Intellectual Freedom." https://www.ala.org/aboutala/offices/oif.

———. "Top 10 Most Challenged Books and Frequently Challenged Books Archive." https://www.ala.org/bbooks/frequentlychallengedbooks/top10/archive.

American Psychological Association. "Developmental Psychology Studies Humans across the Lifespan." American Psychological Association, https://www.apa.org/education-career/guide/subfields/developmental#:~:text=Developmental%20Psychology%20Studies%20Humans%20Across,perceptual%2C%20personality%20and%20emotional%20growth.

Anderson, Linda. *Autobiography*. New York: Routledge, 2001.

Arab American National Museum. "The Arab American Book Award." https://arabamericanmuseum.org/book-awards/.

Aronson, Marc. "Originality in Nonfiction." *School Library Journal* 52, no. 1 (2006): 42-42.

———. "Nonfiction Windows So White." *The Horn Book Magazine* 97, no. 2 (2021): 12-16.

Asheim, Lester. "Not Censorship but Selection." https://www.ala.org/advocacy/intfreedom/NotCensorshipButSelection.

Asian/Pacific American Librarians Association. "Literature Award Guidelines & Nominations." https://www.apalaweb.org/awards/literature-awards/literature-award-guidelines/.

Association for Library Service to Children. "Mildred L. Batchelder Award." https://www.ala.org/alsc/awardsgrants/bookmedia/batchelder.

Association for Library Service to Children. "Book & Media Awards Shelf." https://alsc-awards-shelf.org/.

———. "Pura Belpré Award." https://www.ala.org/alsc/awardsgrants/bookmedia/belpre.

———. "Children's Book Awards - from Other Organizations." https://www.ala.org/alsc/awardsgrants/bookmedia/childrens-book-awards-other-organizations.

———. "Robert F. Sibert Informational Book Medal." https://www.ala.org/alsc/awardsgrants/bookmedia/sibert.

Association of College and Research Libraries. "Framework for Information Literacy for Higher Education." Association of College and Research Libraries, https://www.ala.org/acrl/standards/ilframework.

Association of Jewish Libraries. "Award Overview." https://jewishlibraries.org/sydney_taylor_book_award/.

Audio Publishers Association. "APA 5-Year Industry Date." https://www.audiopub.org/apa-5-year-data.

Avery, Gillian. "The Beginnings of Children's Reading to C.1700." In *Children's Literature: An Illustrated History*, edited by Peter Hunt, 1–25. Oxford, UK: Oxford University Press, 1995.

Baldick, Chris. *Genre*. Oxford Concise Dictionary of Literary Terms. New York: Oxford University Press, 2004.

Bamford, Rosemary A., and Janice V. Kristo, eds. *Making Facts Come Alive: Choosing & Using Nonfiction Literature K–8*. Second ed. Norwood, MA: Christopher-Gordon, 2003.

Bang, Molly. *Picture This: How Pictures Work, Revised and Expanded 25th Anniversary Edition*. San Francisco, CA: Chronicle Books, 2016 (1991).

Bascomb, Neal. *The Nazi Hunters: How a Team of Spies and Survivors Captured the World's Most Notorious Nazi*. New York: Scholastic Inc., 2013.

Beers, Kylene, and Robert E. Probst. *Reading Nonfiction: Notice & Note Stances, Signposts, and Strategies*. Portsmouth, NH: Heinemann, 2016.

Bishop, Rudine Sims. "Mirrors, Windows, and Sliding Glass Doors." *Perspectives: Choosing and Using Books for the Classroom* 6, no. 3 (1990): n.p.

Boatright, Michael D. "Graphic Journeys: Graphic Novels' Representations of Immigrant Experiences." *Journal of Adolescent & Adult Literacy* 53, no. 6 (2010).

Bodart, Joni. "Student Booktalks Can Motivate Readers." *Book Report* 13, no. 5 (1995): 21–23.

Bodart, Joni Richards. "Booktalking Tips from a Pro." In *The Whole Library Handbook: Teen Services*, edited by Heather Booth and Karen Jensen, 110–15. Chicago: ALA Editions, 2014.

Booth, Heather. *Serving Teens through Readers' Advisory*. Chicago: American Library Association, 2007.

Boston Globe–Horn Book Awards. https://www.hbook.com/story/about-the-boston-globe-horn-book-awards.

Bound to Stay Bound Bookstore. "Mission." https://www.btsb.com/about-us/mission/.

Brenner, Robin. "Comics and Graphic Novels." In *Handbook of Research on Children's and Young Adult Literature*, edited by Shelby Anne Wolf, 256–74. New York: Routledge, 2011.

Bruner, Jerome. "Life as Narrative." *Social Research* 71, no. 3 (2004): 691–710.

Brzozowski, Bonnie. "Drawing on Reality." *Library Journal* (Feb. 1, 2012): 32–35.

Buckingham, David. "The Uselessness of Literacies." https://davidbuckingham.net/blog/.

Buell, Ellen Lewis. "A War-Time Handbook for Young Americans." Review of A War-Time Handbook for Young Americans. *The New York Times Book Review*, 1942.

Burnett, Kathleen, and Eliza T. Dresang. "Rhizomorphic Reading: The Emergence of a New Aesthetic in Literature for Youth." *The Library Quarterly* 69, no. 4 (1999): 421–45.

Cahill, Maria, and Jennifer Moore. "A Sound History: Audiobooks Are Music to Children's Ears." *Children and Libraries*, no. Spring (2017): 22–29.

Cahill, Maria, and Jennifer Richey. "What Sound Does an Odyssey Make? Content Analysis of Award-Winning Audiobooks." *Library Quarterly* 85, no. 4 (2015): 371–85.

Callanan, Maureen, Christi Cervantes, and Molly Loomis. "Informal Learning." *WIREs Cognitive Science* 2 (2011): 646–55.

Carpenter, Humphrey, and Mari Prichard. *The Oxford Companion to Children's Literature*. Oxford, UK: Oxford University Press, 1999.

Carr, Jo, ed. *Beyond Fact: Nonfiction for Children and Young People*. Chicago, IL: American Library Association, 1982.

Cart, Michael. *Young Adult Literature: From Romance to Realism*. Fourth ed. Chicago: ALA Neal-Schuman, 2022.

Carter, Betty, and Richard F. Abrahamson. *Nonfiction for Young Adults from Delight to Wisdom*. Phoenix, AZ: Oryx Press, 1990.

Case, Donald O., and Lisa M. Given. *Looking for Information: A Survey of Research on Information Seeking, Needs, and Behavior*. Studies in Information. Edited by Jens-Erik Mai. Fourth ed. Bingley, UK: Emerald Group Publishing Limited, 2016.

Chance, Rosemary. *Young Adult Literature in Action: A Librarian's Guide*. Westport, CT: Libraries Unlimited, 2008.

Charles, Jane V. "Get Real! Booktalking Nonfiction for Teen Read Week." *Young Adult Library Services* 4 (Fall 2005): 12–16.

Chauvin, B. A. "Visual or Media Literacy?" *Journal of Visual Literacy* 23, no. 2 (2003): 119–28.

Cherry, Kendra. "Erikson's Stages of Development." Verywell Mind, https://www.verywellmind.com/erik-eriksons-stages-of-psychosocial-development-2795740.

———. "Piaget's 4 Stages of Cognitive Development Explained." Verywell Mind, https://www.verywellmind.com/piagets-stages-of-cognitive-development-2795457.

Chung, Sunah, and Amina Chaudhri. "Biographies of Women in the Robert Sibert Award: A Critical Content Analysis." *Journal of Children's Literature* 47, no. 1 (2021): 62–72.

CLCD. "CLCD Supporting Content." https://clcd.com/clcd-supporting/.

———. "Children's Literature."

Cleveland Public Library. "Norman A. Sugarman Children's Biography Award." https://cpl.org/aboutthelibrary/subjectscollections/youth-services/norman-a-sugarman-childrens-biography-award/.

Colman, Penny. "Nonfiction Is Literature, Too." *The New Advocate* 12, no. 3 (1999): 215–23.

———. "A New Way to Look at Literature: A Visual Model for Analyzing Fiction and Nonfiction Texts." *Language Arts* 84, no. 3 (2007/1// 2007): 257–68.

———. "Point of Departure." In *Handbook of Research on Children's and Young Adult Literature*, edited by Karen Coats Shelby Wolf, Patricia Enciso, and Christine Jenkins, 299–301. New York: Routledge, 2011.

Common Sense. "Media Choice." https://www.commonsensemedia.org/what-we-stand-for/media-choice.

Consortium of Latin American Studies Programs. "Américas Award." http://claspprograms.org/americasaward.

Conway, Jill Ker. *When Memory Speaks: Exploring the Art of Autobiography*. New York: Random House, 1998.

Cooke, Nicole A. "White Kids Need Diverse Books, Too." *Young Adult Library Services* 17, no. 4 (2019): 27–31. https://yalsa.ala.org/blog/wp-content/uploads/2020/03/YALS_Summer2019.pdf.

Cooper, Linda Z. "Children's Information Choices for Inclusion in a Hypothetical Child-Constructed Library." In *Youth Information-Seeking Behavior: Theories, Models, and Issues*, edited by Mary K. Chelton and Colleen Cool, 181–210. Lanham, MD: Scarecrow Press, 2004.

Cooperative Children's Book Center. "Charlotte Zolotow Award." https://ccbc.education.wisc.edu/literature-resources/charlotte-zolotow-award/.

———. "CCBC Recommended-Books Overview." https://ccbc.education.wisc.edu/literature-resources/ccbc-recommended-books-2/.

Copeland, Clayton A., and Karen Gavigan. "Examining Inclusive Programming in a Middle School Library: A Case Study of Adolescents Who Are Differently- and Typically-Able." *The Journal of Research on Libraries and Young Adults* 6, no. 4 (2015): 1–19. https://www.yalsa.ala.org/jrlya/2015/11/

examining-inclusive-programming-in-a-middle-school-library-a-case-study-of-adolescents-who-are-differently-and-typically-able/.

Coretta Scott King Book Awards Round Table. "Coretta Scott King Book Awards." https://www.ala.org/rt/cskbart.

Council on Interracial Books for Children. "10 Quick Ways to Analyze Children's Books for Racism and Sexism." Worlds of Words, https://wowlit.org/links/evaluating-global-literature/10-quick-ways-to-analyze-childrens-books-for-racism-and-sexism/.

Crawley, S. Adam. "Who's Out? Who's In? (Re)Presentations of LGB+ Individuals in Picturebook Biographies." *Taboo: The Journal of Culture & Education*, no. Winter (2020): 128-59.

Crisp, Thomas. "A Content Analysis of Orbis Pictus Award-Winning Nonfiction, 1990-2014 241." *Language Arts* 92, no. 4 (2015).

Crisp, Thomas, Roberta Price Gardner, and Matheus Almeida. "The All-Heterosexual World of Children's Nonfiction: A Critical Content Analysis of LGBTQ Identities in Orbis Pictus Award Books, 1990-2017." *Children's Literature in Education* 49, no. 3 (2018/9// 2018): 246-63.

Crisp, Thomas, Suzanne Knezek, M., and Roberta Price Gardner, eds. *Reading and Teaching with Diverse Nonfiction Children's Books: Representations and Possibilities*. Champaign, IL: National Council of Teachers of English.

Dávila, Denise, and Sarah Elovich. "Evaluating the Narrative Authenticity of Informational Nonfiction for Children." In *Reading Teacher*, 2022.

Diverse BookFinder. "Our Vision & Mission." https://diversebookfinder.org/our-missionvision/.

Doiron, Ray. "Boy Books, Girl Books: Should We Re-Organize Our School Library Collections?" *Teacher Librarian* 30, no. 3 (2003): 14-16.

Dresang, Eliza T. *Radical Change: Books for Youth in a Digital Age*. New York: H. W. Wilson, 1999.

———. "Radical Change." In *Theories of Information Behavior*, edited by Karen E. Fisher, Sanda Erdelez and Lynne (E. F.) McKechnie, 298-302. Medford, NJ: Information Today, Inc., 2005.

Druin, Allison. "What Children Can Teach Us: Developing Digital Libraries for Children with Children." *Library Quarterly* 75, no. 1 (2005): 20-41.

EBSCO. "Book Review Digest Plus." https://www.ebsco.com/products/research-databases/book-review-digest-plus.

———. "About Novelist." https://www.ebsco.com/novelist/about/our-curated-content.

Englert, Carol S., and Elfrieda H. Hiebert. "Children's Developing Awareness of Text Structures in Expository Materials." *Journal of Educational Psychology* 76, no. 1 (1984).

Erikson, Erik H. *Identity: Youth and Crisis*. New York: W. W. Norton & Company, 1968.

Fang, Zhihui, and Suzanne Coatoam. "Disciplinary Literacy: What You Want to Know About It." *Journal of Adolescent & Adult Literacy* 56, no. 8 (2013): 627-32.

Feminist Task Force and Social Responsibilities Round Table. "Rise: A Feminist Book Project for Ages 0–18." https://risefeministbooks.wordpress.com/.

Fisher, Karen E., Sanda Erdelez, and Lynne (E. F.) McKechnie. "Preface." In *Theories of Information Behavior*, edited by Karen E. Fisher, Sanda Erdelez and Lynne (E. F.) McKechnie, xix–xxii. Medford, NJ: Information Today, Inc., 2005.

Fisher, Margery. *Matters of Fact: Aspects of Non-Fiction for Children*. New York: Crowell, 1972.

Gale. "Gale Literature Resource Center." https://www.gale.com/c/literature-resource-center.

Gardner, Roberta Price, Suzanne Knezek, M., and Thomas Crisp. "Introduction: Diverse Nonfiction in Prek-8 Classrooms." In *Reading and Teaching with Diverse Nonfiction Children's Books: Representations and Possibilities*, edited by Thomas Crisp, Suzanne Knezek, M. and Roberta Price Gardner, xv–xxi. Champaign, IL: National Council of Teachers of English, 2021.

Genette, Gérard. *Paratexts: Thresholds of Interpretation*. New York: Cambridge University Press, 1997.

Giblin, James Cross. "More Than Just the Facts: A Hundred Years of Children's Nonfiction." *The Horn Book Magazine* 76, no. 4 (2000): 413–24.

Gill, Sharon Ruth. "What Teachers Need to Know About the "New" Nonfiction." *The Reading Teacher* 63, no. 4 (2009).

Gingerich, Monica. "Literary Activism: A New Type of Book Club." *Young Adult Library Services* 19, no. 2 (2021): 38–40. http://yalsjournal.ala.org/publication/?m=53337&i=709838&p=1&ver=html5.

Goodreads. "Goodreads." https://www.goodreads.com/?ref=nav_home.

Grafelman, Kate, and Sarah Barriage. "No Finish Line: Creating Inclusiveness in Children's Programs." *Children and Libraries* 20, no. 3 (2022): 3–11. https://journals.ala.org/index.php/cal/article/view/7906.

Graff, Jennifer M., and Courtney Shimek. "Revisiting Reader Response: Contemporary Nonfiction Children's Literature as Remixes." *Language Arts* 97, no. 4 (2020).

Grenby, M. O. "The Origins of Children's Literature." In *The Cambridge Companion to Children's Literature*, edited by M. O. Grenby, and Immel, Andrea, 3–18. Cambridge, UK: Cambridge University Press, 2009.

Grenby, M. O., and Andrea Immel, eds. *The Cambridge Companion to Children's Literature*. Cambridge, UK: Cambridge University Press, 2009.

Gross, Melissa. "The Imposed Query." In *RQ*, 1995.

———. "The Imposed Query and Information Services for Children." In *Journal of Youth Services in Libraries*, 8, 2000.

Gross, Melissa, and Don Latham. "The Peritextual Literacy Framework: Using the Functions of Peritext to Support Critical Thinking." *Library and Information Science Research* 39, no. 2 (2017): 116–23.

Gross, Melissa, Don Latham, Jennifer Underhill, and Hyerin Bak. "The Peritext Book Club: Reading to Foster Critical Thinking About Steam Texts." *School Library Research* 19(2016): 1–17. https://www.ala.org/sites/default

/files/aasl/content/aaslpubsandjournals/slr/vol19/SLR_Peritext%20Book%20Club_V19.pdf.

Gross, Melissa, Cindy Mediavilla, and Virginia A. Walter. *5 Steps of Outcome-Based Planning & Evaluation for Youth Services*. Chicago: ALA Editions, 2022.

Guiness World Records. In *Guiness World Records*. London: Guiness World Records, 1955–.

Guzzetti, Barbara J., and Marcia A. Mardis. "From Dickens to 9/11: Exploring Graphic Nonfiction to Support the Secondary-School Curriculum." *The Journal of Research on Libraries and Young Adults* (May 2014).

———. "The Potential of Graphic Nonfiction for Teaching and Learning Earth Science." *School Libraries Worldwide* 23, no. 1 (2017): 15–29.

Hamilton, Nigel. *Biography: A Brief History*. Cambridge, MA: Harvard University Press, 2007.

Harper, Meghan. *Reference Sources and Services for Youth*. New York: Neal-Schuman, 2011.

Harris, Frances Jacobson. "Gimme Shelter: Informal and Formal Learning Environments in Library Land." *The Journal of Research on Libraries and Young Adults* 2, no. 1 (2011): n.p., https://www.yalsa.ala.org/jrlya/2011/11/gimme-shelter-informal-and-formal-learning-environments-in-library-land/.

Hartel, Jenna. "Serious Leisure." In *Theories of Information Behavior*, edited by Karen E. Fisher, Sanda Erdelez and Lynne (E. F.) McKechnie, 313–17. Medford, NJ: Information Today, Inc., 2005.

Hartnett, Liz. "Intellectual Freedom: Serving up Outreach with a Side of Information Literacy." *Children and Libraries* 18, no. 3 (2020): 35–36. https://journals.ala.org/index.php/cal/article/view/7438.

Havighurst, Robert J. *Human Development and Education*. New York: Longmans, Green and Co., 1953.

Hintz, Carrie, and Eric L. Tribunella. *Reading Children's Literature: A Critical Introduction*. Boston, MA: Bedford/St. Martin's, 2013.

Hirth, Paul. "From the Secondary Section: What's the Truth About Nonfiction?" *The English Journal* 91, no. 4 (2002).

Horning, Kathleen T. *From Cover to Cover: Evaluating and Reviewing Children's Books*. Rev. ed. New York: HarperCollins, 2010.

Hotta, Ann. "Meaning Makers: Leading Book Discussions That Actually Work." *Children and Libraries* 19, no. 4 (2021): 20–21.

Howard, Vivian, and Shan Jin. "Teens and Pleasure Reading: A Critical Assessment from Nova Scotia." In *Youth Information-Seeking Behavior II: Context, Theories, Models, and Issues*, edited by Mary K. Chelton and Colleen Cool, 133–63. Lanham, MD: Scarecrow Press, Inc., 2007.

Hughes-Hassell, Sandra, and Denise E. Agosto. "Modeling the Everyday Life Information Needs of Urban Teenagers." In *Youth Information-Seeking Behavior II: Context, Theories, Models, and Issues*, edited by Mary K. Chelton and Colleen Cool, 27–61. Lanham, MD: Scarecrow Press, Inc., 2007.

Hunt, Jonathan. "Where Do All the Prizes Go? Thoughts on the State of Informational Books." *The Horn Book Magazine* 81, no. 4 (July/August 2005): 439–45.

Hunt, Peter, ed. *Children's Literature: An Illustrated History*. Oxford, UK: Oxford University Press, 1995.

Irvin, Vanessa. "Book Tweets and Happy Reads: Booktalking to Engage Millennial Teens." *The Journal of Research on Libraries and Young Adults* 16 (November 2015): 1–16. https://www.yalsa.ala.org/jrlya/2015/11/book-tweets-and-snappy-reads-booktalking-to-engage-millennial-teens/.

Jane Addams Peace Association. "What Is the Jane Addams Children's Book Award." https://www.janeaddamschildrensbookaward.org/book-award/.

Jenkins, Steve. "The Importance of Being Wrong." *The Horn Book Magazine* 87, no. 2 (2011): 64–68.

Johnson, Abby. "Nonfiction Programming." *American Libraries* (May 2013): n.p., https://americanlibrariesmagazine.org/2013/05/28/nonfiction-programming/.

Johnson, Aeriale N., and Clare Landrigan. "'I Wanna Learn More About That!' Providing Access to Scientific Literacy for All through Inclusive Nonfiction Science Texts." *Language Arts* 100, no. 4 (2023): 338–43.

Johnson, Eric J. "Chronology." In *The Cambridge Companion to Children's Literature*, edited by M. O. Grenby and Andrea Immel, xvii–xxv. Cambridge, UK: Cambridge University Press, 2009.

Jones, Patrick, Michele Gorman, and Tricia Suellentrop. *Connecting Young Adults and Libraries: A How-to-Do-It Manual for Librarians*. Third ed. New York: Neal-Schuman, 2004.

Katz, Stephanie. "Publishing Teen Writers: Amplify Teen Voices through Library Publications." *Young Adult Library Services* 19, no. 2 (2021): 32–37. http://yalsjournal.ala.org/publication/?m=53337&i=709838&p=1&ver=html5.

Kelly, Laura B. "Welcoming Counterstory in the Primary Literacy Classroom." *Journal of Critical Thought and Praxis* 6, no. 1 (2018).

Kelly, Laura Beth. "An Analysis of Award-Winning Science Trade Books for Children: Who Are the Scientists, and What Is Science?" *Journal of Research in Science Teaching* 55 (2018): 1188–210.

Kersten-Parrish, Sara, and Ashley K. Dallacqua. "Three Graphic Nonfiction Series That Excite and Educate." *The Reading Teacher* 71, no. 5 (2018): 627–33.

Kesler, Ted. "Evoking the World of Poetic Nonfiction Picture Books." *Children's Literature in Education* 43, no. 4 (2012).

Kidd, Kenneth. "'Not Censorship but Selection': Censorship and/as Prizing." *Children's Literature in Education* 40 (2009): 197–216.

Kidd, Kenneth B., and Joseph T. Thomas. *Prizing Children's Literature: The Cultural Politics of Children's Book Awards*. New York: Routledge, 2017.

———. "A Prize-Losing Introduction." In *Prizing Children's Literature: The Cultural Politics of Children's Book Awards*, edited by Kenneth B. Kidd and Joseph T. Thomas, 1–18. New York: Routledge, 2017.

Kiefer, Barbara, and Melissa I. Wilson. "Nonfiction Literature for Children: Old Assumptions and New Directions." In *Handbook of Research on Children's and Young Adult Literature*, edited by Shelby Anne Wolf, Karen Coats, Patricia Enciso and Christine Jenkins, 290–301. New York: Routledge, 2010.

Kirkus Media LLC. "Kirkus Reviews." https://www.kirkusreviews.com/.

Kleeman, David. "Books and Reading Are Powerful with Kids, but Content Discovery Is Challenging." *Publishing Research Quarterly* 32 (2016): 38–43.

Kociubuk, Jacqueline. "Branching Out: Promoting Genre Diversity in Storytime." *Children and Libraries* 19, no. 3 (2021): 11–13.

Krashen, Stephen D. *The Power of Reading: Insights from the Research*. Second ed. Westport, CT: Libraries Unlimited, 2004.

Kuhlthau, Carol Collier. *Seeking Meaning: A Process Approach to Library and Information Services*. Westport, CT: Libraries Unlimited, 2004.

———. "Kuhlthau's Information Search Process." In *Theories of Information Behavior*, edited by Karen E. Fisher, Sanda Erdelez and Lynne (E. F.) McKechnie, 230–34. Medford, NJ: Information Today, Inc., 2005.

Kumasi, Kafi. "Cultural Inquiry: A Framework for Engaging Youth of Color in the Library." *The Journal of Research on Libraries and Young Adults* 1, no. 1 (2010): n.p., https://www.yalsa.ala.org/jrlya/2010/11/cultural-inquiry-a-framework-for-engaging-youth-of-color-in-the-library/.

Laffrado, Laura. *Hawthorne's Literature for Children*. Athens: University of Georgia Press, 1992.

Lamb, Mary R. "Teaching Nonfiction through Rhetorical Reading." *English Journal* 99, no. 4 (2010): 43–49.

Latrobe, Kathy H., and Judy Drury. *Critical Approaches to Young Adult Literature*. New York: Neal-Schuman, 2009.

Lear, Bernadette A., and Andrea L. Pritt. "'We Need Diverse E-Books:' Availability of Award-Winning Children's and Young Adult Titles in Today's E-Book Platforms." *Collection Management* 46, no. 3–4 (2021): 223–47.

Lee, Hermione. *Biography: A Very Short Introduction*. New York: Oxford University Press, 2009.

Lerer, Seth. *Children's Literature: A Reader's History from Aesop to Harry Potter*. Chicago: University of Chicago Press, 2008.

Levine-Rasky, Cynthia. "Creative Nonfiction and Narrative Inquiry." *Qualitative Research Journal* 19, no. 3 (2019).

Levinson, Cynthia, Melissa Stewart, and Jennifer Swanson. "Soapbox: 'Hey, Grownups! Kids Really Do Like Nonfiction'." *The Publishers Weekly* (2021).

Lewison, Mitzi, Amy Seely Flint, and Katie Van Sluys. "Taking on Critical Literacy: The Journey of Newcomers and Novices." *Language Arts* 78, no. 5 (2002): 382–92.

Livingston, N., C. Kurkjian, T. Young, and L. Pringle. "Nonfiction as Literature: An Untapped Goldmine." *The Reading Teacher* 57, no. 6 (2004): 582–91.

Lounsberry, Barbara. "Anthology Introduction." In *Writing Creative Nonfiction: The Literature of Reality*, edited by Gay Talese and Barbara Lounsberry, 29–31. New York: HarperCollins, 1996.

Lukenbill, W. Bernard. *Biography in the Lives of Youth: Culture, Information, and Society*. Westport, CT: Libraries Unlimited, 2006.

Lukens, Rebecca J. *A Critical Handbook of Children's Literature*. Fifth ed. New York: HarperCollins, 1995.

Lyons, Reneé. "Creating Environmental Stewards: Nonfiction Prompting a Sustained Planet." *Children and Libraries* 17, no. 2 (2019): 14-19. https://journals.ala.org/index.php/cal/article/view/7021.

Mackey, Thomas P., and Trudi E. Jacobson. *Metaliteracy: Reinventing Information Literacy to Empower Learners*. Chicago: Neal-Schuman, 2014.

MacLeod, Anne Scott. "Children's Literature in America from the Puritan Beginnings to 1870." In *Children's Literature: An Illustrated History*, edited by Peter Hunt, 102-29. Oxford, U. K.: Oxford University Press, 1995.

Marcus, Leonard A. *Minders of Make-Believe: Idealists, Entrepreneurs, and the Shaping of American Children's Literature*. New York: Houghton Mifflin, 2008.

Mardis, Marcia A. "It's Not Just Whodunnit, but How: 'The CSI Effect,' Science Learning, and the School Library." *Knowledge Quest* 35, no. 1 (2006): 12-17.

Martin, Michelle H. *Brown Gold: Milestones of African American Children's Picture Books, 1845-2002*. New York: Routledge, 2004.

Maslow, Abraham H. *The Psychology of Science: A Reconnaissance*. New York: Harper & Row, 1966.

Mather, Cotton. "A Token, for the Children of New-England." https://collections.library.yale.edu/catalog/15497368.

Matthews, Jay. "Read It and Weep: Students Still Aren't Embracing Nonfiction, Despite Campaign." *The Washington Post*, November 24, 2017.

———. "Will My Grandkids Still Love Me If I Buy Them Nonfiction? The Movement to Deepen Childhood Reading Faces the Challenge of Captain Underpants." *The Washington Post*, December 11, 2020.

May, Laura, Thomas Crisp, Gary E. Bingham, Renée S. Schwartz, Mario T. Pickens, and Kate Woodbridge. "The Durable, Dynamic Nature of Genre and Science: A Purpose-Driven Typology of Science Trade Books." *Reading Research Quarterly* 55, no. 3 (2019): 399-418.

May, Laura A., Teri Holbrook, and Laura E. Meyers. "(Re)Storying Obama: An Examination of Recently Published Informational Texts." *Children's Literature in Education* 41, no. 4 (2010): 273-90.

McCloud, Scott. *Understanding Comics: The Invisible Art*. New York: HarperCollins, 1993.

McClure, Amy. "Censorship." *Children's Literature Association Quarterly* 8, no. 1 (1983): 22-25.

McKechnie, Lynne (E. F.). "Becoming a Reader: Childhood Years." In *Reading Matters: What the Research Reveals About Reading, Libraries, and Community*, edited by Catherine Sheldrick Ross, Lynne (E. F.) McKechnie and Paulette M. Rothbauer, 63-100. Westport, CT: Libraries Unlimited, 2006.

McMath, Joan Scanlon, Margaret A. King, and William Earl Smith. "Young Children, Questions and Nonfiction Books." *Early Childhood Education Journal* 26, no. 1 (1998).

Meltzer, Milton. "Where Do All the Prizes Go? The Case for Nonfiction." The Horn Book, https://www.hbook.com/story/where-do-all-the-prizes-go-the-case-for-nonfiction-2.

———. "Notes on Biography." *Children's Literature Association Quarterly* 10, no. 4 (1986): 172-75.

Meltzer, Rachel. "Memoir vs. Autobiography: What's the Difference?" Grammarly, 2022.

Merriam-Webster.com. "Autobiography." https://www.merriam-webster.com/dictionary/autobiography.

Merriam-Webster.com. "Format." https://www.merriam-webster.com/dictionary/format.

MetaMetrics. "Lexile Framework for Reading." https://lexile.com/educators/tools-to-support-reading-at-school/tools-to-determine-a-books-complexity/the-lexile-analyzer/.

Meyers, Eric M., Karen E. Fisher, and Elizabeth Marcoux. "Making Sense of an Information World: The Everyday-Life Information Behavior of Preteens." *The Library Quarterly: Information, Community, Policy* 79, no. 3 (2009): 301-41.

Mitchell, Brooks, Claire Radcliffe, and Kelliann LaConte. "Steam Learning in Public Libraries: A 'Guide on the Side' Approach for Inclusive Learning." *Children and Libraries* 18, no. 3 (2020): 7-10. https://journals.ala.org/index.php/cal/article/view/7432.

Mohr, Kathleen. "Children's Choices for Recreational Reading: A Three-Part Investigation of Selection Preferences, Rationales, and Processes." *Journal of Literacy Research* 38, no. 1 (2006): 81-104.

Moller, Karla J. "Integrating Graphic Nonfiction into Classroom Reading and Content Area Instruction: A Critical Literacy Focus on Selection Issues." *Journal of Children's Literature* 41, no. 2 (2015).

Moore, Jennifer, and Maria Cahill. "Audiobooks: Legitimate 'Reading' Material for Adolescents?" *School Library Research* 19 (2016): 1-17.

Morgan, Kristin, and Jamie Anderson Collett. "Steam Success: Utilizing Picturebook Biographies." *Children and Libraries* 16, no. 3 (2018): 14-17. https://journals.ala.org/index.php/cal/article/view/6795.

Moyer, Jessica E. "What Does It Really Mean to 'Read' a Text?" *Journal of Adolescent & Adult Literacy* 55, no. 3 (2011/11// 2011): 253-56.

National Book Foundation. https://www.nationalbook.org/.

National Council for the Social Studies. "Notable Social Studies Trade Books for Young People Books 2000-2019." https://www.librarycat.org/lib/NCSS.

National Council of Teachers of English. "Orbis Pictus Award." https://ncte.org/awards/orbis-pictus-award-nonfiction-for-children/.

———. "Definition of Literacy in a Digital Age." National Council of Teachers of English, https://ncte.org/statement/nctes-definition-literacy-digital-age/.

———. "Position Statement on the Role of Nonfiction Literature (K-12)." https://ncte.org/statement/role-of-nonfiction-literature-k-12/.

National Science Teaching Association. "Outstanding Science Trade Books for Students K-12." https://www.nsta.org/outstanding-science-trade-books-students-k-12.

New London Group. "A Pedagogy of Multiliteracies: Designing Social Futures." *Harvard Educational Review* 66, no. 1 (1996): 60–92.

New York Times. "New York Times Book Review." https://www.nytimes.com/column/childrens-books.

Nichols-Besel, Kristen, Cassandra Scharber, David G. O'Brien, and Deborah R. Dillon. "A Space for Boys and Books: Guys Read Book Clubs." *Children and Libraries* 16, no. 2 (2018): 19–26. https://journals.ala.org/index.php/cal/article/view/6682.

Nodelman, Perry. *Words About Pictures: The Narrative Art of Children's Picture Books*. Athens: The University of Georgia Press, 1988.

———. *The Pleasures of Children's Literature*. Second ed. White Plains, NY: Longman, 1996.

Oxford English Dictionary. Oxford, UK: Oxford University Press, 2023, s.v. "literacy."

Page Publishing. "Ebooks Vs. Print Books: Pros and Cons." https://pagepublishing.com/ebooks-vs-print-books-pros-and-cons/.

Palmer, Lois. "While Susie Sleeps." Review of While Susie Sleeps. *The New York Times Book Review*, April 4, 1948.

Pappas, Christine C. "The Information Book Genre: Its Role in Integrated Science Literacy Research and Practice." *Reading Research Quarterly* 41, no. 2 (2006).

Pecoskie, Jen, and Nadine Desrochers. "Hiding in Plain Sight: Paratextual Utterances as Tools for Information-Related Research and Practice." *Library and Information Science Research* 35, no. 3 (2013).

Penguin Teen. "Book Trailers." https://www.youtube.com/playlist?list=PL52482DB99ABC834E.

Phelps, Stephen. "Critical Literacy: Using Nonfiction to Learn About Islam." *Journal of Adolescent & Adult Literacy* 54, no. 3 (2010).

Pierce, Jennifer Burek. "Picking the Flowers in the 'Fair Garden': The Circulation, Non-Circulation, and Disappearance of Young Adult Nonfiction Materials." *School Libraries Worldwide* (2007).

———. *Sex, Brains, and Video Games: Information and Inspiration for Youth Services Librarians*. Second ed. Chicago: American Library Association, 2017.

PWxyz LLC. *Publishers Weekly*. https://www.publishersweekly.com/pw/home/index.html.

Reynolds, Kimberly. *Children's Literature: A Very Short Introduction*. New York: Oxford University Press, 2011.

Riot New Media Group. "About Book Riot." https://bookriot.com/about/.

Roman, Susan, and Carole D. Fiore. "Do Public Library Summer Reading Programs Close the Achievement Gap? The Dominican Study." *Children and Libraries* 8, no. 3 (2010): 27–31.

Rosenblatt, Louise M. *Literature as Exploration*. Fifth ed. New York: Modern Language Association, 1995 [1938].

Rothbauer, Paulette M. "Young Adults and Reading." In *Reading Matters: What the Research Reveals About Reading, Libraries, and Community*, edited by Catherine Sheldrick Ross, Lynne (E. F.) McKechnie and Paulette M. Rothbauer, 101-31. Westport, CT: Libraries Unlimited, 2006.

Sableski, Mary-Kate. "Stretching Stem: Using Picturebooks to Connect Stem and Literacy." *Children and Libraries* 17, no. 3 (2019): 23-26. https://journals.ala.org/index.php/cal/article/view/7111.

Sanders, Joe Sutliff. *A Literature of Questions: Nonfiction for the Critical Child*. Minneapolis, MN: University of Minnesota Press, 2018.

Savolainen, Reijo. "Everyday Life Information Seeking: Approaching Information Behavior in the Context of 'Way of Life'." *Library and Information Science Research* 17 (1995): 259-94.

Scholastic. "Book Trailers." https://www.youtube.com/playlist?list=PL0A3EC21903A84659.

School Library Journal. "About Us." https://www.slj.com/page/About-Us.

———. "Series Made Simple." https://www.slj.com/section/reviews/seriesmadesimple.

Serafini, Frank. "Reading Multimodal Texts: Perceptual, Structural and Ideological Perspectives." *Children's Literature in Education* 41 (2010): 85-104.

———. "Expanding Perspectives for Comprehending Visual Images in Multimodal Texts." *Journal of Adolescent & Adult Literacy* 54, no. 5 (2011).

———. *Reading the Visual: An Introduction to Teaching Multimodal Literacy*. New York: Teachers College Press, 2014.

Shaulskiy, Stephanie Levitt, Janet L. Capps, Laura M. Justice, Lynley H. Anderman, and Columbus Metropolitan Library. "Motivational Attributes of Children and Teenagers Who Participate in Summer Reading Clubs." *The Journal of Research on Libraries and Young Adults* 4 (May 2014): n.p., https://www.yalsa.ala.org/jrlya/2014/05/motivational-attributes-of-children-and-teenagers-who-participate-in-summer-reading-clubs/.

Shea, Logan. "Finding What's Right: Readers' Advisory for Middle Grades." *Children and Libraries* 21, no. 3 (2023): 13-15. https://journals.ala.org/index.php/cal/article/view/8106.

Shimek, Courtney. "Sites of Synergy: Strategies for Readers Navigating Nonfiction Picture Books." *The Reading Teacher* 72, no. 4 (2018): 519-22.

———. "Recursive Readings and Reckonings: Kindergartners' Multimodal Transactions with a Nonfiction Picturebook." *English Teaching* 20, no. 2 (2021).

Short, Kathy G. "What's Trending in Children's Literature and Why It Matters." *Language Arts* 95, no. 5 (2018): 287-98.

Shtivelband, Annette, Lauren Riendeau, and Robert Jakubowski. "Building Upon the Stem Movement: Programming Recommendations for Library Professionals." *Children and Libraries* 15, no. 4 (2017): 23-26. https://journals.ala.org/index.php/cal/article/view/6510.

Silvey, Anita. "Where Do All the Prizes Go?" https://www.anitasilvey.com/blog/2016/09/19/where-do-all-the-prizes-go/.

———, ed. *Children's Books and Their Creators: An Invitation to the Feast of Twentieth-Century Children's Literature.* New York: Houghton Mifflin, 1995.

Simons Laufer Mathematical Sciences Institute. "Mathical Book Prize." https://www.mathicalbooks.org/.

Sipe, Lawrence R. "How Picture Books Work: A Semiotically Framed Theory of Text-Picture Relationships." *Children's Literature in Education* 29, no. 2 (1998): 97–108.

Smith, Michael W., and Jeffrey D. Wilhelm. *"Reading Don't Fix No Chevys": Literacy in the Lives of Young Men.* Portsmouth, NH: Heinemann, 2002.

Snowball, Diane. "Building Literacy Skills through Nonfiction." *Teaching pre K–8* 25, no. 8 (1995): 62–62.

Society of Children's Book Writers and Illustrators. "The Golden Kite Awards." https://www.scbwi.org/awards-and-grants/for-pal-published/golden-kite-awards.

STARnet. "Starnet." https://clearinghouse.starnetlibraries.org/32-collections.

Steuter, Erin. "Not Just for Laughs – Using Comics to Burst the Fake-News Bubble." *Media Literacy and Academic Research* (2023).

Stewart, Melissa, ed. *Nonfiction Writers Dig Deep: 50 Award-Winning Children's Book Authors Share the Secret of Engaging Writing.* Champaign, IL: National Council of Teachers of English, 2020.

Stone, Tanya Lee. "The Art of Visual Storytelling in Long-Form Nonfiction." *The Horn Book Magazine* 98, no. 5 (2022): 20–25.

Subramaniam, Mega. "Designing the Library of the Future for and with Teens: Librarians as the 'Connector' in Connected Learning." *The Journal of Research on Libraries and Young Adults* 7, no. 2 (2016): 1–18. https://www.yalsa.ala.org/jrlya/2016/06/designing-the-library-of-the-future-for-and-with-teens-librarians-as-the-connector-in-connected-learning/.

Suen, Anastasia. "Focus on Stem: Family Recipes." Booklist, https://www.booklistonline.com/Focus-on-STEM-Family-Recipes-Suen-Anastasia/pid=9796228?_zs=5G01k1&_zl=AwQc9.

Suico, Teri. "'I've Got a Story You Haven't Heard': Conversation About the Art and Craft of Nonfiction with Candace Fleming." *Bookbird: A Journal of International Children's Literature* 55, no. 3 (2017).

Sullivan, Ed. "Some Teens Prefer the Real Thing: The Case for Young Adult Nonfiction." *The English Journal* 90, no. 3 (2001).

Table, Rainbow Round. "Stonewall Book Awards." https://www.ala.org/rt/rrt/award/stonewall.

Taylor, Melissa. "60 Inspiring Women's History Month Biographies for Kids." Imagination Soup, https://imaginationsoup.net/childrens-books-biographies-womens-history/.

Teaching for Change. "Social Justice Books." https://socialjusticebooks.org/booklists/.

TeachingBooks. "Norman A. Sugarman Children's Biography Award, 1998–2022." https://www.teachingbooks.net/tb.cgi?wid=142.

Tewell, Eamon C. "The Practice and Promise of Critical Information Literacy: Academic Librarians' Involvement in Critical Library Instruction." *College and Research Libraries* 79, no. 1 (2018).

The Bulletin of the Center for Children's Books. "About the Bulletin." https://bccb.ischool.illinois.edu/about-us/.

The Children's Book Guild of Washington, DC. "Nonfiction Award." https://www.childrensbookguild.org/nonfiction-award.

The Children's Book Review. "The Children's Book Review." https://www.thechildrensbookreview.com/.

The Horn Book. "Guide/Reviews Database." https://www.hornbookguide.com/site/.

———. "How Do You Solve a Problem Like Nonfiction?" *The Horn Book* 96, no. 3 (2020): 24-31.

Thimmesh, Catherine. *Team Moon: How 400,000 People Landed Apollo 11 on the Moon.* New York: Houghton Mifflin, 2006.

Through the Looking Glass Children's Book Reviews. "Through the Looking Glass Children's Book Reviews." https://lookingglassreview.com/books/.

UNESCO. "What You Need to Know About Literacy." https://www.unesco.org/en/literacy/need-know.

United States Board on Books for Young People. "2023 Outstanding International Books List." https://www.usbby.org/outstanding-international-books-list.html.

Vardell, Sylvia, and Janet Wong. "The Symbiosis of Science and Poetry." *Children and Libraries* 13, no. 1 (2015): 15-18. https://journals.ala.org/index.php/cal/article/view/5620.

Vardell, Sylvia M. *Children's Literature in Action: A Librarian's Guide.* Westport, CT: Libraries Unlimited, 2008.

———. "Connecting Science and Poetry." *Book Links* (November 2013): 16-20.

Vaughn, Margaret, Vera Sotirovska, Janine J. Darragh, and Mohamed Elhess. "Examining Agency in Children's Nonfiction Picture Books." *Children's Literature in Education* 53, no. 1 (2022).

Visser, Marijke. "Libraries Ready to Code: Past, Present, and Future." *Young Adult Library Services* 17 (Winter 2019): 14-15. https://yalsa.ala.org/blog/wp-content/uploads/2019/11/YALS_Winter-2019-Final.pdf.

Vygotsky, Lev S. *Mind in Society: The Development of Higher Psychological Processes.* Cambridge, MA: Harvard University Press, 1978.

Watson, Jamie, and Jennifer Stencel. "Reaching Reluctant Readers with Nonfiction." *Young Adult Library Services* (Fall 2005): 8-11.

Watson, Victor, ed. *The Cambridge Guide to Children's Books in English.* Cambridge, UK: Cambridge University Press, 2001.

We Need Diverse Books. "The Walter Awards." https://diversebooks.org/programs/walter-awards/.

Weatherford, Carole Boston. "More Than a Footnote: Challenges for BIPOC Nonfiction Authors. (Guest Commentary)." *The Horn Book Magazine* 97, no. 2 (2021): 18-22.

Wenzel, Evelyn L. "Historical Backgrounds." In *Beyond Fact: Nonfiction for Children and Young People*, edited by Jo Carr, 16-26. Chicago: American Library Association, 1982.

Wikipedia. "Golden Kite Award." https://en.wikipedia.org/wiki/Golden_Kite_Award.

———. "Data Literacy." https://en.wikipedia.org/wiki/Data_literacy.

Wilson, Sandip. "Getting down to Facts in Children's Nonfiction Literature: A Case for the Importance of Sources." *Journal of Children's Literature* 32, no. 1 (2006).

Wilson, T. D. "Human Information Behavior." *Informing Science* 3, no. 2 (2000): 49-55.

Wolf, Shelby Anne, ed. *Handbook of Research on Children's and Young Adult Literature*. New York: Routledge, 2011.

Wolfson, Gene. "Using Audiobooks to Meet the Needs of Adolescent Readers." *American Secondary Education* 36, no. 2 (2008): 105-14.

Young Adult Library Services Association. "YALSA Award for Excellence in Nonfiction for Young Adults." https://www.ala.org/yalsa/nonfiction.

———. "Book Finder." http://booklists.yalsa.net/.

Zarnowski, Myra. "The Craft of Historical Nonfiction Writing: Learning from Mentor Texts." *Journal of Children's Literature* 34, no. 2 (2008): 43-50.

———. "History Writing That's 'Good to Think With': *The Great Fire*, *Blizzard!* and *An American Plague*." *Children's Literature in Education* 40, no. 3 (2009): 250-62.

———. "Reading for the Mystery in Nonfiction Science Books." *Journal of Children's Literature* 39, no. 2 (2013): 14-21.

———. "Shaping Nonfiction: Making the Facts 'Dance Together'." *Journal of Children's Literature* 40, no. 2 (2014): 6-14.

———. "'How One Person Sees Another Person': Focusing on the Author's Perspective in Picturebook Biographies." *Language Arts* 96, no. 3 (2019): 145-52.

Zarnowski, Myra, and Susan Turkel. "Nonfiction Literature That Highlights Inquiry: How Real People Solve Real Problems." *Journal of Children's Literature* 37, no. 1 (2011): 30-37.

———. "How Nonfiction Reveals the Nature of Science." *Children's Literature in Education* 44, no. 4 (2013): 295-310.

———. "How History as Mystery Reveals Historical Thinking: A Look at Two Accounts of Finding Typhoid Mary." *Language Arts* 94, no. 4 (2017): 234-44.

Zhang, Meilan. "Supporting Middle School Students' Online Reading of Scientific Resources: Moving Beyond Cursory, Fragmented, and Opportunistic Reading." *Journal of Computer Assisted Learning* 29, no. 2 (2013).

Zipes, Jack, Lissa Paul, Lynne Vallone, Peter Hunt, and Gillian Avery, eds. *The Norton Anthology of Children's Literature: The Traditions in English*. New York: W. W. Norton & Company, 2005.

Zunshine, Lisa. "What to Expect When You Pick up a Graphic Novel." In *SubStance*, 2011.

Index

Abbott, Jacob, 7, 9-10
Abbott, John, 7
Aberg-Riger, Ariel, 63
Abirached, Zeina, 97
Aboriginal America (Abbott), 7
Abrahamson, Richard, xv-xvi
accessibility, 7, 44, 47, 119, 126
ACRL. *See* Association of College and Research Libraries
Actes and Monuments (*Book of Martyrs*) (Foxe), 5-6
A.D. (Neufeld), 97
Ada Lovelace, Poet of Science (Stanley), 91
Adams, Ansel, 61-62
adolescence, 39-40, 41, 76, 96-97
adults, nonfiction for, xi, 10, 27, 77, 128
advice books, 5, 41, 69-70
African Americans, 2, 23, 66, 78-79, 90-91, 115; authors, 8-9, 22, 76-77. *See also* civil rights movement
agency, 79-80, 90
age ranges, recommended, 28-29, 31
Agostini, Alliah L., 116
Agosto, Denise, 41, 44
A Is for Australian Reefs (Lessac), 93
Akim Aliu (Vega, Williams, M.,), 96-97
ALA. *See* American Library Association
Alia's Mission (Stamaty), 97
Alko, Selina, 92
All Rise (Conyngham), 25

All the Water in the World (Lyon, Tillotson), 115
All Thirteen (Soontornvat), 79
Almeida, Matheus, 49
Almost Astronauts (Stone), 74
alphabet books, 3-4, 40
Alphabet City (Johnson, S.), 40
ALSC. *See* Association for Library Service to Children
Amazon, 32
American Association of School Librarians, 55
American Indian Library Association, 23
American Library Association (ALA), 18-19, 22-23, 26-27, 30, 125-27
American Murderer (Jarrow), 58, 110-11
An American Plague (Murphy), 113
Americans with Disabilities Act, U.S., 66
American Wings (Smith, S., Wein), 78
America Redux (Aberg-Riger), 63
Américas Award, 23-24
Amos Fortune, Free Man (Yates), 8
Anderson, Laurie Halse, 113
Anderson, Marian, 8
Andrews, Troy "Trombone Shorty," 92
Angel of Greenwood (Pink), 113
Angelou, Maya, 76
animal books, 10, 81-82, 93, 109
Annie Sullivan and the Trial of Helen Keller (Lambert), 96

APALA. *See* Asian/Pacific American Librarians Association
appropriateness for intended audiences, xv, 28–29, 31, 41, 88
Arab American Book Award, 24
Arab American National Museum, 24
Aronson, Marc, 19, 48, 70, 78, 116
Aserr, Olivia, 24
asexuality, 49, 97
Asheim, Lester, 127
Asian/Pacific American Librarians Association (APALA), 23
Association for Library Service to Children (ALSC), xi–xiii, 21–22, 25
Association for Library Service to Children, ALA, 19
Association of College and Research Libraries (ACRL), 55–56
Association of Jewish Libraries, 24
Astronauts (Ottaviani, Wicks), 96
atomic bomb, 83, 98
audiences, xix, 32, 36–41, 45–49, 66, 93; appropriateness for intended, xv, 28–29, 31, 41, 88
audiobooks, 98–101
Audio Publishers Association, 99–100
author and illustrator library visits, 117–18
authors, xv, xv–xvi, xvii–xviii, 1–2, 24, 48, 71–74, 81; African American, 8–9, 22, 76–77; Latino/Latina, 22, 74
autobiographies, 75–77
Avery, Gillian, 5
Award for Excellence in Nonfiction for Young Adults, YALSA, xiii, 19–20
awards, nonfiction, 12, 17–26, 32, 108. *See also specific awards*
¡Ay, Mijah! (Suggs), 96
Aydin, Andrew, 21

The Babees Book ('Lytyl Reporte' of How Young People Should Behave) series, 4
Baker, Alia Muhammad, 97
Bang, Molly, 89
Bank Street College of Education, 1–2
Banned Books Week, 127
Barker, Meg-John, 98
Bartoletti, Susan Campbell, 60, 70
Bascomb, Neal, 64–65
Bechdel, Alison, 97
Beckerman, Nell Cross, 93
Bedford, Francis D., 6
Beers, Kylene, xiii, xvi–xviii, 59–60
Bell, Cece, 49, 101
Belpré, Pura, 91
Ben-Barak, Idan, 92–93
Bergum, Candace R., 109
Bertozzi, Nick, 98
Bewick, Thomas, 10
Beyond Fact (Carr), xv
biases, xvi, 127–28
Biographical Stories for Children (1842), 7
biographies, xv, 2, 5–8, 10, 46, 82, 112–13; awards for, 18–20, 24; as genre, 70, 72–77, 87; picturebook, 29, 73–74, 90–91, 95–96; of women, 44–45, 73
Biography in the Lives of Youth (Lukenbill), 73
BIPOC (Black, Indigenous, People of Color) authors, 48, 81
Bishop, Nic, 11, 57–58, 82, 108, 113
Bishop, Rudine Sims, 47–48, 71, 76
Bite by Bite (Aronson, Freedman), 116
Black, Indigenous, People of Color (BIPOC) authors, 48, 81
Black Birds in the Sky (Colbert), 48–49, 78
Blue Ribbon Awards, *The Bulletin of the Center for Children's Books*, 30
Blumenthal, Karen, 118
Bodart, Joni Richards, 110–11
Bolden, Tanya, 92

Bomb! (Sheinkin), 83, 98, 108
Bontemps, Arna, 8–9
book club programming, 112–14
book displays, 18, 108
Book Finder, YALSA, 21–22
Booklist, 27, 30
Book of Curtesye (Caxton), 4
The Book of Knowledge (*The Children's Encyclopedia*) (Mee), 4
Book of Martyrs (*Actes and Monuments*) (Foxe), 5–6
The Book of the Knight of the Tower (Caxton), 4
The Book Rescuer (Macy, Innerst), 24
Book Review Digest Plus, 31
booktalks and book trailer programming, 110–12
Booth, Heather, 107–8
Bootman, Colin, 115
Boots on the Ground (Partridge), 78
Boreman, Thomas, 9–10
Bosarges, Liz, 30
Boston Globe–Horn Book Award, xvii, 20–21
Bowen, Fred, 79
The Boy Who Harnessed the Wind (Kamkwamba), 77
brain science research, 39–40
Brazen (Bagieu), 96
Breaking the Mold (Levy), 82
Bronski, Michael, 78
Brothers and Sisters (Lacovara, Pinto, Varejão), 40
Brown, Don, 97
Brown, Louisa, 9
Brown Girl Dreaming (Woodson), 29, 76–77
The Brownies' Book (magazine), 8
Bruner, Jerome, 75
Brzozowski, Bonnie, 96
Buckingham, David, 53
Buckley, Arabella B., 10
Budhos, Marina, 78
Buell, Ellen Lewis, 5

The Bulletin of the Center for Children's Books, 30
Bunting, Philip, 92–93
Burnett, Kathleen, 48
Butler, Octavia, 24
Butzer, C. M., 82

Cabrera, Cazbi, 91
Cahill, Maria, 99
Callanan, Maureen, 42
Call and Response (Chambers), 79
The Cambridge Guide to Children's Books, xiii, 89
Canada, xviii, 26
Careers (DK Publishing), 41
Carnegie Medal for Illustration (Kate Greenaway Medal), U.K., 26
Carnegie Medal for Writing, U.K., 26
Carpenter, Nancy, 58
Carr, Jo, xi, xv
Carson, Mary Kay, 112
Carter, Betty, xv–xvi
The Cartoon History of the United States (Gonick), 97–98
Case, Donald, 37
Caves (Beckerman, Chock), 93
Caxton, William, 4
CCBC-Recommended Book Search, 32
censorship, xx, 125–28
Center for Children's Books, University of Illinois Urbana-Champaign, 30
Cervantes, Christi, 42
Chambers, Veronica, 79
Chance, Rosemary, xiv, 126
Charles, Jane, 110
Charles and Emma (Heiligman), 19–20
Charlotte Zolotow Award, 22
Chasing Cheetahs (Bishop, N., Montgomery), 82
Chasing Lincoln's Killer (Swanson), 108
Chaudhri, Amina, 73
Chevat, Richie, 78

childhood, 1, 37–41, 62, 75–77, 90
children, xi, xix, 8, 32, 105–6; cognitive development and, 39–41; information needs of, 37–38
children, nonfiction for, xi–xii, xix, 2–4, 47–48, 58–66, 99; censorship and, 125–28; library programming for, 108–18
Children's Book Council, 20
Children's Book Guild of Washington, xvii, 18
The Children's Book Review, 32
Children's Books and Their Creators (Silvey), xviii
The Children's Encyclopedia (*The Book of Knowledge*) (Mee), 4
children's literature, xiv, xvii, 1–13, 88
Children's Literature, 32
Children's Literature Comprehensive Database, 31
Chin, Jason, 48, 57, 91
China, 21
Chinese Menu (Lin), 79, 101, 116
Chitrakar, Manu, 95
Chock, Kalen, 93
choice, 46–48, 73, 127–28
Choosing Brave (Joy, Washington), 25, 91
Christensen, Andrew, 114–15
Chung, Sunah, 73
civil rights movement, U.S., 2, 21, 71, 73, 77–78, 90–91, 97
Clarion Books, 57
CLASP. *See* Consortium of Latin American Studies Programs
class, social, 1, 4–5, 9
Classified (Donovan, Sorell), 23
Claudette Colvin (Hoose), 73
Coatoam, Suzanne, 57
Cocca-Leffler, Maryann, 66
cognitive development, 38–41, 43
Colbert, Brandy, 48–49, 78, 113
Cole, Joanna, xii, 11
collections, development, xix, 21–22, 42–43, 45, 47–48, 73; awards and, 17–26, 32; censorship and, 125–28; reviews and, 26–32
collective, biographies, 74 96
Collett, Jamie Anderson, 115
Collier, Bryan, 90
Colman, Penny, xii–xiii, xviii, 27, 29
Comenius, John Amos, 3, 19
comics, 93–95
Common Core State Standards Initiative, U.S., xviii, 111
Common Sense Media, 31
communication skills, 41, 55
comprehension, 45, 100
Congress, U.S., 2, 24
Conkling, Winifred, 66
connectivity, 44, 47
Consortium of Latin American Studies Programs (CLASP), 23–24
Conway, Jill Ker, 75–76
Conyngham, Richard, 25
Cooper, Floyd, 22, 48, 92
Cooper, Linda, 45, 48
Cooperative Children's Book Center, University of Wisconsin–Madison, 22, 31–32
copyright, 111
Coral Reefs (Wicks), 95
Coretta (King, C.,), 92
Coretta Scott King Book Awards, 22
Cosgrove, Brian, 106
Council on Interracial Books for Children, 71
courtesy books, conduct and, 4–5
Crawley, Adam, 73–74
Crawley, Annie, 81
Crisp, Thomas, 28, 49
Critical Approaches to Young Adult Literature (Latrobe, Drury), xii
critical engagement, xiii, xvi–xvii, 28, 60–61, 64–65
A Critical Handbook of Children's Literature (Lukens), xiii
critical literacy, 59, 65–66
Crossing on Time (Macaulay), 82
Crowell Thomas Y., 10–11

Crutcher, Chris, 75
cultural literacy, 28, 53
curiosity, 37, 43

Darwin, Charles, 10
databases, 30-32
data literacy, 57
Dávila, Denise, 71
Day, Nicholas, 79
The Day the River Caught Fire (Wittenstein, Hartland), 92
DDC. *See* Dewey Decimal Classification
deafness, 49, 101
El Deafo (Bell), 49, 101
Deb Haaland (Martinez, Doerfler), 23
decision making, 37, 39, 43
Defending America (Peet, Kredel), 11
Degen, Bruce, xii, 11
Delacre, Lulu, 93
Dembicki, Matt, 98
Denise, Anika Aldamuy, 22, 91
A Description of Three Hundred Animals (Boreman), 10
developmental needs, 36-41, 49, 69, 128
Dewey Decimal Classification (DDC), xiv
digital age, 44, 47, 54-55, 105
digital literacy, 56
Dionne, Evette, 66
disabilities, 45-46, 66, 100
disciplinary literacy, 57
District Comics (Dembicki), 98
Diverse BookFinder, 31
diversity, 2, 24, 28, 48-49, 66, 81, 90, 128; e-books and, 99; in library programs and services, 119
DK Eyewitness Series, xix, 4, 41, 48, 106
Doerfler, Jill, 23
Doiron, Ray, xviii
Donovan, Natasha, 23
A Dream of Freedom (McWhorter), 71

Dresang, Eliza, 43, 47-48
Drowned City (Brown, D.), 97
Drum Dream Girl (López, Engle), 22
Drury, Judy, xii
Duties of a Lady's Maid (1825), 5

Earle, John, 6-7
e-books, 98-101
Eddy, Daniel C., 5
education, xiii, 1-5, 40-41, 45, 116, 118; K-8 classrooms, 19-20, 90; K-12 classrooms, xvi, xviii, 20, 65-66; primary school, xvi, xix, 2, 23-24, 117; secondary school, xvi, xviii, 2, 23-24; teachers and, xvi-xvii, xviii, 100, 113
Ehler, Lois, 76, 92
Eichmann, Adolf, 64
Eisner, Will, 93
Elementary and Secondary Education Act, U.S., 2
ELIS. *See* Everyday Life Information Seeking
Elovich, Sarah, 71
Elrod, Taffy, 116
Emberley, Michael, 41
Emmanuel's Dream (Thompson), 101
encyclopedias, xviii, 4, 106
England, 1, 3-5, 8-10, 74
Engle, Margarita, 22
English language, 3, 24, 94
Enigma Girls (Fleming), 74
Environmental Protection Agency, U.S., 92
epitext, 63
erasure, 29-30, 49
Erdelez, Sanda, 42
Erikson, Erik, 38-39
Escobar, 91
Esquivel! (Wood), 101
ethics, 39, 83
evaluations of nonfiction, xi, xvi, xix, 72-73, 88, 94, 100-101, 118-20; awards and, 17-26; book reviews and, 26-32

Index   **175**

Every Bone Tells a Story (Rubalcaba, Robertshaw), 60
Everyday Life Information Seeking (ELIS), 43–44
expository writing, xiii, 29, 46, 80–81, 90
Exquisite (Cabrera, Slade), 91
Eye to Eye (Jenkings), 93

facts, xi, xiii–xv, 26–28, 60, 77, 95
The Fairy-Land of Science (Buckley), 10
fake news, 56
Family Style (Pham), 96
Fang, Zhihui, 57
Fauset, Jessie Redmon, 8
The Feathered Tribes of the British Isles (Mudie), 10
Fetter-Vorm, Jonathan, 98
Fever 1793 (Anderson), 113
fiction, xii, xiv–xv, xvii, xviii, 29, 59, 69, 80, 95, 101; awards and, 20, 22–25, 101; demand for, 128; graphic, 93; library programming and, 109; science book and, 11
The 57 Bus (Slater), 79
Fighting for YES! (Mildenberger, Cocca-Leffler), 66
Fiore, Carole, 117
First Book of Africa (Hughes), 9
The First Book of the Negroes (Hughes), 9
The First Dinosaur (Lendler, Butzer), 82
A First Time for Everything (Santat), 25
Fisher, George, 5
Fisher, Karen, 44
Fisher, Margery, xiv–xv
Flack, Roberta, 92
Fleming, Candace, 74
Flint, Amy Seely, 65
Floca, Brian, 93, 115
Flowers, Arthur, 95
formal learning, 42–44, 105
formats, nonfiction, xix–xx, 27. See also specific formats

Fortune, Amos, 8
Four-and-Twenty Toilers (Lucas, Bedford), 6
Foxe, John, 5
Freedman, Russell, 7, 74, 116
free voluntary reading (FVR), 46
Freire, Paolo, xvi–xvii
Fritz, Jean, 18–19
From Cover to Cover (Horning), 27
Fry Bread (Martinez-Neal, Maillard), 29
Fun Home (Bechdel), 97
Funny Bones (Tonatiuh), 24
Furnivall, Frederick, 4
FVR. See free voluntary reading

Gall, Chris, 93
A Game for Swallows (Abirached), 97
Gantos, Jack, 75
Gardner, Roberta Price, 28, 49
Gatty, Margaret, 10
Geary, Rick, 98
gender, xviii, 1, 4–5, 44–45, 49, 75–76, 90–91; biographies and, 7–8, 73; sexuality and, 125–26
Gender Queer (Kobabe), 49, 97
General History of Quadrapeds (Bewick), 10
Genette, Gérard, 63
genres, nonfiction, xix, 69–72, 87, 125. See also specific genres
Gerlach, Peter K., 6
Giblin, James Cross, 27, 113
Giedd, Jay, 39
Gigantick Histories (Boreman), 9–10
Gill, Sharon Ruth, 89
Gingerich, Monica, 113
Girls Think of Everything (Thimmesh, Sweet), 45
The Girl Who Drew Butterflies (Sidman), 82
The Girl Who Thought in Pictures (Mosca, Rieley), 29
Given, Lisa, 37

Glubok, Shirley, 21
Go (Kidd, C.), 63, 114
Godwin, William, 9
Go Forth and Tell (McDaniel, Harrison), 91
The Golden Kite Awards, 21
Goldman, Susan Rubin, 79
Goldsmith, Oliver, 9
Gonick, Larry, 97-98
The Good, the Bad, and the Barbie (Stone), 78
Good Brother, Bad Brother (Giblin), 113
Goodreads, 32
Goodrich, Samuel G., 9
Gorman, Michele, 109-10
Grace Hopper (Wu, Wallmark), 115
Grand Canyon (Chin), 48, 91
graphic design, 62-63
graphic nonfiction, 49, 62, 93-98
graphic novels, 88, 93-94
The Great Little Madison (Fritz), 18-19
Great Society Program, U.S., 2
The Great Stink (Carpenter, Paeff), 58
Grenby, M. O., 6
Gross, Melissa, 42, 63-64, 109, 114, 119
Growing Friendships (Kennedy-Moore, McLaughlin), 41
Guts (Telgemeier), 96

Hale, Nathan, 95
Handbook of Research on Children's and Young Adult Literature (Kiefer, Wilson), xii
hands-on library programming, 115-16, 118
Hardcourt (Bowen, Ransome), 79
Harper, Meghan, 106
Harris, Benjamin, 3-4
Harris, Frances Jacobson, 105
Harris, Robie H., 41
Harrison, April, 91
Harrison, Vashti, 45
Hartland, Jessie, 91-92

Havighurst, Robert J., 38-39
Hawthorne, Nathaniel, 7
Hazardous Tales series (Hale), 95
Heat, Light, Force (Abbott), 10
Heiligman, Deborah, 19-20
Helquist, Brett, 79
Here and Now Storybook (Sprague), 1-2
Hidden Systems (Nott), 98
Hidden Worlds (Kunkel, Kramer), 114
Higginson, Thomas Wentworth, 9
Hintz, Carrie, 127
Historical and Miscellaneous Questions for the Use of Young People (Mangnall), 4
Historical Questions on the Kings of England, in Verse (Brown), 9
history books, 9, 70, 77-79, 83, 87, 92, 97, 101
An History of England, in a Series of Letters from a Nobleman to His Son (Goldsmith), 9
The History of England, for the Use of Schools and Young Persons (Godwin), 9
A History of France (Penrose), 9
The History of the Computer (Ignotofsky), 118
A History of the Life and Death, Virtues and Exploits of General George Washington (Weems), 7
Hitler Youth (Bartoletti), 70
Holbrook, Teri, 76, 112-13
Holding Her Own (Wright, Todd), 23
Hole in My Life (Gantos), 75
Holmes, Mike, 95
Honor Girl (Thrash), 97
Hooke, Robert, 10
Hooks, Gwendolyn, 115
Hoose, Phillip, 73, 113
Hopkinson, Deborah, 79
The Horn Book (magazine), xvii, 20-21, 29-30
Horning, Kathleen T., 27, 88

Hosler, Jay, 98
Hotta, Ann, 117
The House Baba Built (Young, E.), 92
How We Got to the Moon (Rocco), 82–83
Hughes, Langston, 8–9
Hughes-Hassell, Sandra, 41, 44
human development, 38–41
Hunt, Jonathan, 21
"hybrid" books, xii–xiii, 29, 88, 90, 95

Ignotofsky, Rachel, 118
I Know Why the Caged Bird Sings (Angelou), 76
illustrations, 3, 5, 10, 22–23, 25–26, 40, 79, 108; evaluations of, 88–90; literacies and, 57–58. *See also* picturebooks
illustrators, 18, 22, 117–18
The Imitation Game (Ottaviani, Purvis), 95
Imposed Query model, 42–43
inclusivity, 55, 71, 81, 128
Indigenous Ingenuity (Havrelock, Kay, Fuller), 81
informal learning, 42–45, 105
"informational books," xii–xv, xviii, 10, 19, 109
information behaviors, xix, 32, 36, 37, 41–45, 49
information literacy, 53–56
information needs, xix, 32, 37–38, 46, 49, 69
Information Search Process, 42–43
Innerst, Stacy, 24
instruction, books of, 2–5, 40
The Instructor (Fisher), 5
intellectual freedom, 126–27
Intellectual Freedom Manual, OIF, 126
International Board on Books for Young People, 25
International Digital Library for Children, 106
internment camps, 61–62, 78
Invincible Louisa (Meigs), 8
Iraq War, 97

Irvin, Vanessa, 111
Isaac the Alchemist (Losure), 82
I See the Promised Land (Chitrakar, Flowers), 95
Islam, 24
It's Perfectly Normal (Emberley, Harris), 41

Jacobson, Trudi, 56
Jakubowski, Robert, 115
Jandu, Allison, 40
Jane Addams Children's Book Award, 24–25
Jane Addams Peace Association, 24–25
Janeczko, Paul B., 114
Janeway, James, 6
Japanese American internment camps, 61–62, 78
Jarrow, Gail, 58–110
Jenkins, Steve, 80
John Newbery Medal, 7–9, 18, 21
Johnson, Aeriale, 81
Johnson, Jane, 4
Johnson, Katherine, 77
Johnson, Lyndon, 2
Johnson, Stephen T., 40
Jones, Patrick, 109–10
Joy, Angela, 25, 91
Judaism, 24–25, 97
Jumbo (Gall), 93
The Juneteenth Cookbook (Agostini, Elrod), 116
Jupiter (Simon), 11
Just a Girl (Levi), 25
The Juvenile Plutarch (Tabart), 6

Kakapo Rescue (Bishop, N., Montgomery), 11, 82, 113
Kamkwamba, William, 77
Keating, Jess, 115
Kelly, Laura Beth, 81, 90
Kendi, Ibram X., 101
Kersten-Parrish, Sara, 95
Kesler, Ted, 90
Kidd, Chip, 63, 114

Kidd, Kenneth, 17–18, 22, 126
Kiefer, Barbara, xii, 8, 27
King, Coretta Scott, 92
King of Mild Frontier (Crutcher), 75
Kirkus Reviews, 30
Knezek, Suzanne, 28
Knots in My Yo-Yo String (Spinelli), 76
Kobabe, Maia, 49, 97
Kobrin, Beverly, xviii
Kociubuk, Jacqueline, 109
Kramer, Stephen, 114
Krashen, Stephen, 46
Kredel, Fritz, 11
Krosoczka, Jarrett J., 96
Kuhlthau, Carol, 42–43
Kumasi, Kafi, 113–14
Kunkel, Dennis, 114

Lacovara, Janis, 40
Lambert, Joseph, 96
Landrigan, Clare, 81
Lange, Dorothea, 61–62
Lansky, Aaron, 24
LaReau, Jenna, 114
Latham, Donna, 114–15
Latinitas (Menéndez), 74
Latino/Latina culture, 22–24, 74
Latrobe, Kathy, xii
Lauber, Patricia, 11
Leaf, Munro, 5
Lear, Bernadette, 99
Lee, Hermione, 72–73
Lendler, Ian, 82
Lerner Publications, 56
Lessac, Frané, 66, 93
Let's Go to the Potty! (Jandu), 40
Let's Talk About It (Nolan, Moen), 41
Leung, Julie, 23
Levi, Lia, 25
Levinson, Cynthia, xviii–xix
Levy, Dana Alison, 82
Lewis, John, 21, 97
Lewis & Clark (Bertozzi), 96
Lewison, Mitzi, 65
Lexile Measure, 28

LGBTQIA+ books, 22–23, 49, 73, 97–98, 125–26
libraries and librarians, school and public, xi, xiv, xvi, xix, 2, 26, 42–43, 98–99; censorship and, 125–26; makerspaces and, 45, 118. *See also* collections, development; promotion of nonfiction
Lifting as We Climb (Dionne), 66
Lin, Grace, 79, 101, 116
Lincoln (Freedman), 7, 74
Lincoln, Abraham, 7, 74
literacies, literacy frameworks and, xvi, xxix, 1, 39, 49, 53–54, 100, 113, 128; multimodal, 58–66, 94; visual, 2, 28, 52, 55–57, 60, 62. *See also specific literacies*
A Literature of Questions (Sanders), xvi
Literature Resource Center, 31
Little Dreamers (Harrison), 45
Lives of the Noble Greeks and Romans (North, Plutarch), 5–6
Long, Michael G., 78
Look, Listen, Taste, Touch, and Smell (Shipe, Nettleton), 40
Looking Back (Lowry), 76
Loomis, Molly, 42
Loon, Hendrik Van, xvii, 7, 9
López, Rafael, 22
Lora, Loris, 22
Lord Chesterfield's Advice to His Son (1818), 5
Losure, Mary, 82
Lounsberry, Barbara, xiv
Lowery, Lynda Blackmon, 77
Lowry, Lois, 76
Lucas, E. F., 6
Lukenbill, W. Bernard, 46, 73
Lukens, Rebecca, xiii
Lunch Lady series (Krosoczka), 96
Lyon, George Ella, 115
Lyons, Reneé, 113

Index   **179**

'Lytyl Reporte' of How Young People Should Behave (*The Babees Book*) series, 4

MacArthur Foundation, 105
Macaulay, David, 18, 53, 82
Mackey, Thomas, 56
MacLeod, Anne Scott, 1, 6
Macy, Sue, 24
The Magic School Bus series (Cole, Degen), xii, 11
Maillard, Kevin Noble, 29
makerspaces, library, 45, 118
Making Facts Come Alive (Bamford, Kristo), xvi
Mama in Congress (Tlaib, R. Tlaib, A., Paul, Aserr), 24
Mangnall, Richmal, 4
March (Powell, Lewis, Aydin), 21
Marcoux, Elizabeth, 44
Marcus, Leonard, 3-4
Mardis, Marcia, 82, 94
marginalized groups, 2, 24, 65-66
Marian Anderson (Hughes, Tracy), 8
Marrin, Albert, 78
Martin, Michelle, 22
Martín, Pedro, 49, 96, 101
Martinez, Matthew J., 23
Martinez-Neal, Juana, 29
Martin's Big Words (Rappaport, Collier), 90
Mary McLeod Bethune (Peare), 8
Maslow, Abraham, 53
Mathical Book Prize, 20
Matters of Fact (Fisher), xiv-xv
Matthews, Jay, xviii
Maus I, Maus II and (Spiegelman), 94-95, 97
May, Laura, 76, 80
McCloud, Scott, 93-94
McClung, Robert, 21
McClure, Amy, 126
McDaniel, Breanna, 91
McKechnie, Lynne (E. F.), 42
McWhorter, Diane, 71

Mediavilla, Cindy, 109, 119
Mee, Arthur, 4
Meigs, Cornelia, 8
Meltzer, Milton, xvii-xviii, 20-21, 26-27, 72
memoirs, 25, 29, 49, 62, 70, 72-77, 83, 87; in picturebook format, 92, 94-97
Memoirs of Celebrated Female Characters (Pilkington), 8
Menéndez, Juliet, 74
Metaliteracy (Jacobson, Mackey), 56
Mexico, 49, 91, 92, 96
Mexikid (Martín), 49, 96, 101
Meyers, Eric, 44, 112-13
Michael L. Printz Award, 21
Microcosmographie (Earle), 6-7
Micrographia (Hooke), 10
middle class, 1, 4, 9
Miguéns, Marta Álvarez, 115
Mike Morgan and Larry Romans Children's and Young Adult Literature Award, 22-23
Mildenberger, Vivien, 66
Mildred L. Batchelder Award, 25
"Mirrors, Windows, and Sliding Glass Doors" (Bishop), 47
misinformation, 56
Mitchell, Brooks, 116
Mitchell, Lucy Sprague, 1-2
Miyatake, Toyo, 61-62
Moen, Erika, 41
Mohr, Kathleen, xix
The Mona Lisa Vanishes (Day, Helquist), 79
Monstrous (Myer), 96
Montgomery, Sy, 11, 57-58, 82, 113
Moonshot (Floca), 93, 115
Moore, Jennifer, 99
morality, 1, 4-5, 7, 126
More Than a Dream (Williams, Y., Long), 78
"More Than Just the Facts" (Giblin), 27
Morgan, Kristin, 115

Mosca, Julia Finley, 29
Mudie, Robert, 10
multimodal literacy, 58-66, 94
Murphy, Jim, 77-78, 113
Muslim people, 24
Myer, Sarah, 96
Myers, Walter Dean, 76

National Book Awards, xvii, 25
National Council for the Social Studies, 20
National Council of Teachers of English (NCTE), xii, 20, 54-55, 65-66; Orbis Pictus Award, xiii, 18-19, 89-90
National Council of Teachers of Mathematics, 20
National Defense Education Act, U.S., 2, 10-11
National Geographic Kids Look and Learn, 40
National Science Teaching Association, 20, 80
National Social Studies Standards Theme, 20
Native Americans, 29, 66, 81, 92
Nazi Germany, 64, 70, 74, 92, 94-95, 97
The Nazi Hunters (Bascomb), 64
NCTE. *See* National Council of Teachers of English
Nelson, Kadir, 79, 101
Nettleton, Pamela Hill, 40
Neufeld, Josh, 97
neuroscience, 39-40
neutrality, 28
Newbery, John, 6, 9
Newbery Me, xvii
Newbery Medal, 7-9, 18, 21
The New England Primer (Harris), 3-4
A New History of England (Newberry), 9
New London Group, 54
Newman, Catherine, 41
Newman, Patricia, 81

New York Times, 27, 31
New York Times Book Review, 5, 31
Nichols, Nichelle, 91
Nina (Todd, Robinson), 91
Nodelman, Perry, 89
Nolan, Matthew, 41
nonbinary people, 49, 97
nonfiction. *See specific topics*
Nonfiction for Young Adults from Delight to Wisdom (Carter, Abrahamson), xv-xvi
"Nonfiction Windows So White" (Aronson), 48
Nonfiction Writers Dig Deep (Stewart), xiii
nonlinear reading, 48
Norman A. Sugarman Children's Biography Award, 20
North, Thomas, 5-6
The Norton Anthology of Children's Literature, 3
Notable Social Studies Trade Books for Young People list, 20
"Not Censorship But Selection," Wilson Library Bulletin, 127
The Notorious Benedict Arnold (Sheinkin), 73
Nott, Dan, 98
NoveList, 31

Obama, Barack, 76, 112-13
Odyssey Award, 101
Office for Intellectual Freedom (OIF), ALA, 125-26
¡Olinguito, de la A A La Z! (Delacre), 93
Orbis Pictus Award, NCTE, xiii, 18-19, 49, 89-90
Orbis Sensualium Pictus (*The Visible World in Pictures*) (Comenius), 3-4
Ordinary Hazards (Grimes), 77
Osborne, Linda Barrett, 79
Ottaviani, Jim, 95-96
outer space, 11, 82-83, 96, 114

Outstanding Science Trade Books for Students K–12 list, 20, 80, 90
Oxford Concise Dictionary of Literary Terms, 69
Oxford English Dictionary, 54

Paeff, Colleen, 58
Paper Son (Leung, Sasaki), 23
Parables from Nature (Gatty), 10
parents, xvii, 116, 126–27
Parrots Over Puerto Rico (Roth, Trumbore), 90
participatory design, 105–6
Partridge, Elizabeth, 61–62, 78
Patricelli, Leslie, 40
Paul, Miranda, 24
Peare, Catherine Owens, 8
"A Pedagogy of Multiliteracies" (New London Group), 54
Peeper, First Voice of Spring (McClung), 21
Peet, Creighton, 11
Peña, Zeke, 95–96
Penrose, Elizabeth, 9
people of color, 8, 22–24, 48, 66
peritextual literacy, 59, 63–65, 114
Peritextual Literacy Framework (PLF), 63–65
Persepolis (Satrapi), 97
Pham Thien, 96
Phelps, Stephen, 65
Phenomenal AOC (Denise, Lora), 22
Photographic (Quintero, Peña), 95–96
photography, 2, 61–63, 65, 74, 95–96
physical books, 47, 87, 98–99
Piaget, Jean, 38–39
picturebooks, xii, 3, 6–7, 21–24, 48, 72, 87–89, 101; biography, 29, 73–74, 90–91, 95–96; science, 81, 92–93, 115–16
Picture This (Bang), 89
Pierce, Jennifer Burek, 39–40
Pilkington, Mary, 8
Pink, Randi, 113
Pinto, Anthony, 40

Planet Ocean (Newman, Crawley), 81
Planting Stories (Denise, Escobar), 91
PLF. See Peritextual Literacy Framework
poetry, xiv, 21–22, 29, 76–77, 90, 115–16
The Poetry of Science (Vardell, Wong), 116
The Polite Academy (1762), 5
Popular (Wagenen), 77
Posada, José Guadalupe, 23–24
"Position Statement on the Role of Nonfiction Literature (K–12)," NCTE, 65–66
Potty (Patricelli), 40
Powell, Nate, 21
Pride (Stevenson), 22–23
primary school, xvi, xix, 2, 23–24, 117
Primates (Ottaviani, Wicks), 96
Pritt, Andrea, 99
Prizing Children's Literature (Kidd, Thomas), 17
problem solving, 43, 79–80
Probst, Robert, xiii, xvi–xviii, 59–60
promotion of nonfiction, xix, 125; programs, 105, 108–20, 128; services, 105–8, 118–20
The Protestant Tutor (1683), 3
psychology, 38–39, 126
Publishers Weekly, 27, 30–31, 78
publishing, publishers and, 1–5, 10–11, 25, 28, 99, 125
Pura Belpré Award, 22
Purvis, Leland, 95

Queer (Barker, Scheele), 98
queer erasure, 49, 125–26
A Queer History of the United States for Young People (Bronski, Chevat), 78
The Quilts of Gee's Bend (Goldman), 79
Quintero, Isabel, 95–96

race, 2, 7-8, 22-25, 48-49, 66, 78-79, 96-97
The Race to Save the Lord God Bird (Hoose), 113
racism, 8, 66, 71, 96-97, 101
Radiant Child (Steptoe), 115
Rainbow Round Table, ALA, 22-23
Randolph Caldecott Medal, 18, 21
Random House, 9
Ransome, James E., 79
Rao, Kate, 30
Rappaport, Doreen, 90
Ratcliffe, Claire, 116
Reaching for the Moon (Johnson, K.), 77
readers' advisory, 107-8, 117
"Reading Don't Fix No Chevys" (Smith, Wilhelm), 45
reading levels, 28-29
Reading Nonfiction (Beers, Probst), xvi, xviii
reading practices, 45-49
Reading the Visual (Serafini), 61
Reed, William Maxwell, 10
Reference Sources and Services for Youth (Harper), 106
relationship building, 40-41
religion, religious instruction and, 7, 19-20, 24, 75, 97
reluctant readers, xix, 46
representation, 28, 47-49, 81, 99
reviews, book, 26-32
Reynolds, Jason, 101
Reynolds, Kimberly, 69
Richards, Laura, 8
Rieley, Daniel, 29
Riendeau, Lauren, 115
Rise (Amelia Bloomer Project), ALA, 23
Robert F. Sibert Informational Book Medal, ALSC, xiii, 73
Robert F. Sibert Medal, ALA, 19
Robertshaw, Peter, 60
Rocco, John, 82-83
Rochman, Hazel, 27

Roman, Susan, 117
Rosenblatt, Louise, 46-47, 59, 90
Roth, Susan L., 90
Rothbauer, Paulette, 46
Rubalcaba, Jill, 60
Run and Hide (Brown, D.), 97
Rusch, Elizabeth, 79, 114
Ryan, Pam Muñoz, 91

Sanders, Joe Sutliff, xiii, xvi-xvii, 28, 59-60
Sandler, Martin W., 58
Santana, Carlos, 91
Santat, Dan, 25
Sasaki, Chris, 23
Satrapi, Marjane, 97
Saturn (Simon), 11
Saving the Ghost of the Mountain (Montgomery, Bishop), 57-58
Savolainen, Reijo, 43
Scheele, Jules, 98
Scheider, Nina, 6
School Library Journal, 25, 30
science and technology books, 10-12, 57-58, 70, 79-83, 91-93, 98
The Scraps Book (Ehlert), 76, 92
secondary school, xvi, xviii, 2, 23-24
second language learners, 46, 100
Secret Coders series (Yang, Holmes), 95
Secret Engineer (Dougherty), 91
Seen and Unseen (Tamaki, Partridge), 61-62
self-help books, 5, 41, 69-70
Selznick, Brian, 91
Sensorimotor stage, 38
Separate Is Never Equal (Tonatiuh), 25, 92
Serafini, Frank, 54, 58-59, 61
Series Made Simple, 30
Sex, Brains, and Video Games (Pierce), 39-40
sexism, 71
sexuality, 41, 73, 125-26
Shark Lady (Miguéns, Keating), 115

Shaulskiy, Stephanie Levitt, 117
Shea, Logan, 107
Sheinkin, Steve, 73, 83, 98, 108
Shimek, Courtney, 89-90
Shipe, Becky, 40
Shipwrecked! (Sandler), 58
Short, Kathy, 87
Shtivelband, Annette, 115
Sidman, Joyce, 82
Silvey, Anita, xvii-xviii
Simon, Seymour, 11
Simone, Nina, 91
Simons Laufer Mathematical Sciences Institute, 20
Sipe, Lawrence, 89, 93
Sir Walter Ralegh and the Quest for El Dorado (Aronson), 19
Sisters (Telgemeier), 96
Skyscraper (Christensen, Latham), 114-15
Slade, Suzanne, 91
Slater, Dashika, 79
slavery, 8, 78
Sluys, Katie Van, 65
Smile (Telgemeier), 96
Smith, E. Boyd, 7
Smith, Sherri L., 78
Snakes (Bishop, N.), 108
social justice, 31, 91-92
social media, 111-12
Social Responsibilities Round Table, ALA, 23
Society of Children's Book Writers and Illustrators, 21
Soontornvat, Christina, 79
Sorell, Traci, 23, 66, 92
sources, information, 70-71, 77-78
South Africa, 25
Spiders (Bishop), 11
Spiegelman, Art, 94-95, 97
Spinelli, Jerry, 76
Sputnik (Soviet satellite), 2
Stamaty, Mark Alan, 97
Stamped (Reynolds, Kendi), 101
Stanley, Diane, 91

Star Child (Zoboi), 24
STARnet website, 115
The Stars for Sam (Reed), 10
Stars of the Night (Stetson, Alko), 92
Stebbins, Robert, 44
Stencel, Jennifer, xix
Steptoe, Javaka, 115
stereotypes, 8, 65-66, 71
Stetson, Caren, 92
Steve Jobs (Blumenthal), 118
Stevenson, Robin, 22-23
Stewart, Melissa, xiii, xviii-xix, 109
Stewart, Potter, xiv
Stiles, Charles, 58
St. Nicholas (magazine), 8
Stone, Tanya Lee, 74, 78
Stonewall Book Awards, 22-23
The Story of Ferdinand (Leaf), 5
The Story of Mankind (Loon), xvii, 7, 9
The Story of Pocahontas and Captain John Smith (Smith), 7
The Story of the Greek People (Tappan), 9
The Story of the Negro (Bontemps), 9
The Story of the Roman People (Tappan), 9
story-telling, xv, 63, 89, 91, 98, 108-9
Subramaniam, Mega, 105-6
Suellentrop, Tricia, 109-10
Sugar Changed the World (Aronson, Budhos), 78
Suggs, Christine, 96
summer reading programs, 116-17
Swan, Susan, 115
Swanson, James, xviii-xix, 108, 113
Sweet, Melissa, 45
Sydney Taylor Book Award, 24

Tabart, Benjamin, 6, 10
Takei, George, 62
Tales of Peter Parley about America (Goodrich), 9
Tamaki, Lauren, 61-62
Tamarin, Alfred, 21
Tappan, Eva March, 9

Taylor, Melissa, 44–45
teachers, xvi–xvii, xviii, 100, 113
Team Moon (Thimmesh), 65, 82–83, 114
technology, 81–83, 93, 115, 118; digital, 47, 54–56; printing, 1–2, 11, 87
teenagers, 39–41, 56, 58, 74, 79, 99, 105–6, 117. *See also* adolescence
Telgemeier, Raina, 96
10 Quick Ways to Analyze Children's Books for Racism and Sexism (Council on Interracial Books for Children), 71
Theories of Information Behavior (Fisher, Erdelez, McKechnie), 42
Theory of Radical Change, 43, 47
They Called Themselves the K.K.K (Bartoletti), 60
They Called Us Enemy (Takei), 62
Thimmesh, Catherine, 45, 65, 114
This Land Is Our Land (Osborne), 79
Thomas, Joseph, 17–18, 22
Thompson, Laurie Ann, 101
Thrash, Maggie, 97
Through the Looking Glass Children's Book Reviews, 32
Till, Emmett, 25, 91
Tillotson, Katherine, 115
Tiny Stitches (Bootman, Hooks), 115
Titanic (Hopkinson), 79
To Boldly Go (Dalton, Semmer), 91
Todd, Traci N., 23
A token, for the children of New-England, or, Some examples of children, in whom the fear of God was remarkably budding, before they dyed, in several parts of New-England (Mather), 6
A Token for Children being an Exact Account of the Conversion, Holy and Exemplary Lives, and Joyful Deaths, of Several Young Children (Janeway), 6

Tonatiuh, Duncan, 24–25, 92
Top Secret (LaReau, Janeczko), 114
Tornado Scientist (Carson, Uhlman), 112
Tracy, Steven C., 8
trade nonfiction, xix, 20
translation, 25
transportation, modes of, 9, 82
travel books, 9–10
Tribunella, Eric, xiv, 127
Trinity (Fetter-Vorm), 98
Trombone Shorty (Andrews), 92
Trumbore, Cindy, 90
truth, xiii, 61, 95
Truth, Sojourner, 8
Tuchman, Barbara, xii
Tulsa Race Massacre (1921), U.S., 22, 48–49, 78, 92, 113
Turing, Alan, 95
Turkel, Susan, 78–80
Turning 15 on the Road to Freedom (Lowery), 77
The 21 (Rusch), 79

Uhlman, Tom, 112
"umbrella" literacy, 57
Understanding Comics (McCloud), 93–94
Under the Snow (Bergum, Stewart, M.), 109
United States (U.S.), xiv, xviii–xix, 1–2, 4–5, 7–10, 19–21, 63, 79, 95; civil rights movement, 2, 21, 71, 73, 77–78; Common Core State Standards Initiative, xviii, 111; Gonick on, 97–98
United States Board on Books for Young People (USBBY), 25
The Universe in You (Chin), 57
University of Illinois Urbana-Champaign, 30
University of Maryland, 107
University of Wisconsin-Madison, 22, 31–32

Unspeakable (Weatherford, Cooper), 22, 48, 92
upper-class, 5
Uprooted (Marrin), 78
USBBY. *See* United States Board on Books for Young People

Vardell, Sylvia, 4, 19, 115–16, 126
Varejão, Carlos, 40
Vaughn, Margaret, 90
Vega, Karen De la, 96–97
Vietnam War, 96
The Visible World in Pictures (*Orbis Sensualium Pictus*) (Comenius), 3–4
Visser, Marijke, 118
visual literacy, 2, 28, 52, 55–57, 60, 62
Volcano (Lauber), 11
Volcano Rising (Rusch, Swan), 115
Votes for Women! (Conkling), 66
Voyaging to Cathay (Glubok), 21
Vygotsky, Lev, 38, 40

Wagenen, Maya Van, 77
Wallmark, Laurie, 115
Walter, Virginia, 109, 119
Walter Dean Myers Awards, 24
War of the Revolution (Abbott), 7
War Relocation Authority (WRA), U.S., 62
A War-Time Handbook for Young Americans (Leaf), 5
Washington, Janelle, 25, 91
Water and Land (Abbott), 10
Watson, Jamie, xix
The Way We Work (Macaulay), 53
We Are Still Here! (Lessac, Sorrell), 66
We Are the Ship (Nelson), 79, 101
Weatherford, Carole Boston, 22, 48, 92
web resources, 30–32
Weems, Mason Locke "Parson," 7

We Go Way Back (Ben-Barak, Bunting), 92–93
Wein, Elizabeth, 78
Wenzel, Evelyn, 10–11
What Can I Say? (Newman), 41
What Kids Are Reading report (Renaissance Learning), xviii
Wheatley, Phillis, 8
When Angels Sing (Mahin, Ramirez), 91
When Marian Sang (Ryan, Selznick), 91
When Memory Speaks (Conway), 75
"Where Do All the Prizes Go?" (Silvey), xvii–xviii
"Where Do All the Prizes Go? The Case for Nonfiction" (Meltzer), xvii, 20–21, 26–27
While Susie Sleeps (Scheider), 6
white men, 7–8, 81
Wicks, Maris, 95–96
Wilhelm, Jeffrey, 45
Will Eisner Comic Industry Award, 96
Williams, Bert, 8
Williams, Marcus, 96–97
Williams, Yohuru, 78
Wilson, Melissa, xii, 8–9, 27
Wilson, Sandip, 70–71
Wilson, Thomas D., 41–42
Wilson Library Bulletin, 127
Wise, Daniel, 5
Wittenstein, Barry, 92
Wolfson, Gene, 100
women, 8, 44–45, 66, 73, 76–79
The Wonders of the Microscope (Tabart), 10
Wong, Janet, 116
Wood, Susan, 101
Woodson, Jacqueline, 29, 76–77
Words About Pictures (Nodelman), 89
working class, 5
World War II, 5, 11, 25, 74, 78, 97
WRA. *See* War Relocation Authority

Wright, Shannon, 23
The Wright Brothers (Freedman), 74
writers, nonfiction. *See* authors, nonfiction
Wu, Katy, 115

YALSA. *See* Young Adult Library Services Association
Yang, Gene Luen, 95
Yates, Elizabeth, 8
Young, Ed, 92
Young Adult Library Services Association (YALSA), xi-xiii, xiii, 19-20, 21-22

young adults, xi, xvi, xix, 41, 96-97, 99-100, 108-18
Young Folks' History of the United States (Higginson), 9
The Young Lady's Counsellor (Wise), 5
The Young Man's Friend (Eddy), 5
YouTube, 111
Yuen, Anastasia, 116

Zaldarriaga, Millo Castro, 22
Zarnowski, Myra, 59, 61, 72-73, 77-80
Zoboi, Ibi, 24
Zone of Proximal Development, 38, 40

About the Author

Don Latham is professor in the School of Information at Florida State University. His research focuses on information behavior of children and young adults, information literacy, and digital literacy. He is co-editor of *Literacy Engagement Through Peritextual Analysis* (2019), *The Information Literacy Framework: Case Studies of Successful Implementation* (Rowman & Littlefield, 2020), and *From Text to Epitext: Expanding Students' Comprehension, Engagement, and Media Literacy* (2021). He has published extensively in journals such as *Children's Literature*, *Children's Literature Association Quarterly*, *Children's Literature in Education*, *College & Research Libraries*, *Library & Information Science Research*, *Library Quarterly*, and *Public Library Quarterly*. He has received funding from the Institute of Museum and Library Services, the ALAN Foundation, OCLC/ALISE Research Grants, and the Florida State University Council on Research and Creativity.

www.ingramcontent.com/pod-product-compliance
Lightning Source LLC
Chambersburg PA
CBHW021141230426
43667CB00005B/214